APR 2 3 2007

The Sociology of African American Language

The Sociology of African American Language

A Language Planning Perspective

Charles DeBose
California State University

First published 2005 by
PALGRAVE MACMILLAN
Houndmills, Basingstoke, Hampshire RG21 6XS and
175 Fifth Avenue, New York, N. Y. 10010
Companies and representatives throughout the world

PALGRAVE MACMILLAN is the global academic imprint of the Palgrave Macmillan division of St. Martin's Press, LLC and of Palgrave Macmillan Ltd. Macmillan® is a registered trademark in the United States, United Kingdom and other countries. Palgrave is a registered trademark in the European Union and other countries.

ISBN-13: 978–1–4039–3970–8   hardback
ISBN-10: 1–4039–3970–5   hardback

This book is printed on paper suitable for recycling and made from fully managed and sustained forest sources.

A catalogue record for this book is available from the British Library.

Library of Congress Cataloging-in-Publication Data
DeBose, Charles E., 1939–
    The sociology of African Americans language : a language planning perspective / Charles DeBose.
        p. cm.
    Includes bibliographical references and index.
    ISBN 1–4039–3970–5 (cloth)
    1. African Americans–Languages. 2. English language–Social aspects–United States. 3. English language–Variation–United States. 4. Language planning– United States. 5. Black English. I. Title.

PE3102.N42D43 2005
427'.973'08996073–dc22   2005046314

10   9   8   7   6   5   4   3   2   1
14 13 12 11 10 09 08 07 06 05

Transferred to Digital Printing in 2005

Dedication

This book is dedicated to the speakers of African American language, especially the nameless persons who encouraged me from porches and doorways as I walked down the streets of Ardella Homes, the housing project in Akron Ohio where I spent many of my formative years. Seeing that I was on my way to or from school they would shout the following memorable words of encouragement.

Git that education, boy, cause caint nobody take it from you.

It was a wonderful community of people recently arrived from various locations in the South, speaking the accents of their former homes. I am thankful to them all: my Akron neighbors, playmates, first cousins and running buddies; my extended family from Louisiana of DeBoses, Alfords, Watsons and McDaniels; and my Bay Area in-laws, the Orrs, Gardners and Hardins; for the lasting influence of their wisdom, courage and strength on my becoming who I am today.

I cherish the memory of my mother, Marie DeBose, whom I was blessed to see on her 90th birthday, a few months before she went to join my father, Samuel DeBose, brother, Jerry and sisters Emma and Cora Sue in Glory. I dedicate this book to all of them, as well as my living siblings, Sammy, Paul, Patricia and Renee; my sons, Fred and Charles Jr. and my wife, Jackie, all of whom I dearly love.

Charles DeBose, April 9, 2005

Contents

Acknowledgments

I thank the faculty, staff, administration and students of California State University, East Bay, for providing a supportive environment for the ideas developed in this book. Although it is an institution dedicated primarily to a mission of teaching, it recognizes and values the kind of faculty development that results from research and publication. I received several grants from California State University sources of money and released time from teaching which enabled me to further my work on African American language. A recent generous award from the Dean of the College of Arts Letters and Social Sciences was applied directly to the work of completing the manuscript for this book.

I acknowledge the continuing encouragement and help of colleagues in the field of linguistics, especially those who maintain contact through dinner meetings at professional conferences, and list-serve messages, and have gone by different names, including the Committee of Linguists of African Descent, and more recently, TOPS. Finally, I acknowledge the singular importance of my collaboration with Nick Faraclas which culminated in our frequently cited article. (DeBose and Faraclas 1993)

Charles DeBose, April 8, 2005

Introduction

After the Egyptian and Indian, the Greek and Roman, the
Teuton and Mongolian, the Negro is a sort of seventh son,
born with a veil, and gifted with second-sight in this American
world, – a world which yields him no true self-consciousness,
but only lets him see himself through the revelation of the
other world. It is a peculiar sensation, this double-consciousness, this sense of always looking at one's self through the
eyes of others, of measuring one's soul by the tape of a world
that looks on in amused contempt and pity. One ever feels his
two-ness, an American, a Negro; two souls, two thoughts, two
unreconciled strivings; two warring ideals in one dark body...
W. E. B. DuBois, 1999.

Academic scholarship is typically motivated by an urge to explore new
frontiers of knowledge, and guided by a time-honored tradition that
values *objectivity* – that is, a point of view on the subject matter as free as
possible of bias – totally unaffected by myth, misconception, hyperbole,
and other "contaminating" features of "unscientific" thought. Such was
undoubtedly the primary incentive for linguists who, in the 1960s,
began to produce books, articles and other academic material on a
variety of language called *Black English*.[1] An unavoidable source of bias,

---

[1] It would be more precise to say that Black English came to be the generic label
for a variety that has been referred to by several different labels, corresponding
in part to changes in the preferred group name for African Americans, e.g.,
Nonstandard Negro English; Negro dialect; and more recently, African American
Vernacular English. An in-depth exploration of these naming practices is undertaken in chapter four.

however, which applies to the case at hand, is the stigma associated with membership in a marginalized social group.

According to the American Heritage Dictionary of the English language, the noun *stigma*, related etymologically to the Greek word for "tatoo mark," has expanded in meaning over time to signify "a mark burned on a criminal or slave; a brand;" and more generally, "a mark or token of infamy, disgrace or reproach." The verb *to stigmatize*, is defined as "To characterize or brand as disgraceful or ignominious." (Morris et al. ed. 1976)

The approach to African American language developed in the following pages takes, as a primary point of departure, frank acknowledgment of the fact that it is stigmatized – and furthermore, that it is part and parcel of the general stigmatization of African American identity in American society. In calling attention to that fact, I further contend that the stigmatization of Black American identity has functioned historically to exclude persons of African descent from full participation in American life. The stigmatization in question is so deeply embedded in the fabric of American society that its full significance has tended to escape the attention of scholars of African American language.

The social location factor

W. E. B. DuBois, in his inimitable way, uses the metaphor of a "veil," in his classic formulation of African American identity where he characterizes "the Negro" as "a seventh son, born with a veil, and gifted with second sight in this American world." When scholars from the dominant social group engage in academic study of some aspect of the Black experience, the existence of the veil may well be an insurmountable obstacle to objectivity. Such scholars are limited, by virtue of their *social location*, in their capacity to know what it is like to experience, in DuBois' words, "this sense of always looking at one's self through the eyes of others, of measuring one's soul by the tape of a world that looks on in amused contempt and pity."

In order for the scholar of African American language to attain the pinnacle of true objectivity, he or she must not only rise above the emotions of contempt, pity, amusement and such, but, further, must empathize sufficiently with the duality of selfhood through which the emotions must pass, before they replicate the essence of Black identity. In recent years, a growing number of scholars take the position that objectivity is an unattainable ideal. The best that one can do, in the view of such scholars, is to announce one's social location "up front," so to speak, so that readers and critics may take that into account in evaluating the claims of a given piece of scholarship. In that spirit, I divulge my identity as an African American with Southern roots, who spent many of my formative years in an all-Black housing project in the urban North. I further claim to be a native speaker of the variety known as Black English.

The issue of social location and how it affects the objectivity of academic work is informed by the sociology of knowledge – which affords theoretical status to the distinction between academic knowledge and the "real world" of everyday experience. A fundamental claim of *the sociology of knowledge* is that what ordinary men and women take for granted as "real" is *socially-constructed*. According to the sociologist W. I. Thomas,

Things that people believe are real are real in their consequences.

Research conducted from such a perspective seeks, thus, to explicate how knowledge of the "real world" is maintained through the collective efforts of members of society. Berger and Luckmann (1966) develop a framework for investigation of "the reality of everyday life" as having its origins in the "thoughts and actions" of "ordinary members of society," and maintained by them as real. Berger and Luckmann formulate their "primary task" as

to clarify the foundations of knowledge in everyday life, to wit, the objectivations of subjective processes (and meanings) by which the intersubjective commonsense world is constructed. (Berger and Luckmann 1966: 19, 20)

A crucial difference exists between academic knowledge and everyday experience in terms of the type and amount of conscious and deliberate thought that is devoted to questioning and critical analysis of the crucial variables according to which reality is constructed. The characterization of everyday experience as "taken-for-granted" is a fair indication of the absence of critical examination of that aspect of the world in which we find ourselves. Aspects of that experience which might involve unfair or unequal distribution of rights and privileges are just as likely to escape being submitted to critical examination, if it is part of what is taken-for-granted as just the way that things are.

The privileged position of males in American society was seen as so obvious that the Founding Fathers were able to proclaim liberty in the words "all men are created equal," without seeing the blatant contradictions in their own behavior of owning slaves and denying equal rights to women. Most Americans today take it for granted that Standard English is supreme, and nonstandard varieties of English are inherently "bad." In fact, such beliefs lie at the core of language policies presently upheld by law and custom in the United States, based on *the hegemony of Standard English*.

Hegemony

Gramsci (1971) defines hegemony as a function of "civil society;" and one of two ways in which the dominant group of a society maintains its dominant position. The other is "direct domination." In other words, in addition to the coercive means of state power used by ruling groups to maintain direct control of society; hegemony is exercised through ideas, attitudes, myths, and values, perpetuated through education and socialization.

Gramsci's notion of hegemony is implicit in the current practice of military strategists who characterize the "pacification" stage of a military conquest as a struggle for the "hearts and minds" of the conquered. Hegemonic ideas and values often function to legitimate the existing social order by providing justifications for inequalities in the distribution of social goods. In the realm of lifestyle and culture, the customs and practices of elite groups and individuals come to symbolize the benefits of membership in the elite and to serve as desirable objects of persons striving to attain elite status. When a particular language, or way of speaking the common language of a society, is associated with persons of elite status, the ability to speak the language, and to speak it "correctly," may serve a legitimating function. That is, the superior position of the dominant group is justified by their "proper" speech; and the subordinate position of marginalized groups is legitimated by the characterization of their language in such pejorative terms as "poor," "slovenly," "broken," "bastardized," and "corrupt."

Throughout the history of racist oppression of African Americans, hegemonic ideas have functioned to legitimate the unequal position of Black persons, and reconcile it with prevailing democratic ideals. In slave society, direct domination often took the form of a whip, in the hand of the overseer; or barking bloodhounds, hot on the heels of runaway slaves – while hegemony was exercised through the power of words like "savage," "primitive" and "heathen," used in conjunction with the presupposition that being "civilized" is a prerequisite to full participation in American democracy. After emancipation, the continued subordination of Blacks to the lower tier of a color caste system was justified by the stigmatization of key features of Black identity, including language. In the present Post Civil Rights era, the stigmatization of Blackness as a rationale for denial of full and equal status in American democracy has outlived its purpose. Nevertheless, the idea that African American language is tantamount to "Bad English" remains embedded in the hearts and minds of the public.

Visceral reactions to nonstandard language

The association of the idea of "Bad English" with low social status is so firmly entrenched in the hearts and minds of the American people that the mere presence of certain features in a person's language is sufficient to elicit a strong and visceral reaction of disapproval.

The adjective *visceral*, derived from *viscera*, a plural form of the Latin noun, *viscus*, "body organ," retains the sense of an intensely emotional reaction to an experience, as opposed to a cool, thoughtful, rational or intellectual response. It is equivalent to the more common term *gut*, especially when used to describe the basis of a feeling as a *gut reaction*. A noteworthy characteristic of commonsense – as opposed to academic – knowledge is its visceral nature, the sense in which it is experienced by the whole body. It is *intuition* in the sense of "the act or faculty of knowing without the use of rational processes; immediate cognition," and "[k]nowledge so gained; a sense of something not evident or deducible." (Morris et al. ed. 1976) Discussions of intuition by my students inevitably bring out the idea of "gut reaction," as well as the assertion that it is something that "you just know."

The tendency for Americans to react viscerally to nonstandard language in general, and African American language in particular, is based on the commonsense notion that it consists of mistakes committed by persons attempting to speak "correctly." Such a characterization of nonstandard language happens to be at odds with the current state of linguistic knowledge, according to which all human language is systematic and rule-governed.

The conflicting perspectives of linguistics and everyday experience are boldly highlighted by the claims of academic scholarship on African American language. A dynamic tension between the academic construct of Black English, and the equivalent real world construct of "bad English" has been a recurring source of controversies, the

Grandmother of which is the so-called *Ebonics firestorm*. It is of such historic proportions that it cannot be ignored in an undertaking of the nature of this book.

Recalling the firestorm

On December 18 1996, the public School Board of Oakland California passed a resolution recognizing a variety of language referred to as Ebonics as a language, the public reaction to which has frequently been described as a "firestorm of controversy." In the days and weeks following the resolution, the level of public interest expressed in the subject of Ebonics was nothing short of phenomenal. It dominated the discussion of radio talk shows and late night TV programs; newspaper headlines and the nightly news.

Colleges and universities put on workshops and forums on the subject. An Ebonics Forum at my home institution, California State University, Hayward, drew a very large audience that included news reporters, TV cameramen, children transported in busloads from local elementary and secondary schools, and a wide cross-section of the surrounding community. Everybody from the High and Mighty to the Average Joe weighed in on the subject. The Reverend Jesse Jackson characterized it as "ungrammatical;" and the poet Maya Angelou called it "an embarrassment." When guests at a dinner party in Washington, D.C. that my wife and I attended, found out that I am a linguist, the discussion shifted to Ebonics, pitting my expertise against the experiences, feelings and mother wit of several guests.

Interest in Ebonics continued at a high level as late as August 1997, when I presented a seminar entitled "Ebonics 101," on the campus of the University of South Carolina, Columbia, at the request of the Chair of African American Studies. The turnout was so great that the event had to be moved from the lecture hall in which it was originally scheduled to a small auditorium that could barely accommodate the standing-room-only crowd.

I could give many more examples of the Ebonics firestorm, which document the considerable extent to which it consisted of visceral reactions to the incongruous juxtaposition of what is commonly known as "bad" or substandard English, slang, or by some comparably pejorative term, with the idea of somehow using it in the classroom – as a subject, if not medium, of instruction. Either way, for the average American – accustomed to experiencing the language variety in question in a variety of ways: as the medium of performance of ethnic humor, in the lyrics of a

Hip Hop record, in overheard conversations of baggy-pant-wearing young men in animated street corner conversation, or as evidence that the persons from whose mouth it emanates is poor or uneducated – the idea of "Ebonics in the classroom" is patently ridiculous.

Language planning perspective

While a good part of the Ebonics firestorm consisted of visceral reactions, magnified by international media exposure, to what was perceived as an incongruous proposal to use "bad English" in the classroom, there are other aspects of it that are not so easy to explain, and that is the content of the Ebonics resolution itself, which, among other things, recognizes Ebonics as a language. The actions of School Board members, linguists and other persons who came out in support of the resolution also resist easy explanation. I devote a good deal of the following pages to what purports to be a principled and comprehensive account of what I call the Ebonics Phenomenon, which I characterize metaphorically as an iceberg. The firestorm itself is treated as the tip of the iceberg, while the totality of the phenomenon is analyzed as a case study of language planning.

Readers familiar with Black English scholarship may find it surprising that I include it as an integral part of the metaphorical iceberg. My rationale for including it is discussed in the next section where I provide a number of examples of ongoing concerns of Black English scholarship that qualify as language planning issues. At this introductory stage of the discussion, I define language planning simply as *language change that occurs as a consequence of conscious and deliberate decision-making*. I not only include change in the internal structure of a language, such as the coining of new words or creation of a writing system, but also change in the attitudes of users and ways in which their languages are typically used. Change of the first kind is known as *corpus planning*, whereas the latter kind of change is called *status planning*.

A familiar example of corpus planning is the recent proliferation of gender-neutral occupational titles, such as *firefighter* and *flight attendant* to replace such traditional terms as *fireman* and *stewardess*, in response to demands of the feminist movement. The word *Kwanzaa*, appropriated from KiSwahili by Dr. Maulana Karenga, in creating the Afrocentric holiday of the same name, is a noteworthy example of language change resulting from the conscious and deliberate action of a particular individual. It qualifies as such as language planning.

Language planning issues of Black English scholarship

Linguists engaged in the academic study of African American language, by virtue of their recognition of its systematic and rule-governed nature, and publication of the findings of research based on that premise, are engaged in status planning. As a consequence of linguistic scholarship, the commonsense belief that Black language consists of mistakes and failure, has been superceded by knowledge to the effect that it is correct according to the rules of a different grammar. The traditional status of "Bad English," and the implication that it is inferior, has been replaced by that of a *dialect*, in the technical sense used in linguistics which simply means one of several different, but equal, varieties of the same language. There are ongoing debates among scholars concerning a number of disputed claims about the nature of African American language, including its classification as a dialect of English, and those are taken up further below. My immediate aim is to support the basic point that it merits study as a case of language planning.

In characterizing the entire body of scholarship on African American language as a case of language planning, I acknowledge that the linguists involved in it have not considered themselves to be engaged in language planning. The point is made, however, that their work qualifies as such, in a manner that becomes clear when attention is called to specific ongoing actions and behaviors in which Black English scholars have been engaged, which are, in essence, language planning issues.

Corpus planning issues

One type of decision-making that repeatedly thrusts itself upon scholars of African American language, and which, to that extent, qualifies as corpus planning, involves questions about how to represent tokens of Black speech and language on the printed page in a manner that faithfully represents salient features of pronunciation. The most common response has been to use conventional English spelling modified in accordance with established practices of literary writers faced with the need to represent dialectal or vernacular speech in print. A common example of such *modified conventional orthography* is the use of apostrophes to represent contracted and abbreviated word forms. The casual pronunciation of *talking*, for instance, is commonly spelled *talkin*.

One problem with the use of modified conventional English orthography to represent casual or dialectal speech is its lack of standardization, in the sense of consistency. A cursory review of the literature on Black English reveals many examples of spelling decisions that have been thrust upon scholars in the course of reporting the findings of their research, and the ways in which they have dealt with them. Labov explicitly characterizes as "dialect spelling, " *inte'ested*, "interested", and *Ca'ol*, "Carol," cited as examples of "r-lessness" in the speech of informants for a study carried out in Harlem, New York. (Labov 1972: 14) In the same article, Labov uses dialect spelling to represent "[v]arious forms derived from *going to*" which "are quite frequent" in Black language "*gonna, gon', 'on', gwin*, and with *I, I'm'na* and *I'ma* [amənə, amə]." (25) His use of phonetic symbols to more precisely represent the last two variants calls attention to a potential trade-off between precision and reader-friendliness that a scholar must consider when discussing Black English research with diverse audiences. It also raises the question of why researchers tend to opt for dialect spelling, notwithstanding its imprecision and lack of standardization.

Fasold and Wolfram discuss the form *gonna* in a section of an article on linguistic features of Black English dealing with how future time is expressed. While they use the same spelling of *gonna* as Labov in the above-cited article, they write the reduced variant, which Labov spells *gon'*, without an apostrophe. They note that in Black English "there are three reductions not possible in standard English, *mana* (*I'mana go*), *mon* (*I'mon go*), and *ma* (*I'ma go*). When the subject is something other than *I*," they continue, "Negro dialect may give the reduced form *gon* (*He gon go*)." (Fasold and Wolfram 1975: 68) Another spelling issue raised by the form *gon* is the difficulty of modifying conventional spelling in a manner that accurately represents how it is pronounced. Using a phonetic alphabet, the sequence of sounds that occur in the pronunciation of *gon* can be precisely described as beginning with a voiced velar stop, represented by the symbol /g/, followed by the nasalized vowel, /õ/, i.e., /gõ/.

A reader unfamiliar with Southern American English, and the dialect spelling conventions applied to representation of its typical forms in print, would probably be mislead by the "n" in the spelling of *gon* to assume that the form is pronounced like *gone*. The full set of options to be considered, therefore, in decisions about the spelling of African American language, should not only include modified conventional, or, "dialect" spelling, with and without the traditional use of apostrophes; but also, the use, whenever needed, of symbols of the phonetic alphabet to make explicit the pronunciation of forms that cannot otherwise be adequately represented on the printed page.

The question of how African American language should be spelled is one of several specific, often interlocking, issues discussed in the following pages that qualify as language planning issues. The variation in apostrophe usage just noted in the spelling of the clipped form *gon'* calls attention to another language planning issue that interfaces with that of spelling. A central feature of the stigmatization of Black language is its characterization as failure or inability to speak Standard English. The use of apostrophes serves to reinforce that attitude by suggesting that whatever is replaced by an apostrophe is something that should be present in the "correct" form of the word or expression. A conscious decision to avoid apostrophe use in the spelling of African American language forms may be seen as a language-planning decision insofar as it seeks to affect one of the traditional ways in which African American language is used, i.e., to stigmatize African American identity.

The issue of how Black language should be spelled also interfaces with the issue of how its basic grammatical structure is best characterized; and whether or not it has the same system of rules as other varieties of American English. The argument that it has the same grammar, characterizes *gonna*, as a variant of the Standard English *be going to* construction. One of the most intensely studied grammatical features of African American language, known as "copula deletion" (Labov 1969) and by other terms discussed below, is marked by the frequent absence of present tense forms the copula/auxiliary forms *be*, illustrated by examples 1–4.

1. *She nice.*
2. *They at home.*
3. *He my brother.*
4. *We dancing.*

Labov and other adherents to the "same system" view of Black English grammar invoke a copula-deletion rule to account for the absence of any trace of *is* or *are*; not only in sentences like 1–4, but also in sentences like (5) and (6)

5. *She gonna meet us at the Mall.* "She is going to meet us at the Mall."
6. *We gonna miss the train.* "We are going to miss the train."

Such scholars – in crafting arguments against the position that Black English has a different grammar than Standard American English – find it significant that although the copula forms *is* and *are* rarely co-occur with the future marker *gon*, the copula is practically always present, at least in the contracted form of *am*, spelled *'m*, when *gon* occurs with the first person singular subject pronoun, *I*, as in

> 7. *If I don't hurry, I'm'on miss the train.*
> "If I don't hurry, I'm going to miss the train."

The second apostrophe in 7, represents the initial /g/ which the rules of Black English permit to be suppressed when *gon* follows *I'm*. The specific focus on the presence or absence of forms of *be* and its relationship to whether or not the subject is *I*, is motivated by the generalization that wherever Standard English can contract the copula/auxiliary *be*, Black English can delete it (Labov 1969) One acknowledged exception to that generalization is that the contracted form *'m* is generally present under conditions where the contracted forms *'s* and *'re* are frequently absent in Black English sentences, e.g., sentences 1–4 above. The contracted form *'s* is also rarely "deleted" from the pronoun forms *it's*, *that's*, and *what's*. Thus, while it is common to hear an African American say, *We dancing*, the same person would never say **I dancing*, but rather, *I'm dancing*. (The asterisk is used in linguistic argumentation to indicate that a cited string of words is ungrammatical, in the technical sense of not sounding right to a native speaker) Likewise, the sentence, *She nice*, is acceptable Black English with the copula "deleted." Deletion of the *'s* from *It's nice* or *That's nice*, however, results in an ungrammatical string; i.e., **It nice, *That nice*.

The specific issue of whether or not the copula/auxiliary *be* is in the underlying structure of sentences like 1–4 is a language planning issue insofar as it relates to the more general question, *What is the grammar of Black English?* When scholars such as Labov, Fasold and Wolfram speak of the grammar of Black English, what they seem to have in mind is *a systematic and exhaustive account of the ways in which Black English diverges from Standard American English in pronunciation, vocabulary and grammar*. In existing descriptions of that kind, each point of divergence from the Standard is referred to as a *feature*, and given a name, such as r-lessness, or copula deletion. Another such feature is known as habitual or invariant *be* (Fasold 1969) illustrated by examples 8, and 9.

> 8. *Most mornings, they be at home.*
> 9. *Every time she call, we be dancing.*

The action or event expressed by the invariant *be* feature is understood as not occurring at the present time, but habitually, or on occasions. The action of "dancing" expressed in sentence 5 is understood as occurring at the present time, whereas in sentence 10, the time frame for our "dancing" is the recurring occasion when whoever "she" is calls. Another feature commonly attributed to Black English is illustrated by the verb *call* in example 9. It is the absence of the suffix *–s* that attaches to present tense verb forms in other varieties of American English in agreement with a third-person singular subject, e.g., *she calls*.

The so-called lack of subject-verb agreement in the verb *call* in example (9) is sometimes seen in the speech of working class Americans of other races, although its occurrence tends to be restricted to special constructions such as the negated form *don't*, in sentences like 10.

10. *He don't have no change.*

In African American language, however, any verb may occur without the *–s* suffix – including positive forms of the auxiliary *do*, as in (11) and the main verb of a clause as in (12).

11. *Do she still smoke?*
12. *She smoke when she at home.*

The past tense–*ed* suffix also tends to be absent from verb forms under conditions where it would be present in other varieties, e.g.,

13. *I cook a mess of greens yesterday.*
"I cooked a measured quantity of greens yesterday."

The tendency for the *–ed* suffix to be absent where it would be expected to occur in Standard American English is related to a feature of African American pronunciation, commonly described as a tendency for final consonant clusters to be "reduced" or "simplified," with the result that pairs of words such as *lost: loss*; and *ask: ass* tend to be pronounced the same. The same process may affect a past tense verb formed by addition of *–ed* to a verb like *cook* that ends in a consonant, in which cases the suffix consists of a single sound, /t/, and the resulting past tense form ends in a consonant cluster, /kt/. Such facts have led some scholars to claim that the *–ed* suffix is present in the underlying structure of the verb in sentences such as 12, but has been deleted from the surface structure as a consequence of the final consonant cluster simplification feature.

One way in which contributions to such an account constitute language planning is the fact that once a given feature has been identified and described, the mere naming of it has implications for ongoing issues such as the extent to which Black English is a "separate system." (Labov 1972: 36–64)

Scholars such as Labov, in arguing that Black English is *not* a separate system, refer to the variable absence of present tense forms of the copula/auxiliary *be* as "copula deletion." Scholars who contend that it is a different system tend to use a different name, such as "zero copula," or "copula absence." The selection of particular names for the features selected for inclusion in the grammar of Black English also qualifies as language planning. Insofar as the names have a tendency to evoke attitudes of one kind or another toward African American language, they have implications for status planning as well as corpus planning.

There is a notable tendency for feature names to employ words that construe it as the absence of something present in Standard English. All of the terms for the copula feature currently in widespread use include a word of that nature, i.e., "deletion," "zero," "absence." Indeed, all of the above-listed features, and others not yet discussed, are similarly named, "r-lessness," "l-lessness," "final consonant clusters simplification," etc. Even the prefix *in-*, meaning "not" in the first word of the feature label, "invariant *be*" is a subtle instance of the tendency to characterize Black English as the absence or opposite of what is normal or expected in non-stigmatized varieties.

Status planning issues

The work of describing the internal structure of African American language, by whatever means, clearly qualifies as corpus planning. The very idea that Black English has grammatical structure is unprecedented, however, and the antithesis of the traditional characterization of it as Bad English. The mere act of endowing it with grammar, therefore, not only affects its corpus, but also its status; particularly, the manner in which it traditionally functions in the stigmatization of African American identity.

One aspect of the status of African American language that is clearly language planning involves ongoing decision-making regarding what it should be called. The term *Black English* is one of a variety of names that have been proposed and used by scholars since the academic study of African American language began in the sixties. Most of the names conform to the model of combining the currently preferred group name with "English," or the name of a particular language type such as "dialect." The term "Negro dialect," in the above quote from Fasold and Wolfram (1975) is typical. An indication of how much the naming of the variety was subject to conscious decision-making is found in the preface to a 1969 work in which Wolfram reveals his inner turmoil on the issue,

> Somewhat apologetically, I have used the term "Nonstandard Negro English" to refer to the linguistic system of working-class Negroes. In other publications, I have used the term "Black English", first suggested to me by my colleague Ralph W. Fasold. (Wolfram 1969: X)

Inasmuch as the various names by which African American language is known are the result of conscious decisions of scholars, the decision-making processes by which they are formed qualify as status planning. To grasp the full significance of this fact, it should be remembered that at the same time that scholars were debating whether to call the variety "Black English" or some other name; none of the proposed names meant anything to most African Americans.

Several years ago, when I undertook a pilot study of African American language – and sought to involve friends and acquaintances as sources of tape-recorded data – it was necessary to explain the goal of the study to them in a roundabout way that did not use the term "Black English." Instead of asking our prospective informants to "talk some Black English," we had to say,

> *We're not interested in "proper" English. We just want you to "talk normal."*

In fact, one informant is heard on tape saying to a visitor, who happens to drop in on a taping session,

> *Come on in! We just in here talkin normal.*

Since that time, a different name for Black language has caught on, and virtually become a household word. Were I to find myself in a similar situation today, I could ask a similar group of African

Americans to, *Talk some Ebonics*, and they would know exactly what I meant.

The names Ebonics, and Black English, correspond to two different academic approaches to the study of African American language, i.e., *Black English studies*, and *Ebonics scholarship*. The main contributors to Black English studies are linguists, whereas Ebonics scholars represent a variety of academic disciplines, and are united by a critical and Afrocentric approach to the subject; an approach that predates by over two decades the public controversy ignited by the Oakland School Board resolution.

Few people watching the Ebonics controversy unfold were aware of the fact that the name *Ebonics* had existed, in an embryonic state, since January 1973 when it was adopted by a group of Black scholars attending a conference in Saint Louis on "cognitive and language development of the black child." The psychologist R. L. Williams is credited with having created the word *Ebonics* as a blend of "Ebony" and "phonics," intended to evoke the idea of "black sounds." In the introduction to a collection of articles on the subject, Williams describes the immediate context in which the Ebonics concept crystallized:

A significant incident occurred... . . The black conferees were so critical of the work on [Black English] done by white researchers, many of whom happened to be present, that they decided to caucus among themselves and define black language from a black perspective. (Williams ed. 1975 ii).

One of a number of issues that Ebonics scholars have with orthodox Black English scholarship is its characterization of Black English as a nonstandard dialect. A typical way that Ebonics scholars express that concern is by insisting that Ebonics is not the same thing as Nonstandard English. (c.f. Williams and Brantley 1975) The details of the argument are discussed further below. One point of a general nature, that is relevant to the present discussion of status planning issues is a claim advanced by some Ebonics scholars to the effect that the linguistic repertoire of the African American community includes two different varieties (in addition to Standard English) corresponding to the names Ebonics, and Black English. The opposing view of Black English scholars tends to characterize the African American linguistic repertoire as *bidialectal*, further characterizing the two component varieties Black and Standard English as coexisting in a pattern of *class stratification*.

The linguistic repertoire of a speech community offers its members a set of choices in the form of different languages, or different varieties of the same language, that may be selected for various situations of use. It may be characterized informally by the analogy of a wardrobe. A typical American would think of a tuxedo as appropriate for wearing to a formal ball, and blue jeans as appropriate for a barbecue. The *incongruity* of wearing clothing that is inappropriate for a given the situation, e.g., wearing a tux to a barbecue, calls attention to the act, and elicits predictable reactions of shock, humor, amazement, and such.

Two aspects of African American language that are at the center of ongoing status planning issues are its *typological status* and its *social function*. The question frequently raised during the Ebonics firestorm as to whether the variety is a dialect, or a separate language is a question about its typological status. The controversy over its typological classification in Black English literature as a nonstandard dialect was mentioned above. The decision of Black English scholars to classify it thusly constitutes status planning insofar as it involves change from the traditional pejorative characterization of Black language as "bad," or substandard English. One other relevant aspect of the typological status of African American language, which is at the center of ongoing discussions of its origin, is the issue of whether or not it was at some earlier time a creole. The question about whether or not Ebonics should be taught in the schools concerns its social function.

Linguists have developed several useful and interesting ways of analyzing the social function of language varieties. One is by matching the ways in which a variety corresponds to one or more of the categories on a list of language functions, such as: *official, religious, literary, group, medium of education, school subject*, etc. (Stewart 1968)Another approach that seems well suited for expressing relevant dimensions of use of African American language is based on the notion of *societal domains*. According to such a model African American language is often characterized as normal and acceptable in such domains of use as Black home and community life, the church and the performing arts; but unacceptable – due to its stigmatized status – in the spheres of business, government and education.

While the use of African American language is normal and acceptable within the African American speech community, speaking in a markedly standard way – known traditionally as "talkin proper," and in recent times as talking "bougie" – has the effect of distancing oneself from the in-group. A student in a modern English grammar class that I recently taught, confided that although her family commonly speaks

"Ebonics," she found herself making a conscious effort to speak "correct" English; an effort that provoked her sister to ask her in all seriousness,

> *How come you talkin all bougie?* "Why are you speaking in such a Bourgeois manner?"

The complementary roles of Standard English and African American, highlighted by the above example are enforced by visceral reactions such as that of the students' sister to incongruities in the use of a variety with a particular situational context.

The number one question of the Great Ebonics debate, "Do you think Ebonics should be taught in the classroom?" may be seen as a reaction to the incongruity of African American language, in the minds of many persons, with the domain of education – as well as a challenge to explain to the questioner how anyone in their right mind could propose such a thing.

Black English scholars have been involved in several ways in actions and decisions that involve the use of African American language in the Domain of education. Scholars who hold faculty positions at colleges and universities began to infuse the findings of Black English research into the content of the courses they teach, and even launch new courses on the subject of African American language. The decision to offer college courses on Black English qualifies as a status planning decision in that it expands the list of societal functions of Black language to include that of school subject.

Some Black English scholars enthusiastically endorsed a proposal for using so-called *dialect readers* to facilitate the teaching of initial reading skills. (Baratz and Shuy eds 1969) The fact that the proposal never got the crucial backing of Black parents and community leaders, necessary for them to have any chance of success, however, speaks to the incongruity – in the minds of many persons – of African American language with the functions of school subject and medium of instruction. The proposal qualifies nonetheless as language planning insofar as it sought to use Black English in an unprecedented way, by producing children's textbooks written in it.

In the foregoing discussion, several instances of conscious and deliberate decision-making have been identified that affect either the internal structure of African American language, or the ways in which it is used in society, and qualify as such as language planning. They are summarized on Table I.1.

Table I.1   Summary of Language Planning Issues

Corpus planning issues
How should African American language be spelled?
• Modified conventional orthography
• Phonemic alphabet
• Consequences of apostrophe usage for stigmatization

How is its grammatical structure best characterized?
• List of features representing points of divergence from Standard English
• Autonomous, self-contained system, described without reference to Standard English

Status planning issues
What typological categories best describe African American language?
• Dialect/vernacular
• Separate language

In what situations is the use of African American language acceptable?
• Black home and community
• Literature and performing arts

In what situations is the use of African American language stigmatized?
• School subject/medium of instruction
• Business and government

What should African American language be called?
• Ebonics
• Black English

Those issues are further examined in the next section, in which I focus on issues of language policy.

Language policy issues

The terms "language planning" and "language policy" are frequently employed in the literature in ways that are, if not synonymous, at least similar enough that they may be used interchangeably as it best suits the stylistic interests of a writer at a given moment. In the present context, I use the term language policy in reference to issues that go beyond the scope of the definition of language planning, given above, as planned change, and raise questions in the area of law and ethics as they pertain to the rights and privileges to which speakers of a variety of language are entitled under the laws and administrative regulations of a given social order, and how such concerns relate to goals and objectives in the sphere of education with respect to speakers of the various language varieties maintained in that society's linguistic repertoire.

Some of the major language planning issues embedded in Black English scholarship were reviewed in the previous section, sub-classified as corpus planning and status planning issues. A pervasive concern, or underlying issue, is the stigmatization of African American identity, and the manner in which it is maintained through the construction of Black language as "Bad English." A dynamic tension between the "real world" construct of Bad English, and the construction of Black English as systematic and rule-governed, characterizes ongoing dialogue between linguists and members of the general public. The tension is resolved when someone "gets it." That is, they get the linguists' point that there is nothing wrong with African American language.

People who are still at the "don't get it" stage may react to the experience of being introduced to African American Vernacular English (or AAVE) as the variety is currently known, with head-scratching confusion. Those who eventually get around to reacting verbally may pose a rhetorical question of the form, *"Do you mean to say that I should accept this kind of language coming from students in my classroom?"* At that point it is clear that material presented with the aim of describing the linguistic features of a language variety that may be spoken by some students in some American classrooms, so that teachers will be able to do their jobs in a manner that is informed by the current state of linguistic knowledge, has had the effect of raising a different concern, the *policy question* of *What should be done about African American language, in the classroom, and in society?*

As the discussion focuses on the policy question, typical audiences express a great deal of concern about the fact that African American language is stigmatized, although the word "stigma" is rarely spoken. Frequent references tend to be made, however, to the "real world," and how important it is to be able to speak Standard English is a job interview situation. Persons making such references to the real world, and the hypothetical job interview requirements would probably agree, if pressed, that what most concerns them about the real world is the fact that African American language is stigmatized as Bad English. They would probably not want to go on record as in favor of the right of employers to discriminate against job applicants on the basis of their dialect, or grant preference to applicants who speak non-stigmatized varieties of the common language. Nevertheless, such concerns translate into strong and overwhelming support for the current policy in which Standard English reigns supreme.

The crucial variables

A general account is developed in the following pages of how contrasting orientations to the policy question tend to correspond to the contrasting academic approaches of Ebonics and Black English scholarship. A key explanatory concept is the above-mentioned social location hypothesis. Within that framework, attention is focused on a tendency for scholars of African American language, and members of the general public as well, to deal with what I call *the crucial variables*, i.e., the *stigmatization of African American language*; and *the Hegemony of Standard English*, in predictable ways, characterized in the following discussion as policy options, with specific reference to the theoretical construct of hegemony:

1) *Active support* of the Hegemony of Standard English;
2) *Acquiescence* to it; and
3) *Resistance* to it while calling for Full recognition.

In the world of everyday experience, the construction of Standard English as superior is supported by the stigmatization of African American language as consisting of mistakes and random deviations from what is expected to occur in Standard English. For uncritical members of the general public, the crucial variables function to justify the unequal treatment and marginal status typically afforded to speakers of Black language. For linguists, however, the stigmatization of African American language, and its role in supporting the Hegemony of Standard English has to be weighed against its incompatibility with the current state of linguistic knowledge.

The policy option of full recognition of African American language is strongly supported by the consensus of linguistic scholars that to be human is to be a native speaker of a particular dialect of some particular language. Furthermore, linguists hold that all dialects are equally suited to the demands of the societies in which they exist, and that, to such an extent, all languages, and all dialects of such languages are equal. One particular aspect of the equality of dialects is their systematic and rule governed nature. The stigmatization of African American language as failure to perform according to the rules of a different language variety, Standard English, and the implication that it has no rules of its own, is totally contrary to the current state of linguistic knowledge.

In view of the fact that the current state of linguistic knowledge effectively refutes both of the foundational ideas of the hegemony of

Standard English, i.e. – the stigmatization of African American language; and the superiority of Standard English – one might predict that linguists would come out strongly in support of a policy of full recognition. As a matter of fact, however, the most typical response of linguists has been to opt for what I have previously characterized as a policy of limited recognition, and characterize here as acquiescence to the Hegemony of Standard English.

A working hypothesis, introduced here and further discussed in the following pages and chapters, is that the tendency for Black English scholars to opt for a policy of acquiescence to Standard English is, motivated by a sincere commitment to academic objectivity, and a corresponding obligation not to cross the boundary from objective scholarship to advocacy. "Is it the my role?" a scholar might sincerely ask, "to condemn the way in which Black language is constructed in the real world, and actively campaign for its recognition as a language in its own right? Or am I required to maintain a detached and unobtrusive perspective, stating the facts and leaving it to prophets and firebrands to condemn any evils and injustices my research might bring to light." It is the kind of ethical dilemma faced by medical researchers who attempt to advance knowledge of a dread disease by withholding treatment to patients in a control group whose lives might be saved by it.

The ethical conflicts sometimes faced by scholars engaged in the study of phenomena that harbor social inequalities can be exacerbated by the social location of the scholar, inasmuch as the principles and practices in which the inequality resides are part and parcel of the taken-for-granted commonsense world of everyday experience. Such inequality tends to pass "beneath the radar screen" of critical analysis to which scholars submit crucial variables of an academic investigation.

In addition to the points just noted about aspects of the social location of Black English scholars that may explain their policy choices, the social location hypothesis is further supported by a strong tendency for Ebonics scholars to favor a different policy option. The typically marginalized social location, and Afrocentric perspective, of such scholars accounts for a marked tendency on their part to resist the hegemony of Standard English, further characterized by an interest in African American language – *not as an end in itself* – *but as an means of cultural revitalization.*

For present purposes *cultural revitalization* may be defined simply as the reconstruction of negatively defined identity traits in positive terms that imbue them with a sense of dignity and worth. A simple example of it is the slogan "Black is Beautiful," promoted by the Black Freedom Movement of the Sixties, to counter the traditional construction of Black identity in negative terms. Another is the above-mentioned Kwanzaa holiday, insofar as it is the outgrowth of a project to promote an Afrocentric alternative for high celebration during the traditional American holiday season, imbued with rituals explicitly designed to elicit feelings of pride and dignity in persons of African descent.

In general, Ebonics scholarship may be characterized by a central interest in the implications of Black language for the construction of African American identity, an interest which contrasts markedly with the above-noted concern of Black English scholars with the implications of Black English for the employability of its speakers. Such contrasting interests and concerns are amenable to further analysis through the lens of DuBois' model of double consciousness; a model which serves not only as a useful frame of reference for studying Black identity but also as the basis for a more definitive characterization of cultural revitalization.

Within the theoretical framework sketched in above, contrasting positions that the two camps have taken, on a number of crucial issues are highlighted, e.g., what should African American language be called? How should it be classified typologically? And whether or not Black English and Ebonics are different words for the same thing. The willingness of certain Black English scholars to acquiesce to the hegemony of standard English as part of the "real world" as well as the tendency just noted for Ebonics scholars to adopt a policy position of resistance, rather than acquiescence to the hegemony of Standard English add up to strong support for the claim that a scholar's position on the policy question is a function of his or her social location.

I do not fault my fellow linguists for their social location, or its possible effect upon their perception of what is real and normal. Nor do I wish to focus the following discussion on advocacy of my preferred policy position, but, mainly, to make a novel contribution to the academic study of language planning based on the issues raised by the case of Black English scholarship. I draw freely from my own experience as a participant-observer in the phenomenon under study, in which I have, when called upon to state my position on the policy question, expressed my preference for a policy of full recognition. The basic structure of my argument has been to call attention to the overwhelming testimony of linguistic knowledge to the effect that there is nothing wrong with African American language; as well as other persuasive points; and then invoke the logic of the folk proverb, "If it ain't broke don't fix it."

Plan of the book

The real world of everyday experience, and the visionary world of linguistic knowledge with which it coexists in a dynamic tension, are both made explicit by the theoretical perspective of the sociology of knowledge. The fundamental claim that the "real world" is socially constructed is of crucial importance insofar as it allows for the critical study of such variables as "hegemony" "stigmatization" "Bad language" "dialect," and "Standard English," as social constructs, that is, features of everyday reality that seem to be immutably of a particular nature, but are amenable, nevertheless, to change. A case in point is the once firmly established belief that the Earth is flat, which – with the exception of a few reactionary persons affiliated with the Flat Earth Society – has, with the advent of global consciousness, become outmoded.

The socially-constructed nature of the real world is highlighted in Chapter One, through the characterization of *linguists as visionaries.* The chapter begins by calling attention to the role of scientists, inventors and other persons whose visionary ideas place them ahead of their times, and often subject them to laughter and ridicule – but which once accepted entitles them to scoff at the ones who once made fun of them, singing the rhetorical question that is the title of a popular song, "Who's got the last laugh now?" The chapter includes a cursory overview of the field of linguistics, and stresses the overwhelming degree to which linguistic knowledge supports the full recognition of African American language. Chapter Two, "If it ain't broke, don't fix it;" not only suggests a logical answer to the policy question based on the "clean bill of health" given to African American language by linguistic knowledge, it also includes continuing discussion of the effect of the social location of scholars on the policy options with which they chose to align themselves.

Chapter Three focuses on Language Planning as a Field of Inquiry, with special emphasis given to policy issues identified in the foregoing discussion that relate specifically to the case of African American language. The chapter includes a review of the literature on language planning, and the key concepts and analytical perspectives that have characterized its development.

Chapter Four, "What's in a Name?" is an occasion to revisit the theme of the social construction of reality as it informs the phenomenon of *naming,* and the specific question of what African American language should be called. It includes a section on typical naming practices of various groups in Africa and the African diaspora, as well as the diverse names that African Americans use for their own group, and others, in in-group as well as public settings. The chapter also includes discussion of how the changing preferences of African Americans for naming their group is informed by the subject of taboo words and euphemisms. The main focus of the chapter is on names for Black language that have been proposed and adopted by different persons and groups at different times.

A good deal of Chapter Five is organized around the pros and cons of the Creolist Hypothesis of the origin of African American language, and concludes with discussion of the implications of the hypothesis for ongoing issues of language planning and policy. Chapter six adopts the perspective of recent work on the origin of African American language based on insights from approaches to historical linguistics that group language varieties into families of languages based on evidence of their descent from a common parent. Alternative accounts of the origin of African American language are introduced in this chapter which focus on African language influences, and the genetic affiliation of Black language with African and the African diaspora languages. An archaic variety of African American language spoken in the Dominican Republic, known as Samaná English, spoken by descendants of free Africans who migrated from the Northeastern United States to Hispaniola in the early 1800s is a central focus of the discussion.

Chapter Seven, "The Language Situation in the African American Speech Community: The Status of Variety X" compares and contrasts alternate accounts of the language situation based on class-stratification, bilingualism, diglossia, and a speech continuum. The discussion is driven by the insight that the situation in Black America is a microcosm of the general language situation in the United States of America. The question of whether or not Black English and Ebonics are different words for the same linguistic phenomenon permeates the discussion. The contention of some scholars that Ebonics is a different language than English is also discussed.

Chapter Eight, "Cross-Over: From African American to National and World Culture," examines the frequently noted potential for African American culture to transcend established boundaries of cultural identity and nationality. The singular impact upon national and world culture that has been made by such diverse genres of African American creativity and artistic expression as Jazz, Blues, Spirituals, and most recently, Hip Hop music, is examined with the aim of finding a satisfactory explanation for the phenomenon. Specific conceptual tools introduced and developed in previous chapters contribute to a systematic analysis of cross-over, a term that first appeared in the jargon of the sound recording industry. The concept of double-consciousness, alternatively characterized as the "Push versus Pull Syndrome" (Smitherman 1977) is shown to be a major explanatory variable, which accounts for, among other things, the push of commercial forces in Show Business and the recording industry, and how it is countered by a pull toward validation of the dignity and worth of African American identity, and the latent genius and creative power it embodies. Another explanatory variable is a culture of resistance to hegemonic forces that appear relentlessly determined to reduce and contain Black identity within simplistic stereotypical boundaries created for purposes of stigmatization and exclusion.

Chapter Nine, "Ebonics and Black School Achievement: The Language Difference Hypothesis," examines the chronic under-achievement of African American students, and diverse ways in which it has been addressed by academic scholars of various disciplinary backgrounds. At the time that Black English studies emerged in the sixties, a long tradition of academic scholarship had established various kinds of "deficit models" to account for typical patterns of Black behavior, including verbal performance. Although there are a number of possible reasons for this, it is not surprising that the difference between Black and Standard English has been singled out by some scholars as a possible causal factor. Several noteworthy projects have emerged over the years, based explicitly or implicitly on such a *language difference hypothesis.*

A major source of insights into the relationship between the language of African American children and their academic achievement is a research effort which grew out of the politics of the Ebonics controversy called the *African American Culture and Literacy Project,* an effort which brought together scholars from various disciplines to study how the achievement of school literacy by African American children is related to various approaches to teacher development and the design of reading materials that take into account distinctive features of African American culture and the surface features of their language.

The title of Chapter Ten, "The Grammar: We be following rules," appropriates a typical African American language syntactical pattern to introduce the following detailed overview of its grammatical structure, presented as an autonomous system. The chapter includes critical discussion of the "list-of-features" approach to the grammatical description of African American language that has dominated Black English scholarship. The discussion centers on recent contributions that use native speaker intuitions as well as empirical data to describe the variety as an autonomous and self-contained system.

Chapter Eleven, "The Standardization of African American Language" discusses prospects for using language planning to attain an unprecedented level of standardization of African American language, in which it is recognized as a language in its own right and functions as a medium of all kinds of published material including dictionaries, grammars, newspapers, magazines and creative writing for persons of all ages. The options of specific language planning measures are discussed especially in the area of orthography development, and sample texts are presented, written in a proposed phonemic orthography for precisely representing African American language in a manner that highlights its distinctive features of pronunciation and grammar.

1
Linguists as Visionaries

A popular song from the middle of the twentieth century celebrates *visionaries*, persons whose extraordinary ability to imagine a world different from, indeed, ahead of the present state of affairs, inspired them to make claims that seemed utterly ridiculous to their contemporaries. Through their persistence and perseverance – leading to world-changing discoveries, inventions and breakthroughs – they were able to ultimately turn the tables and in so doing raise the rhetorical question,

Who's got the last laugh now?

The first line of the song recalls that, "they all laughed at Christopher Columbus when he said the world was round;" and successive lines and verses allude to various other persons known for their role in world-changing creations, discoveries, and inventions – Edison for recording sound; Hershey for his chocolate bar, etc.

The visionaries highlighted in this chapter are distinguished for their contributions to the field of linguistics, a field noted for its advanced methods, methods capable of describing languages at a level of precision and accuracy that is the envy of the behavioral sciences, and rivals that of the physical sciences. Linguistics is a technical and exacting science; and some of the claims that linguists make about language are contrary to common sense. To that extent they are in the same realm as the more famous inventors and explorers alluded to above.

What is most visionary about linguistics is the profound equality that it endows to language varieties that enjoy vastly differing degrees and amounts of prestige or stigma in the various societies in which they are spoken. That is, regardless of its status in society – whether dialect, standard, or pidgin – all human language is systematic and rule governed.

When linguistic knowledge is applied to existing beliefs about a stigmatized variety such as African American language, it effectively debunks the commonsense notion that it consists of mistakes and deviations from the grammar of a hegemonic standard. Competent linguistic analysis of data samples of persons speaking the variety inevitably results in a concrete set of elements and rules that underlie the grammatical structure of sentences that speakers recognize as tokens of the language variety.

Consider for example the language of the following utterance, produced by one of the informants for the pilot study of Black English mentioned in the introduction:

I ain't pick no cotton! The only cotton I ever pick was off my shirt!.

It can be roughly translated into Standard English:

I haven't ever picked cotton! The only cotton I've ever picked was (picked) off of my shirt!

The context of the utterance is a discussion of the informants' common roots in Louisiana, in families who had in the past engaged directly in the activity of cotton picking to earn a livelihood. The speaker's intent was to deny any personal experience as a cotton picker.

The kind of language highlighted by the above example tends to be characterized as "substandard" or "ungrammatical." Upon close examination, however, although it has features that are stigmatized as "incorrect," such as the word, *ain't,* and the use of so-called double negatives, it is systematic and rule governed nonetheless. The first sentence, for instance, has a subject *I,* and predicate, *ain't pick no cotton.* The predicate can be further analyzed to identify such elements as the transitive verb, *pick,* and the noun phrase *no cotton,* functioning as its direct object. Semantically, the auxiliary *ain't,* functions to negate the meaning of the predicate "pick some cotton." Far from being "ungrammatical," the speaker's language clearly has grammar.

It would never occur to a typical member of American society to analyze the structure of the above sentence in the manner that I just did. A more common response would be to express visceral reactions of horror and disgust, or make fun of the speaker. The ability of linguists to approach stigmatized language varieties in a cool and rational manner, and reach conclusions that are scientifically defensible, but contrary to common sense is befitting of the title, visionary. Our willingness to treat all languages equally places us ahead of our times. Persons seeking better understanding of the visionary perspective of linguists, may begin by focusing on the term grammar and the special meaning that it has as a technical linguistic term.

Grammar as a technical linguistic term

For many laypersons, the subject of grammar calls to mind rules that they have been consciously taught to observe, but about which they feel insecure. We may remember, for example, being taught that it is sometimes correct to use *whom*, instead of *who*. It is such consciously-taught "dos and don'ts" that people often have in mind when they speak of grammar.

As it is used in linguistics, the term *grammar* simply denotes a description of a language. It has none of the connotations of correctness associated with the everyday usage of the word. The rules by which language is judged correct or incorrect are known in linguistics as *prescriptive grammar* rules; and are contrasted to rules of *descriptive grammar*, which account for the patterns that actually occur in the language of native speakers of a language. A key distinction between prescriptive and descriptive grammar is that the former make reference to what speakers "should" or "should not" do in order to be considered correct and proper, whereas the latter simply account for what speakers actually do when they speak. A very important distinction between descriptive and prescriptive grammar is that prescriptive rules are consciously taught and enforced, whereas descriptive rules are unconsciously acquired and automatically followed by native speakers. A third important difference between the two types of rules is that native speakers never break descriptive rules. Native speakers *may* violate prescriptive rules, however, and some do so frequently.

The uses of *ain't* and double negatives, in the above cotton picking example, are violations of prescriptive grammar. At the same time, however, the speaker is following the descriptive rules of the grammar of his native dialect. From the point of view of descriptive grammar, there is nothing wrong with the sentence, *I ain't pick no cotton*. Many of us were consciously taught that we shouldn't use *ain't*, and may have experienced being corrected. Some of us continue to use *ain't* on occasion, nonetheless, although we know that it is considered wrong.

When I was a child, we were often corrected for using *ain't* so frequently that we would playfully correct each other. A person being corrected had the option of making the playful reply:

> <u>*Ain't*</u> *ain't a word cause it ain't in the dictionary.*

Although we would joke that *"ain't* ain't in the dictionary", the last time I checked it was there. The *American Heritage Dictionary of the English Language* characterizes *ain't* as a "Nonstandard" form which is historically derived from the contraction of *am not,* and is "extended in use to mean *are not, is not, have not, has not."* (Morris et al. ed. 1976) As such, it supports the linguists' claim that all language is systematic and rule governed. The designation "Nonstandard" is prescriptive in that it implies that *ain't* should not be used. The dictionary's account of how *ain't* actually is used is descriptive, however. When native English speakers use *ain't*, therefore, they are engaging in rule-governed behavior. They do not use *ain't* indiscriminately. They would never substitute *ain't* for *can't, won't,* and other negated contractions. Part of knowing how to speak English entails knowing how to use *ain't*.

To the extent that a given usage conforms to descriptive grammar rules, it is considered correct from a linguistic perspective; and from such a perspective, features of African American language that violate prescriptive grammar rules may be defended as systematic and rule-governed. Unlike prescriptive grammar rules, which are consciously taught and enforced, descriptive rules are unconsciously acquired, intuitively known and automatically followed.

Native speaker intuitions and grammaticality

For some linguists, the term grammar not only refers to a description of a language, but also to a speaker's internalized knowledge of the language, or *competence* (Chomsky 1965). In that sense of grammar, the speaker of the above cotton picking utterance was following such an internalized grammar of his dialect of African American language.

The structure of the second sentence of the above utterance is extremely complex, and would require advanced skills of syntactic analysis to completely unpack. Suffice it to note that the surface subject noun phrase, *The only cotton I ever pick*, has a relative clause, *(that) I ever pick* embedded within it; from which the relative pronoun *that* has been deleted. On closer scrutiny, the main clause of the sentence appears to be in the passive voice. The active voice equivalent of the sentence would be something like *I pick the only cotton I ever pick off my shirt*. The active voice direct object corresponds to the subject of the passive version, and the auxiliary *was* is preposed to the verb *pick*, as a signal of passive voice, before the verb is deleted from the surface form of the sentence. The speaker's ability to encode the utterance, and the ability of his interlocutors to decode it implies that they share an extremely complex internalized grammar of African American language.

One aspect of the theory of linguistic competence which is elaborated in this section is the use of native speakers' intuitive knowledge of their language as a resource for grammatical description. Although native speakers never violate the descriptive rules of their language, those who lack special training in grammatical analysis are usually incapable of explaining those rules. They have highly reliable intuitions, however, of what is constitutes "native-like" speech, that is, of what "sounds right" to them. When presented with the following examples, (1–4) most native speakers would agree that examples 1 and 2 below sound fine. The same speakers would reject 3 and 4, however, as sounding wrong. Asterisks (*) such as those before examples 3 and 4 are used in linguistics to indicate unacceptability to native speakers.

1. *I cooked too much rice*
2. *I cooked too many apples.*
3. * *I cooked too many corn.*
4. * *I cooked too much noodles.*

Although most native speakers are unable to explain what is wrong with sentences like 3 and 4, the correct usage of *much* vs. *many* is accounted for in descriptive grammars of English by subclassifying certain nouns as "count nouns" and others as "mass nouns." As a rule, English speakers use *many* with count nouns, and use *much* with mass nouns. The fact that native English speakers use *much* and *many* correctly but are incapable of explaining how they do it supports the claim that they are following the rules of an internalized grammar which they know intuitively.

In linguistic argumentation the judgments of native speakers are taken as evidence of *grammaticality*. Sentences that sound right to native speakers are considered *grammatical*, and those that sound wrong are considered *ungrammatical*. Using the facts represented by particular grammatical or ungrammatical examples, we try to arrive at general statements which accurately explain the unconscious and intuitive knowledge that native speakers have of their language.

For many English speaker, sentence 5 is grammatical.

    5. *We didn't tell nobody.*

Although 5 violates the prescriptive rule against *double negatives*, it sounds fine to some people. Furthermore, any English speaker would concede that *it is English*, albeit nonstandard. In that sense, it is grammatical. It is possible, therefore, for a sentence which is considered "incorrect" from a prescriptive point of view to be "correct," from the perspective of descriptive grammar. Sentences which break prescriptive rules might sound wrong to those of us who are well educated and have been taught that they are wrong. It should be clear, however, that the kind of "wrong" involved in breaking prescriptive rules is a different kind of "wrong" than what we represent as an ungrammatical string (e.g.: 6)

    6. * *We nobody tell didn't.*

Linguists explain the grammaticality of sentence 5, in part, by showing how it is systematically related to a positive sentence such as 7

    7. *We told somebody.*

Sentence 5 may be derived from 7 by first inserting the auxiliary *do*, and giving it the past tense of the main verb *told*, resulting in *did tell*. Following that the negated contraction of the auxiliary, i.e., *didn't*, is substituted for *did*. We hardly realize how complex the native speaker's knowledge of the English language is until we try to make it explicit. In fact, to fully describe sentence 5 as a negated version of 7, we need to account for the occurrence of *nobody* in 10 where *somebody* occurs in 12. English restricts the indefinite pronoun *somebody* to positive sentences, when it occurs in the predicate after the main verb, as in 7. When such sentences are negated, English speakers may substitute *nobody*, as in 10, although it results in a violation of the rule against using double negatives. They may also substitute the word *anybody* of course, and be prescriptively correct, as well as grammatical.

The linguistic concept of grammaticality underscores an aspect of the visionary perspective of linguistics which makes it possible for language considered "bad" by the norms of society to be – at the very same time – systematic and rule-governed. It may be difficult for an educated, middle-class American to accept the idea that usages such as *ain't*, or double negatives which they have been taught to abhor, is grammatical. Such persons might benefit from considering the following sentences and indicating whether or not they "sound right."

8. *Who did you give the money to?*
9. *You have to really push it hard!*
10. *He decided to lay down and rest.*

Each of the above three sentences happens to be "wrong" to the extent that it contains a violation of one or more prescriptive rules. Sentence 8 not only violates the rule that prescribes *whom* instead of *who* under certain conditions, it also violates the rule that you should not end a sentence with a preposition. In sentence 9, the occurrence of *really* between *to* and *push* violates the *split-infinitive* rule, and the verb *lie* should be used in 10, instead of *lay* according to prescribed norms of "proper" grammar.

It so happens that the prescriptive rules violated in the above sentences are violated so frequently by educated, middle-class speakers, and so laxly enforced, that they tend to escape the attention of most people. Persons for whom sentence 8–10 are grammatical, but have difficulty accepting the "grammaticality of sentence 5 may be able to at least intellectually accept the idea that it is equivalent to examples 8–10 in being consistent with descriptive grammar at the same time that they violate prescriptive grammar.

The claim that all language is systematic and rule-governed, as illustrated by the difference between descriptive and prescriptive grammar, and the notion of grammaticality, is one of several examples of the visionary nature of linguistic knowledge, and the manner in which it debunks the stigmatization of black language as consisting of mistakes and random deviation from the rules of Standard English. Another aspect of the visionary nature of linguistics is brought out in the next section. It adds additional substance to the general assertion that there is nothing wrong with African American language, by developing the point that *everybody speaks a dialect and, all dialects are equal.*

Everyone speaks a dialect

Linguists, in their encounters with educators, or the general public, often confront the conflict between their visionary perspective and that of the person on the street by initiating a dialogue on dialects[2] built around the point that *Everybody speaks a dialect.* Most Americans think of dialects as what certain people in certain places like the South, Appalachia, Boston and Brooklyn speak. As the dialogue gets under way, participants typically recall experiences in which, while traveling to another part of the country they were told that they "sound funny" by the very people whom they always characterized that way; while the same persons insist that their speech is normal.

Once participants in the dialogue get the point that it is not just "the other guy" who speaks a dialect, and sounds funny, the discussion typically moves to a more technical level and focuses on the idea of *dialect differences.* The claim that everybody speaks a dialect is based on the realization that *whenever a language is spoken by several different groups of speakers – whether in different places, or by different social groups in the same place, differences develop at certain points: in pronunciation, in grammar, as well as in vocabulary; and wherever such differences exist, everybody speaks it one way or the other.* At the level of vocabulary, for instance, Americans have different words for a "soft drink." Some say *soda* and some say *pop.* Several different verbs meaning "to carry," may be heard in different parts of the country. New Yorkers, for example may say *schlepp*, and Southerners often say *tote.* To the extent that everybody says one or the other of the words in the above sets, everybody speaks a dialect.

Dialect differences also exist in the way that particular words are pronounced. Some Americans pronounce the word *syrup*, in such a way that the first vowel sounds like the vowel of *sear*, while others will pronounce the same vowel like the vowel of *sir.* Some African Americans, including Yours Truly, pronounce *syrup* with just one syllable, in a manner that rhymes with *burp.* The fact that everybody pronounces *syrup* in one or another of the above ways, is further proof that everyone speaks a dialect. Phonetic symbols come in handy when it is necessary to represent on paper the different pronunciations of a word, i.e.: /sɪrəp/, /sɛrəp/, and /sʌrp/.

An interesting example of dialect differences in grammar is seen in the contrasting patterns in the sentences,

---

[2] A publication of the Center for Applied Linguistics entitled *Dialogue of Dialects was developed and disseminated in the 1960s by linguists affiliated with the center for the purpose of raising the awareness of teachers, parents and educators of the nature of dialects.*

a) *My car needs washed,* and
b) *My car needs washing.*

In most dialects of American English, only the pattern represented by (b) occurs; and to such speakers the pattern of sentence (a) sounds funny. To other speakers, sentences with the pattern of (a) sound completely normal, so much so that they are seldom aware of saying anything unusual. The crucial point is that just as in the case of the examples of vocabulary and pronunciation differences, wherever there are grammatical differences such as the syntactic patterns just considered, everybody's usage conforms to one pattern or the other.

The equality of dialects

After participants in the dialogue accept the idea that everybody speaks a dialect, the conversation moves to the most difficult and visionary point of the dialogue: Not only does everyone speak a dialect, but *all dialects are equal.* Participants typically accept the point that all dialects are equal when it applies to such lexical pairs as *tennis shoes* and *sneakers,* or the varying pronunciations one may hear of words like *roof,* pronounced with the vowel of either *cook* or *coop.* The dialect that pronounces it one way is equal to the one that says the other. Problems arise, however, when an example like *creek* is given. Although most Americans have heard *creek* pronounced *crick,* many of them strongly resist the idea that the dialect that says *crick* is equal to the one that says *creek.*

The reader new to the field of linguistics needs to understand that the term *dialect,* as used by linguists, does not imply an inferior type of speech, the way that it sometimes does in everyday usage. Speakers of certain dialects may use English in a way that would be judged by speakers of other dialects to be "incorrect," either because it is contrary to the rules of standard English, or because it just sounds "funny." An example of the first type is the use of so-called double negatives in sentences like *I don't have no change.* An example of the latter type is the above sentence *My car needs washed,* and other sentences with the same pattern. There is nothing in the traditional grammar book that prohibits a combination of verbs like "needs washed," but for many Americans it just doesn't sound right, and for them, the alternative *My car needs washing* sounds much better.

Yet another specific way in which there is nothing wrong with African American language comes into view when we shift our perspective from the manner in which a linguistic system is organized, to the ways in which it changes over time. A significant generalization about language change is that it is constant, inevitable, and absolutely normal. That perspective is advanced in the next section.

The normalcy of language change

Sometimes, dialect features reflect ongoing changes in the language. In such cases, the status of the persons leading the change may contribute to negative reactions typically evoked by the feature. A case in point is the verb *ask*, which has the variant pronunciation *axe*, in certain dialects, a variant which is spreading in youth culture. Although some persons react viscerally to hearing *ask* pronounced /æks/, by cringing in outrageous indignation, it is systematic and rule governed nonetheless. It continues to be a verb, and its pronunciation is still accounted for by the same three phonemes as in the standard pronunciation: /æ/, /s/ and /k/. They just happen to be arranged in a different order.

Another recent innovation in the language of American youth involves the forms *hecka* and *hella*. Persons who see such words as deterioration of the language might take some comfort in the assurance that they are among the latest instances of the kind of change that all languages undergo at all stages of their history. When new words enter the language, they are used according to an already established system. In the case of hecka and hella, they are new members of the class of words called *qualifiers*, the most common of which is *very*. In the sentence, *I was hella tired*, hella has the same form and grammatical function as *very* in *I was very tired*.

As noted above, the Average Jane or Joe may greet language change with alarm, and as a sign of deterioration; and describe innovative features of languages with pejorative adjectives such as "corrupt," and "bastardized." Several such features are presently spreading in American English, especially among younger speakers. The above noted use of *hecka*, or *hella*, to modify the intensity of a quality expressed by an adjective, is one of many illustrations of such change. Another involves the use of variants of *to be like* as a discourse marker to set off direct quotes in a narrative sequence, e.g.: *I was like, "I'm hecka hungry," and she was like, "Me too. Let's go to Micky Dee's."*

For the linguist, language is always changing. The idea that a language has deteriorated from a former state of pristine purity, is a myth. One of the main reasons that language changes is because the reality that we talk about, through language, changes. When something new is invented, a new word is needed to name it, and other words may be needed to talk about the actions or behaviors involved in using it. The word *refrigerator*, for example, was created for the electric powered food storage container that replaced the *icebox*, which served the same purpose by using a block of ice to keep an insulated interior area cold until it melted and had to be replaced. From the noun *refrigerator*, a verb *to refrigerate* was created by a process known as *back formation*. Another verb that is a product of back formation is *edit* which was created to describe what an *editor* does.

The advent of the computer age and high technology brought with it a virtual onslaught of new vocabulary, which represent a variety of typical ways that new words enter a language. The word *mainframe* is an example of the process of *compounding*, as is *download, touchpad* and *motherboard*. Change in the vocabulary often takes the form of adding prefixes and suffixes to existing words, resulting in new words such as *digital*, and *debug*. The same process of *affixation* accounts for certain words created for the special purpose of advertising such as *uncola*, for a popular soft drink, and the verb *nutracize*, created by the advertising department of a weight loss enterprise with product name Nutra-Systems.

Other common word-formation processes are *blending*, represented by the combination of *smoke* and *fog*, to create *smog*; *clipping*, a common example of which is *doc*, from *doctor*; and *acronyms*, such as *AIDS*, for "acquired immune deficiency syndrome," and *scuba*, for "self-contained underwater breathing apparatus."

Students are often surprised to learn that the recently popularized word *PHAT* meaning "attractive," "good-looking" is an acronym, created by college boys of my generation from four words for parts of the female anatomy. The word is now frequently seen in ads for products targeting the younger generation produced by marketers who are oblivious to the word's etymology.

Change in the vocabulary often takes the form of extending the meaning of an existing word as in the case of *monitor, keyboard* and *mouse*. Even when linguists are confronted with the especially outrageous kinds of new words that strike fear in the hearts of defenders of the purity of the language, they see the results of normal process of change such as the ones discussed above.

Some words, like *humongous*, meaning "very large," do not fit easily into any of the above types. It may be explained, however, partly as a case of *analogy* with the existing word *tremendous*. A possible source of the stem, *humong–*, to which the adjective-forming suffix, *–ous* attaches, is blending of two words like *huge* and a word like *long, strong* or possibly *throng*. The stem *humong–* could also be the result of the process of *coinage*, through which new words are created from scratch. Another new word, ending in *–ous*, adopted as the name of the female singing group, *Bootylicious*, may be adequately explained as a blend of the last part of *delicious* with the noun *booty*, which includes in its range of meaning "plunder," and "buttocks."

Languages change not only in vocabulary, but also in pronunciation and grammar. The pronunciation of the verb *ask*, in some dialects of English as *axe* is the result of a sound change process known as *metathesis*, in which a word keeps the same sounds, but switches the order in which two of them occur, i.e., the sounds spelled "s" and "k." Many people react viscerally, with annoyance and even disgust to the "axe" pronunciation. The fact that it is presently spreading among young people who identify with the Hip Hop generation, may raise the concern of such persons that the language is "going to the dogs," but such fears are unfounded. It is just another instance of the normal processes of change that all languages experience all the time.

Implications for language planning

The points made in the above sections – about the systematic and rule-governed nature of all human language, the equality of dialects, and the normalcy of language change have profound implications for the traditional stigmatization of African American language – for it undergirds the premise that all human language, regardless of its status in society; whether dialect, standard, or pidgin is systematic and rule governed. It follows, therefore, that the traditional hegemonic status of Standard English is unfounded.

Such a premise has guided my own thinking on African American language from a language planning perspective, which may be traced to the experience of hearing a lecture by Joshua Fishman at a conference on bilingual education held at the University of San Francisco in 1979. (subsequently published as Fishman 1980)

In the Fishman lecture, the Bilingual education movement in the United States is analyzed from a language planning perspective. Shortly after hearing Fishman's talk, I wrote "Language planning in the United States: the status of Black English." (DeBose 1979)

A major focus of DeBose 1979 is the largely untapped potential for using language planning to change the attitudes of society towards Black English so that it is no longer thought of as a liability. As a prelude to making that point, I call attention to a tendency, discussed in the next chapter, for linguists to acquiesce to Standard English Hegemony. I make the point that a desirable alternative to such a policy would use language planning to bring about a change in attitudes toward African American language such that it is no longer seen as a liability.

> A linguist, in his role as citizen, might adopt a position, consistent with popular attitudes, that black children should be required to learn [Standard English]; not because there is anything wrong with [Black English], but because popular prejudices against it are so strong. The underlying assumption seem to be that the alternative of trying to change attitudes toward BE is impractical or unrealistic. (DeBose 1979: 4)

I spend a good part of the paper making the point that the alternative of changing attitudes toward Black English is not as unrealistic as linguists imply through their acquiescence to "popular prejudices against it." I call attention to how American attitudes towards race have changed as a consequence of the Civil Rights Movement; and suggest an eight-point program for bringing about a "Planned generational shift of attitudes toward non-standard English."

In the early 1980s, I organized the syllabus for a class, "Afro-American Language Patterns." that I taught at the University of California, Berkeley. The course syllabus was organized around four key questions

> *What is it?*
> *Where did it come from?*
> *Is there anything wrong with it?* and,
> *What should be done about it?*

Discussion of the first three questions sets the stage for the fourth and most crucial question, which I came to refer to as *the policy question*. The four questions set the stage for a process of reasoning which culminates with the conclusion that the current state of linguistic knowledge strongly supports a policy of full recognition. In the intervening year leading up to the firestorm, those four questions came to be the standard outline for lectures and workshops that I was occasionally invited to present.

2

If It Ain't Broke, Don't Fix It: Toward a Policy of Full Recognition of African American Language

How does it feel to be a problem?
W. E. B. DuBois (Gates Jr. et al. eds 1999: 9)

Material reviewed in Chapter One strongly supports the conclusion that there is nothing wrong with African American language – at least from the visionary perspective of linguistic theory. It is a dialect, equal in status to other dialects of American English. It has a grammar. In short, it is an instance of normal language that came into being through normal processes of language change. For all those reasons, and more, there is nothing wrong with it. The "clean bill of health" that Black language receives from the current state of linguistic knowledge supports a policy of leaving it alone.

The chapter title, *If it ain't broke, don't fix it,* is a familiar piece of American folk wisdom, which I came to rely on as a "punch line" in presentations to lay audiences, the standard title of which is the subtitle of this chapter, *Toward a policy of full recognition of African American language.* In one particular version of my "stump speech," presented at the University of South Carolina, Columbia, in the fall of 1997, with the catchy title, "Ebonics 101," I portray the options available to educators and policy makers as points on a continuum (Figure 2.1) ranging from a traditional policy of suppression, at one extreme, to a policy of full recognition, at the other extreme.

Suppression	Limited Recognition	Full Recognition

Figure 2.1 Policy options toward African American language

40

Standard English Hegemony	Acquiescence to Standard English Hegemony	Full recognition/ Resistance to Hegemony Cultural Revitalization

Figure 2.2   Policy options toward African American language (revised)

As a consequence of continued reflection, I have found that the policy options are more adequately characterized with respect to their implications for the hegemony of Standard English. Accordingly, I now use the terms represented in Figure 2.2 in place of the terms corresponding to the same cells in Figure 2.1.

Instead of "suppression," therefore, the traditional policy is now referred to as "Standard English hegemony." I have replaced the term "limited recognition" with "acquiescence to Standard English hegemony."

While I continue to use the term "full recognition," I use it together, or in alternation with, "Resistance to the Hegemony of Standard English," and "cultural revitalization," for reasons elaborated on in the following pages. As a prelude to that discussion, however, in the next section, I examine the traditional policy of outward and active support for Standard English hegemony.

The traditional policy

DuBois' lament about the perennial predicament of the "Negro" in being treated as "a problem" may serve as a reminder of how the social location of a scholar can affect the manner in which an issue is experienced, perceived or handled. In the case at hand – where the essence of the "problem" is stigmatization – DuBois' point is doubly significant, for there is not really anything wrong with African American language, nothing, that is, except in the hearts and minds of people who insist on characterizing it as "bad," "wrong," or "broken."

The term "suppression," which I previously used in reference to the traditional policy, does not fully and accurately capture the essence of the traditional policy toward African American language. It suggests that the goal of the policy is to discourage the use of varieties of English labeled "substandard," when the real goal, as I now understand it, has been to perpetuate the idea that a language variety characterized as such stigmatizes its users as unqualified for certain rights and privileges to which they would otherwise be entitled.

When attention is focused on individual cases of parents correcting the nonstandard usage of their children, or teachers interacting with Black student speakers in the classroom, such efforts might be perceived as microscopic manifestations of societal efforts to promote the kind of assimilation to mainstream society and upward mobility that tends to be associated with the acquisition of Standard English proficiency. When such efforts are viewed at a macroscopic level, however, paying due attention to established and ongoing patterns for accommodating persons of various cultural ethnic and linguistic backgrounds to American society, the overwhelming majority of African Americans appear to be as marginalized as ever in ethnic enclaves where African American language is alive and well.

One particular feature of American society that was at the center of concerns expressed in the Ebonics Resolution, but tended to be muffled by the clamor of visceral reactions to the idea of Ebonics in the classroom, is the monumental failure of African American students, repeatedly documented by statistics of high rates of drop outs, suspension, retention at grade level and other discouraging indicators of Black school achievement.

Such issues are prominently mentioned in the Oakland School Board Ebonics resolution, and reflected in a variety of concrete ways; including reading test scores, grade point average, and overrepresentation in special education classes. To understand why this is so, we need to keep going back to the concept of hegemony. Most of the inequalities in American society are not maintained by coercive state power so much as by hegemonic ideas. Many of the ideas that have traditionally served to justify the subordination of Black Americans have been discredited, e.g., the doctrine of white supremacy. One idea that Americans still hold dear, however, and many Black people still buy into, is the superiority of Standard English over other varieties.

The goal of the traditional policy, therefore, understood properly, was not suppression of African American language, but its maintenance, as one of a diverse array of features of Black identity which helped to reinforce the hegemonic idea, already deeply imbedded in the hearts and minds of many Americans, that the subordinate status of African Americans is a consequence of their own shortcomings and limitations. One aspect of the traditional role of African American language, which supports the claim that the policy was aimed at maintenance, and not suppression, is its acceptance and promotion in the performing arts.

As far back as the time when white men in blackface sang and danced in Minstrel shows, African American language has been a stock ingredient of American show business. (Rickford, J. and R. Rickford 2000) From the stereotypical imitations and distortions of Black speech in the Amos n' Andy series, to the routines of Black standup comedians making fun of their own life circumstances, Black language – or stereo-typed imitations thereof – has been deeply ingrained in American life. Such examples serve as reminders of the many ways in which language interfaces with other traits, physical as well as cultural, in the construc-tion of group identity, and how all of the above contribute to the final outcome of stigmatization.

The stigmatization of Black identity has functioned throughout the history of persons of African descent in the Western hemisphere to exclude persons so marked from rights and privileges to which they are otherwise entitled. An ideological conflict posed by the slave trade – between the democratic principles of liberty and equality to which American society is committed, and the blatant contradiction of those principles embodied in the deprivation of persons of African descent of their freedom in order to exploit them as a source of cheap labor, is resolved by hegemonic conceptions of Black identity that construct it as pathological and deficient. The idea subsequently took hold that Black people deserve the treatment they receive due to their lack of such virtues as industry, honesty and thrift. The notion of such ethical deficiencies are promoted through stereotypes, including the belief that Blacks lack the intelligence to perform any kind of work but the manual labor and servile domestic tasks they have typically been expected to perform, both before and after emancipation.

In addition to the ways just noted in which the stigmatization of Black identity has been constructed and maintained at the level of common-sense knowledge, there has been a dominant tendency for academic knowledge pertaining to persons of African descent in the Western Hemisphere to employ modes of analysis and exposition that appeal to various kinds of deficiencies and pathologies in order to explain, and ultimately justify, the typical situations in which Black people find themselves. It is a stream of academic work that interfaces in several ways, noted in the next section, with the academic scholarship identified specifically with the Ebonics phenomenon.

Academic perspectives

The first studies of Black English to emerge in the late sixties and early seventies (Bailey 1965; Stewart 1967; Fasold 1969; Labov 1969; Wolfram 1969; Dillard 1971) while addressed primarily to current issues in the field of linguistics, were highly relevant to the education of Black children, and other vital concerns of the Black community. In the context of persistent reports of Black children failing to perform academically at expected levels, the idea of a language barrier between the dialect spoken in black homes and communities and the Standard English of the schools, that was keeping Black children from achieving their maximum potential, became a focal point of academic discussions. One of the first issues to engage scholars in this area – which came to be known as the *difference versus deficiency* debate – pitted educational psychologists claiming that distinctive characteristics of the language output of Black children result from a *cognitive deficit* (Bereiter and Englemann 1966) against linguists arguing that Black language is structured according to rules of its own, which are simply *different* than the rules of Standard English. (Labov 1972) A similar controversy engaged social scientists attempting to account more generally for problems endemic to African American communities, such as urban gangs and juvenile delinquency. In this case scholars who see the problems as grounded in *social pathology* or *cultural deprivation* (Riessman, F. 1962) line up against proponents of a distinctive African American culture in which differences from general American culture may be accounted for in part by retentions from the ancestral cultures of African slaves. (Hale, J. E. 1982) Advocates of the pathology/deprivation view appeal to the brutality of the slave system to support their contention that the slaves' ancestral customs and traditions could not have survived the bruising experience of slavery, which struck at the very core of social organization – the family. According to Levine (1977)

> most scholars until very recently have assumed that because United States slavery eroded so much of the linguistic and institutional side of African life it necessarily wiped out almost all of the fundamental aspects of traditional African cultures.

He cites as an example Robert Park, who "wrote in 1919" and "typifies much of twentieth-century scholarship on this question,"

> The Negro, when he landed in the United States, left behind him almost everything but his dark complexion and his tropical temperament... . Coming from all parts of Africa and having no common language and common tradition, the memories of Africa which they brought with them were soon lost. (Park 1919, cited in Levine 1977: 4)

The metaphor of a *tabula rasa*, or "blank slate," has come to represent this prevalent claim that African institutions and traditions were "lost," "eroded," or "wiped out" by the experience of slavery. Levine notes two "exceptions" to this point of view, "W. E. B. DuBois and Melville Herskovits" (Levine 1977: 4) both of whom acknowledged the continuing influence of Africanisms in the language and culture of African slave descendants in the United States and throughout the Western Hemisphere. Another notable exception is Lorenzo Dow Turner.

Turner (1949) conducted more than a decade of field work in the Sea Islands of the Southeastern United States, and found thousands of African survivals in the English-lexified creole language, Gullah; including personal names, other words used in everyday conversation, and words heard only in songs, stories and prayers. Herskovits' work is wider in scope, looking at populations of persons of African descent throughout the diaspora of persons of African descent in the Western Hemisphere (Herskovits, F. S. ed. 1966).

Herskovits compiled comparative evidence of African survivals in North, South and Central America, and the Caribbean, corresponding to a geographic arc from mainland North America – where he found few if any African survivals among urban Blacks of the United States – to outlying areas of Surinam where he documented Africanisms in abundance in the language, customs and folkways of the so-called Bush Negro. (Gilbert 1993)

The scholarship of both Herskovits and Turner contain the seeds of controversies that more recently have engaged Black English researchers, not only the above-mentioned difference versus deficiency debate, but also the so-called Creolist controversy, which pits scholars who trace the origin of African American language to an earlier creole similar to Gullah against those who trace its origin to varieties of British English spoken by American colonists. That controversy is discussed in detail in Chapter Five.

The totally negative construction of African American identity contin-ued, virtually unabated, until the breakthroughs achieved by the Civil Rights movement. At around the same time that such changes were underway, a serious challenge to the hegemony of Standard English was taking shape in the emergence of Black English scholarship. One result of that challenge which is the main focus of the rest of this chapter, is the change in policy orientation that it precipitated from active support of the Hegemony of Standard English to either resistance, or acquies-cence to it. The discussion is organized in a manner that facilitates comparison of the contrasting features and qualities of Black English and Ebonics scholarship, and evaluation of the hypothesis that the typical social location of Black English scholars accounts in large measure for their tendency to adopt an orientation of acquiescence.

One consequence of juxtaposing the two schools of thought for comparative analysis is the highlighting of the great and continuing power of Standard English Hegemony. To highlight that observation, I alternate, in reference to the third policy option between calling it full recognition, and *resistance to Standard English Hegemony*. The latter designation calls attention to the practical necessity of acknowledging Standard English hegemony as a factor in present day language planning decisions, leaving the policy maker without the option of making it go away, and limited to the choices of resisting it, pushing the envelope, so to speak, as far as possible, or fully acquiescing to it.

Acquiescence

In view of the incompatibility of the doctrine of Standard English hegemony with the current state of linguistic knowledge, one would expect, and even predict, strong opposition to it from members of the linguistic profession, as well as support for a movement to dethrone the Standard. As a matter of fact, however, such is far from the case. The position typically expressed by linguists on the policy question is not opposition to the Hegemony of Standard English, but rather, *acquiescence*, although it is seldom if ever stated thus bluntly. The most common way of stating it is by lamenting, with a shrug of the shoulders, "that's the way things are in the real world."

The American Heritage Dictionary of the English Language offers the following definition of the verb, *acquiesce*:

> *To consent or comply passively, or without protest.*

One of the clearest and most articulate expressions of what I am calling a policy of acquiescence to Standard English hegemony is found in a discussion of policy options in a book by Robbins Burling. After discussing the relative merits of "wiping out nonstandard English," "full acceptance of the dialect," and "encourag(ing) bidialectalism," Burling explains why he cannot support the option of "full acceptance." After conceding that

> The policy of full acceptance of the dialect should appeal to our sense of democracy ...

he proceeds to note what he sees as some of its obvious "dangers"

> It is doubtful that even the most splendidly educated young man ... will find employment ... speak[ing] the language of the black ghetto.

Burling rests his case with an allusion to "the practical if unjust world [which] demands the standard dialect." (Burling 1973: 132)

Although Burling dismisses the policy option of "full acceptance," his mere acknowledgment that there is a range of serious options to simple acquiescence to the hegemony of Standard English – worthy of careful and sustained dialogue – in which long-suppressed issues of justice and language rights are freely discussed, is a welcome improvement on the worn out refrain that "you can't get a job talking like that."

It is not readily apparent why Black English scholars opt for the kind acquiescence to Standard English hegemony represented by the above Burling quote. It is interesting to note, however, how much the policy has in common with the traditional policy. One subtle difference is that it does not consider African American language "substandard," but *nonstandard*. The term nonstandard is intended to convey the idea that African American language is no worse than the standard, only different. It is so similar to "substandard," however, that it is tantamount to compliance with hegemony of Standard English.

One way in which the typical response of Black English scholars to the question of what to do about African American language qualifies as acquiescence is its lack of candor and clarity, its refusal to "tell it like it is," to "call a spade a spade" – in the case at hand, to acknowledge that the essence of the problem is stigmatization. References to the "real world," and the hazards one encumbers by speaking African American language in a job interview situation, are subtle and indirect references to the fact that the language of African Americans is stigmatized. Failure to consciously and critically deal with such crucial variables as hegemony – and the role of stigmatization in its maintenance – in questions of educational policy for speakers of nonstandard varieties, is virtually the same thing as acquiescence to it.

Black English studies occurred at a time of cataclysmic developments in the United States and the world, including the Black Freedom Movement. The direction of Black English scholarship was influenced more by its response to the Chomskian revolution in linguistics, than the Black Revolution that was being heralded by African American leaders. Preoccupied, as they were, with establishing legitimacy for their chosen area of study, in an academic discipline with a strong tradition of "pure" inquiry, Black English scholars were strongly inclined by training as well as their immediate location in academia to imbue their work with the aura of objectivity.

The highly theoretical nature of the major issues on which Black English scholarship is focused, i.e., the nature of linguistic variation, and the question of whether or not Black English has the same system as other varieties of American English, underscores the extent of its disconnectedness from the Black movement with which it coincided. Yet the very fact that it reached an audience which included Black intellectuals insured that a connection would be made, albeit in the dissonant form of critical reaction. One focus of the criticism was the inadequacy of Black English scholarship for dealing with the chronic educational failure of Black children. Another had to do with the fact that linguists had constructed a central component of African American identity as nonstandard English.

While the educational policy implications of the linguists' claims never took center stage, until the Ebonics controversy, they inevitably came up in discussions of the research with lay persons and non-linguists.

When called upon to share their knowledge with educators, Black English scholars advocated sensitivity on the part of teachers toward speakers of nonstandard English while teaching them standard English in a humane fashion, informed by the current state of linguistic knowledge. The calls for sensitivity were often lost, however, on audiences who tended to be distracted by the idea that the linguists were granting a seal of approval to what they considered "substandard" English.

Prior to the sixties, the reigning consensus among scholars of American language was that "Negroes" spoke the same dialect as white Americans of the same regional and social class background. A prevailing taboo on the subject of race enabled otherwise clear-thinking intellectuals to remain in denial of the fact that Black and White Americans were located socially in different color castes, each of which sustained its own separate class structure; and that Black and white Americans of the same regional backgrounds tend to be segregated into different residential sectors of their common region.

When linguists began to acknowledge a distinctive African American variety of English, their claims tended to conflict with long established notions about what constitutes "correct," "proper," or "standard" English; and they did so in a social climate in which issues of African American identity were beginning to be raised in the political arena.

It is interesting to note that when the first studies of African American language emerged in the 1960s, at a time when Blacks were deeply engaged in a monumental struggle for their Civil and Human Rights, the typical demands of the Movement did not include recognition of Black English, nor were there any demands for addressing a language barrier caused by differences between Black and Standard English. African Americans were demanding jobs, and freedom from discriminatory treatment in the workplace, in public accommodations, in housing, education; and increasingly, for recognition of the intrinsic beauty, dignity and worth of blackness. The affirmation of the beauty of blackness rarely applied to black language, however.

The policy option that Burling characterizes as "promote bidialectalism" represents a practical way for African Americans to avoid the consequences of speaking a stigmatized language variety. One point that linguists often overlook, however, in recommending such a solution to the "problem" of talking Black is the fact that African Americans *been* figured that out on their own.[3]

Multiple ambiguities

So there is multiple ambiguity in saying, "If it ain't broke don't fix it," in response to the question of what to do about African American language. First, with respect to the verdict of linguistic knowledge that it is an instance of normal language that came into being through normal processes of language change. Secondly, because of the emptiness of the advice that African Americans learn to switch to Standard English when it suits their needs and purposes. I learned to codeswitch by following the example modeled by my father, whom I frequently observed speaking one way around his Louisiana "homies" and another way in public encounters with outsiders. The practice of codeswitching is part and parcel of the general strategy that African Americans have long employed in dealing with the stigmatization of Black identity in American society.

African American codeswitching is a particular instance – focused on the dimensions of Black identity that is language – of a general strategy

---

[3] The feature of African American language known in the literature as *stressed bin*, locates the event predicated by a sentence in which it occurs in the "remote past." My usage in this sentence is intended to convey the idea that African Americans have long since practiced the kind of switching to Standard English to avoid the stigma of Black English that Black English scholars prescribe.

that African Americans have used in responding to the overall stigmatization of Black identity, by whatever dimension it is measured, by suppressing the "Negro" component of their dual identity, and emphasizing the "American." In a manner analogous to the way that many African Americans will modify their physical identity by straightening their hair, and other cosmetic means of assimilating to mainstream standards of physical beauty; the ability to modify one's speech output so as to sound "proper," is valued, and cultivated.

The third, and most important dimension of the ambiguity of, "If it ain't broke don't fix it," is the obsolescence of the policy of stigmatizing Black identity. Inasmuch as its original purpose was to justify the exclusion of African Americans from the ranks of first-class citizenship, it has obviously outlived its usefulness. When the stigmatization of African American language is viewed in the light of linguistic knowledge in general, and Black English scholarship in particular, it is shown to be unfounded and unsupportable. The policy of acquiescence to Standard English hegemony that has typified the stance of Black English scholars until now, has the effect of allowing a false conception of African American language, which they are imminently qualified to refute, to continue to be the basis of educational and public policies that adversely affect the African American community and the likelihood of its members receiving fair and equitable treatment in such vital areas as the classroom and the workplace. The alternative policy of full recognition, takes the implications of linguistic knowledge as a basis for responding to the stigmatization of Black language in the same way that had come to characterize the response of African Americans to the stigmatization of other aspects of Black identity – by affirming its intrinsic worth and dignity; i.e., through *cultural revitalization*, as well as other forms of resistance to Standard English hegemony.

Resistance/Cultural revitalization

The personal experience of being speakers of a stigmatized language variety tends to elevate the crucial variables of stigmatization and Standard English hegemony to a level of consciousness at which they are submitted to critical reflection, and create a fertile atmosphere for sustained serious dialogue. The critical content of the reactions of Ebonics scholars, especially those who have directly experienced the painful and humiliating consequences of speaking what is considered "Bad" language, is a predictable correlate of their social location, and is one of several justifications for characterizing their orientation to the policy question as one of resistance to Standard English Hegemony.

A prime example of the scholarly orientation of resistance to Standard English hegemony is Geneva Smitherman. The definition of Black language that she offers in her 1977 book reveals a strong interest in cultural revitalization.

> ... an Africanized form of English reflecting Black America's linguistic-cultural African heritage and the conditions of servitude, oppression and life in America.

Scholars of the resistance to hegemony orientation, tend to adopt a very personal tone of involvement in and sympathy with African Americans, as well as love of their language. In the introduction to her 2000 book, under the title of "From Ghetto Lady to Critical Linguist," Smitherman expresses a strong sense of identification and sympathy with the harsh conditions often thrust upon persons of African descent in the United States. After alluding to the Great Migration in which millions of African Americans relocated from the rural south to urban enclaves in the north and west, she identifies herself as a participant whose family made the trek from rural Tennessee to "Southside Chicago," eventually settling in "Black Bottom Detroit" where, as she explains

> I had my first taste of linguistic pedagogy for the Great Unwashed. Teachers who didn't look like me and who didn't talk like me attacked my language and put me back one grade level. (Smitherman 2000: 1)

In the following pages Smitherman describes how she ended up in a "speech therapy class" after she "flunked [a] speech test'" that was required for admission to a "teacher preparation program." She explains that the test results reflected "a bias against [the] different-sounding American English" that she spoke "emanating from the margins."

Ernie Smith, whose characterization of Ebonics as "an African Language System," (1998: 49) is reflected in the Ebonics Resolution of the Oakland School Board, exhibits, in addition to the above-noted earmarks of the resistance/revitalization policy orientation, a sensitivity to issues of fairness and equity embedded in the phenomenon of African American language.

> The imperative ... is to recognize that all pupils are equal ... Limited English Proficient (LEP) ... pupils who come from backgrounds where a language other than English is dominant are provided bilingual

education ... programs to meet their ... needs. LEP African American pupils are equally entitled to be provided bilingual education ... programs to address their ... needs. (Smith 1998: 58)

I express a similar concern in DeBose 1979

A central concern of this paper is that the law, as presently constituted, appears to provide greater protection to children from backgrounds where a different language than English is spoken than it does to children who speak a non-standard variety of English, although parallel educational needs and problems affect both types of children.

One way in which I sometimes signal my resistance to Standard English hegemony is by including the points that African American language is "beautiful," and is "a part of African American culture" in the litany of reasons given in my Ebonics stump speech why there is nothing wrong with Black language.

... Not only is Black English beautiful, it's a part of African American culture. Most educators now accept the idea that the diverse cultures that children bring to school should be honored and respected, and competent teachers should be capable of teaching in a way that is sensitive to cultural differences.

Another way of challenging the Hegemony of Standard English is by codeswitching between African American language and Standard English – in defiance of traditional rules that mark nonstandard English unacceptable for academic discourse. An example of such a codeswitch in my Ebonics 101 speech occurs as I am commenting on how the policy of full recognition is supported by the current state of linguistic knowledge.

All languages, and all dialects of all languages, have structure: they are systematic and rule governed. This includes Ebonics. So, when we talk Black English, it is inaccurate to say that we are trying, but failing, to speak Standard English. We are just following a different set of rules than those which govern Standard English. To put it another way: when we talk that way, *we don't be messin up, we be following rules.*

Such explicit references to issues of Black identity and their policy implications clearly point to a cultural revitalization strand in the policy orientation of the scholars in question. A manifest tendency for African American scholars, and Ebonics scholars in particular, to opt for such a policy orientation strongly supports the working hypothesis that the social location of the scholar is a major determinant of his or her policy orientation. Valuable insight into the notion of cultural revitalization, particularly as it affects the typical policy orientation of Ebonics scholars may be derived from viewing it through the lens of DuBois' double-consciousness.

Double-consciousness and identity politics

An indispensable tool for critical analysis of the accommodation of persons of African descent to American society is DuBois' concept of double-consciousness. Smitherman (1977) calls attention to the extent to which double-consciousness is embedded in the Black experience. She prefers to characterize it as a *"'push-pull' syndrome ... that is, pushing toward White American culture while simultaneously pulling away from it."* She acknowledges its equivalence to DuBois' concept, however.

Smitherman alludes to the emergence of the African Methodist Episcopal Church as the first independent Black Christian denomination in the United States, citing it as *"[a] striking example of the [push-pull] syndrome."* She recalls the famous incident in which Absalom Jones, along with Richard Allen, founder of the AME Church, led a walkout of Black worshippers from St. George Methodist Episcopal Church in Philadelphia in protest of racist treatment by white members.

> Jones took on the white man's religion, and proceeded to practice it. (The "push.") Yet when he attempted to pray in a white church ... , an usher pulled him from his knees and ousted him from the church. Thereupon, Jones, along with another ex-slave, Richard Allen, established the African Methodist Episcopal Church. (The "pull.")

During the crucial years of the Black Freedom movement, double-consciousness functioned to push certain civil rights organizations and their leaders toward opportunity, survival and conformity, at the same time that it pulled others in the opposite direction, toward affirmation of group cohesiveness, pride, dignity and racial identity. The earlier stages of the movement were oriented more toward assimilation, while the latter stages were increasingly characterized by a pull toward pluralism, which ultimately was picked up by other American political groups and movements organized on the basis of other identity features besides race, e.g., women, Latinos, senior citizens, gays and lesbians.

The emergence of identity politics in the wake of the Black Freedom Movement has had the ultimate effect of changing the landscape of American politics in such a manner that the traditional melting pot ethos is often in conflict with a rival ethos of multiculturalism. While supporters of multiculturalism often coincide with the traditional liberal wing of American politics, an adequate analysis of the politics of race in post-colonial America, from a Black perspective, cannot be accomplished within the left to right wing spectrum of options typically applied to majority-group politics. The most important forces affecting decision-making from an African American perspective are best characterized as those which involves a delicate balance between the dynamics of push and pull. Decision-making in the area of language is no exception.

Implications for language planning

The policy option of acquiescence to Standard English Hegemony, identified above as a significant aspect of the policy orientation of many Black English scholars; and the accompanying goal of facilitating the acquisition of Standard English by speakers of African American language is consistent with the goal of assimilation of Blacks into the mainstream of American society. As such, it responds to one of the warring souls of DuBois double-consciousness, the "push" toward opportunity and achievement. The interest in Standard English proficiency adequately symbolizes the "American" component of DuBois' "two-ness." An equally vital interest in recognizing the intrinsic worth and dignity of the variety of language associated with African American home and community life, is effectively sabotaged, however, by the decision of Black English scholars to classify the variety typologically as a nonstandard dialect, and solidify that decision by naming it as a type of English – with the term "vernacular" thrown in for good measure.

In bypassing the opportunity to balance the symbolic value of Standard English, with another positively-valued symbol of the African component of double-consciousness, Black English scholars set the stage for a series of developments that started with the 1973 Ebonics caucus, and culminated thirteen years later in the Ebonics firestorm. They did so by defining a central component of Black identity in negative terms – at the very time in which African Americans were in the throes of a cultural revitalization movement encapsulated in the slogan, Black is beautiful.

3

A Language Planning Approach to African American Language

As the linguistic repertoire of a speech community passes from generation to generation, each of its component varieties may undergo change; both in its *corpus*, or set of structural features, and its *status* relative to other components, i.e., the composite value of its prestige, popularity, utility and function. Whenever such changes result from the conscious and deliberate decisions of persons in authority acting in a policy making capacity, the process is referred to as *language planning*.

(DeBose 1979)

In this chapter I present a general overview of the language planning enterprise, with the ultimate goal of highlighting aspects of Black English scholarship that quality as language planning. The definition of language planning cited above, from my 1979 paper, builds upon the preliminary definition given in the introduction, i.e., "language change that occurs as a consequence of conscious and deliberate decision-making." The explicit reference it makes to the linguistic repertoire of a speech community enhances the basic point that it involves planned change, by specifying at the same time the descriptive parameters for the collection and analysis of data, and relating it to a theoretical construct in which all of the relevant real-world variables of power, status, stigma and authority coexist with the words, morphemes and other structural elements of the internal structure of affected languages. In the remainder of this chapter, I sketch in a brief overview of the emerging academic field of language planning in terms of the kinds of analytical methods and approaches that have been developed in order to make sense of and provide some order to a diverse array of practices, projects, programs and the like that qualify as language planning.

55

Language planning as a field of inquiry

Language planning is a social science, inter-disciplinary in character, but more sociological than linguistic; for it is grounded in real-world knowledge, and by its very nature must be so. The goal of language planning is to study, and seek to understand, a kind of activity that commonly goes on in different societies all around the world. Numerous books and articles on language planning have been written, based primarily on the study of situations in other countries, in which conscious and deliberate changes in one or more languages either in terms of their internal structure, or their role in society are sources of significant insight and understanding. (Haugen 1966a, 1966b; Fishman 1980; Fishman, Ferguson and Das Gupta eds 1968; Rubin and Jernudd eds 1971; Ruiz 1984; Tollefson 1991; Williams 1992; Wiley 1996)

As an academic discipline, language planning may be characterized as the constantly evolving product of ongoing dialogue among scholars and other interested persons about the nature of language planning, and its relevance to a wide range of common and recurring concerns of public and educational policy. This book may be seen as a major effort on my part to contribute to the field by sharing insights gained through reflection on the "Ebonics phenomenon."

The Ebonics phenomenon

The insight for treating the Ebonics phenomenon as a case study of language planning was triggered in my mind by the goodness of fit of Fishman's definition of language planning with the persons, issues and events involved in the firestorm. According to that definition language planning is

> the allocation of resources to language by authorities. (1979 lecture)

The recognition given to Ebonics clearly fits the description of "resources," and the school board members by whom the recognition was given certainly qualify as "authorities." Fishman's definition, brief though it is, and no doubt because of its brevity, places appropriate emphasis on the *authoritative* basis of language planning decisions. In calls to mind a typical routine that I follow, when presenting my standard course unit on language planning. I tend to use Fishman's definition as an opener and then add a second definition, i.e.,

> Language planning aint nothin but politics!

Which I attribute to DeBose.

What is important about acknowledging the extent to which language planning is indeed political in nature may be made explicit by noting once again the socially-constructed nature of reality. Change of the type we are calling language planning is tantamount to change in the nature of what is experienced by people, not only as real, but also as right, necessary, and legitimate. The more conscious we become of what is meant by language planning, the more obvious it becomes that it is something that is going on all of the time, and it becomes obvious, to those of a scholarly inclination, that it is worthy of academic study.

Fishman's concise definition does not make any reference to different types of language planning. The first point that he makes, however, after giving his definition is that *there are two types of language planning: Corpus Planning and Status Planning.* The Ebonics resolution, it quickly occurred to me, is of the latter type, i.e., status planning. The School Board was trying to elevate the *status* of something commonly considered "Bad English" by declaring it a language.

It had occurred to me in the past that certain events and projects inspired by the academic study of Black language were language-planning like; for instance, the above-mentioned Dialect Readers proposal; the so-called Ann Arbor–King Black English decision promulgated in 1979 in the United States District Court of Eastern Michigan (Chambers Jr. 1983) and the idea of applying foreign language teaching methods to the teaching of Standard English to Black-English speaking children. It did not occur to me until later that the entire body of Black English/Ebonics scholarship is amenable to analysis as a case study of language planning. A number of specific aspects of Black English and Ebonics scholarship that qualify as language planning issues were identified in the introduction. They are summarized below to facilitate ongoing discussion of how they interface with particular concepts, definitions and analytical tools commonly employed by language planning scholars. The focus of the next section is on concepts that facilitate identification of specific types of language planning activity.

Types of language planning

I begin this section with the basic twofold classification of language planning activities as corpus planning and status planning; although it has been elaborated in recent years to include additional categories. The term corpus, based on the Latin word for "body," refers to the internal structure of a language, in its spoken or written form. Typical

corpus planning projects include creating new vocabulary, or extending the meaning of existing words; production of dictionaries and
grammars, and development of writing systems. The status of a language is an expression of the role that it plays in society, and the
various ways in which its value to society is expressed. The DeBose
1979 definition of language planning underscores the multidimen-
sional nature of the status of a language in making specific reference to
the dimension of "prestige, popularity, usefulness, and function."
Another important dimension of a language's status is its typological
classification as a dialect, vernacular, standard, creole, etc.

Some typical status planning projects are selection of a national
or official language, selection from among the various spoken varieties of a single language the one that is to serve as the standard for
the society in which they coexist, and offering opportunities for
children of a multilingual society to receive primary instruction in
their mother tongue. One form of status planning that is of direct
relevance to the case of African American language is the act of
naming, applied either to an existing variety, the previous name of
which is considered inadequate or inappropriate, or a newly-created
variety.

Although corpus planning and status planning are conceptually distinct activities; in practice, they are often inextricably intertwined.
(Williams 1992: 124) A decision, for example, to begin offering primary
school instruction in a particular language for the first time, might
necessitate translating textbooks into that language, and even creating
a writing system. A project to designate language X as the national language could create the demand for new vocabulary to accommodate
the various issues and topics that might be addressed in it in its new
function.

Wiley (1996) makes reference to two additional types of language
planning besides corpus and status planning. They are *language acquisition planning*, and *language in education planning*, the latter of which
he characterizes as "the primary form of language acquisition planning." The notion of language acquisition planning was introduced
by Cooper (1989) and is said to involve "decisions concerning the
teaching and use of language." (Cooper 1989: 31) The rationale for
proposing such a category is the limitation of the other two major
types to changes in the structure, function, or level of recognition of a
given language, without consideration of its possible spread to new
speakers through consciously thought-out methods and strategies of
dissemination. Deliberate efforts to spread a language to new speakers

have coincided with such historical events as military conquest and promotion of religion.

Wiley, in the section of his article headed "Language in education planning," alludes to several of the events which I refer to above as "language-planning like events and projects inspired by the academic study of Black language"

> In the United States since the 1960's, controversy has surrounded the status of African-American varieties of language. (211)

Wiley calls attention to three specific issues from that period that have been "hotly debated."

> [T]he extent to which there is a need for specialized training for teachers of African-American children... . whether, and to what extent, they should receive formal instruction in African-American language . . [and] the fact that many of the prescriptions for the education of African-American children have been put forth by white social scientists ... whose intentions and prescriptions have been severely criticized by some commentators. (Wiley 1996: 132–33)

It is interesting to note how the "language in education," issues identified by Wiley, involve a number of the corpus and status planning issues identified in the introductory chapter.

The first of the two major categories of corpus planning issues, which involve the question of orthography, or, *how should African American language be spelled?* is an aspect of the Dialect Reader issue. A chapter in an anthology on the issue (Baratz and Shuy eds 1969) is devoted to the question of what orthography should be used. The consensus reached by contributors to the anthology – after conscious thought and deliberation on a variety of options, including regularized spelling, and a phonemic alphabet – is that the readers should use conventional English orthography. The main rationale given for the choice of conventional orthography is the envisioned purpose of using the dialect readers as a bridge to Standard English literacy. Since conventional orthography is firmly grounded in tradition, and furthermore, since the main differences between the language that Black English speaking children bring to the classroom, and the language of traditional textbooks are not in vocabulary but grammar, such children face no greater challenge than speakers of other varieties of American

English in learning the conventional sound-letter correspondences of individual words. The dialect readers, thus conceived, focus on using markedly African American grammatical features so as to minimize the challenge of a different system in the children's initial exposure to books.

A major implication of the decision to opt for the use of conventional orthography in the creation of dialect readers is that it is consistent with the policy orientation of acquiescence to Standard English hegemony. In the case at hand, it specifically involves the hegemony of established norms of "correct" spelling. Another important aspect of the spelling standardization issue is related to the variety of ways in which cited forms of African American language are represented in technical linguistic literature; such as the future marker, which appears as *gonna*, and *gon'* (with or without the apostrophe) and the pronominal forms *it's that's* and *what's*. Yet another concern stems from anticipation of a future state in which African American language is recognized as a language, and authors of a full range of material published in Black language will seek authoritative answers to questions of orthography. This last comment is a reminder of yet another useful way of typologizing language planning, by highlighting its involvement in literacy. In fact, many of the issues treated above under the rubric of language in education planning might just as well be labeled *Language and literacy planning*.

Language planning and literacy

My interest in looking at language planning and literacy together stems partly from the coincidence of the term literacy being mentioned prominently in several different projects and issues that have recently commanded my attention. One is the African American Literacy and Culture Project (AALCP) a federally-funded research project which grew out of the politics of the Ebonics controversy. One consequence of the turmoil created by the Ebonics resolution was a congressional hearing in which key persons in the controversy: School Board officials, community leaders and linguists, went to Washington D.C. to testify before a congressional committee interested in flushing out the facts and substantial issues on which the government might properly inject itself. As an outgrowth of the hearings a sum of money was appropriated to fund research with the aim of finding out what kind of relationship there might be between the school achievement of African American students and the structural patterns of African

American language. Ultimately the AALCP was organized as a consortium of three educational institutions: the Oakland Unified School District, the University of Pennsylvania, and California State University, Hayward, where I serve on the faculty. The AALCP is discussed in detail in Chapter Nine.

A second project with which I have recently been associated is called the Sea Island Translation and Literacy Project. It is a joint project of the Wycliff Bible Society and Gullah speakers to translate the Bible into Gullah. After a period of over a decade of effort, the translation team completed a Gullah translation of the Gospel according to Luke, which was published in 1995. I recently completed a thesis on the project (DeBose 2003).

One other example of a language planning and literacy issue involves the Papiamentu language. In my dissertation, DeBose 1975, in a section on the language situation in the Netherlands Antilles, where Papiamentu, an Iberian Romance-lexified (i.e. Spanish and Portuguese) creole functions as the national vernacular, the former colonial language, Dutch, continued for a time in the function of official medium of instruction, notwithstanding the fact that Papiamentu was typically the common first language of teachers and pupils. "A frequently given justification for the continuation of the Dutch-medium school system [was] the lack of an official set of orthographic symbols for representing Papiamentu in writing." (DeBose 1975: 22)

One striking similarity of the three cases, that offers insight into the nature of the phenomenon, is a concern with cultural revitalization on the part of a significant segment of the population under study. In the case of the AALCP, cultural revitalization is a clearly identifiable feature of Afrocentric approaches to classroom teaching that some teachers in the Oakland School District had adopted, and that backers of the Ebonics resolution sought to have implemented on a larger scale. The Sea Island Translation and Literacy Project is shown to be a particular instance of a widespread and multi-faceted cultural revitalization movement in which the Sea Island community is presently immersed. In the case of Papiamentu, its growing standardization, concomitant with the emergence of the Antillean people from Dutch colonialism is amenable to analysis as cultural revitalization.

The interest in literacy, represented by each of the above cases is related to a perceived illiteracy on the part of persons who speak a stigmatized language, and must acquire a different language, which exists in a hegemonic relationship with their vernacular in order to have access to written literature. Efforts to promote literacy for speakers of such a vernacular may take either of two forms:

- promotion of bilingual proficiency in the vernacular and the hegemonic standard; or
- standardization of the vernacular.

The policy option toward African American language of acquiescence to Standard English hegemony, i.e., Burling's "promote bidialectalism" option is of the former type. Translation of the Bible into Gullah, and standardization of Papiamentu represent the latter. The only one of the above mentioned African American language proposals that fit the latter type is the dialect readers proposal.

When the three cases of literacy planning are viewed side by side, one striking point of contrast is the relative degree of development – or lack of the same – that characterizes each case. The need to discuss such differences calls to mind a useful dimension along which particular language planning projects and proposals may be described and analyzed, that has not yet been introduced; i.e., by situating them with respect to a set of typical stages of the language planning process.

Stages of language planning

Reference to stages of the language planning process take markedly different forms in the work of different scholars. Fishman (1980) lists the following six stages.

1. Decison-making
2. Codification
3. Elaboration
4. Implementation
5. Evaluation
6. Iteration

Haugen (1966b) identifies the following four stages, three of which overlap with Fishman's list.

1. Selection
2. Codification
3. Elaboration
4. Implementation

The stage of codification is defined in Haugen's account with specific reference to a linguistic code. It involves such decisions as determination of the phonemic inventory corresponding orthographic symbols, and rules of morphology and syntax.

When applied to a status planning issue such as bilingual education in the United States, codification may be interpreted more generally as applying to the stage at which a proposed change attains the status of law either through legislative action such as the Bilingual Education Act of 1987; or a judicial decision such as Lau versus Nichols.

In general, codification is a process of endowing a particular change or set of changes with legitimacy, whether through governmental action, or the governing bodies of private organizations. The need for legitimacy with respect to language planning decisions, highlights the importance of authorities as essential to the phenomenon of language planning.

A good example of a codified orthography is standard English spelling, and the elaborate set of rules and conventions that regulate it, and serve as criteria for judging particular instances of spelling correct, or incorrect. The lack of standardization in the spelling of African American words in technical literature, to the extent that it constitutes a language planning issue, situates it at the decision-making, or pre-codification, stage. If and when discussion of the issue results in a detailed consensus, expressed in some type of formal proclamation of rules and principles for spelling African American language, and accepted as legitimate and binding among a body of users; then, and only then, can it be considered codified, and the stage would be set for the following stages of implementation and elaboration.

The issues summarized on Table I.1 are considered language planning issues on the basis of evidence presented in support of their classification as such. The fact remains, however, that the scholars engaged in the decisions do not identify themselves or their activity as language planning.

When attention is focused on the manner in which language planners, whether scholars, educators, activists or governmental officials approach the issues that engage them, another important analytical dimension is highlighted, studied under the heading of scholarly orientations, and approaches to language planning.

Scholarly orientations and approaches

It was noted above that the choices scholars make with respect to particular language planning issues, such as those summarized in Table I.1, can serve as an indication of their general orientation to one or another of a set of policy options. The notion of *scholarly orientation* is one of several typological schema that have emerged in the ongoing discussion of basic or deep-seated tendencies for language planning scholars to adopt different approaches and perspectives. Ruiz (1984) characterizes the notion of orientation as

> a complex of dispositions toward language and its role, and towards languages and their role in society.

He goes on to characterize such dispositions as

> largely unconscious and pre-rationale because they are at the most fundamental level of arguments about language. (Ruiz 1984: 16)

A tripartite set of orientations identified by Ruiz are: *language as a problem, language as a right* and *language as a resource.*

There is a major tendency in early literature on language planning for it to focus on language situations in so-called developing nations, viewed as affected by problems that stand in the way of their attainment of a level of "modernity" comparable to that of Western societies. (c.f. Fishman, Ferguson and Das Gupta eds 1968). Rubin and Jernudd (1971) define language planning in a way that is explicitly addressed to problem solving. In addition to characterizing it as "*deliberate* language change ... in the systems of language code or speaking or both ... planned by organizations ... established for such purposes or given a mandate to fulfill such purposes," they add,

> As such, language planning is focused on problem solving and is characterized by the formulation and evaluation of alternatives for solving language problems to find the best (or optional, most efficient) decision. (xvi)

A parallel to the tendency to view linguistic issues in developing nations as a problem exists in the United States, where linguistic and cultural diversity may be seen as the source of problems, the solution to which tends to be formulated in terms of efforts to promote proficiency in English among linguistic minorities.

The language as a right orientation stems from a perspective on language issues that adopts a critical attitude toward the function of language policies to maintain established patterns of social stratification, and use literacy in the dominant language of a society as a criteria for full participation and full enjoyment of political and economic benefits. From such a point of view, language planning might justifiably be seen as an instrument of social control. A prime example of language as an instrument of social control is the use of literacy in the American South during the Jim Crow era to deny African Americans the right to vote.

Ruiz's language as a resource orientation strikes a middle ground between the perspectives of viewing language as a problem – which is subject to criticism for a condescending, paternalistic view toward cultural diversity – and that of language as a right; which tends to obscure the boundaries that separate dispassionate scholarship from engaged advocacy and activism. The key feature of the language as resource orientation is a shift of attitude toward cultural diversity from viewing it as a problem to seeing it as a resource.

Similar ways of conceptualizing contrasting perspectives and approaches to language planning have been proposed by other scholars. Tollefson (1991) makes a distinction between

> the neoclassical approach, which emphasizes individual linguistic decisions, and the historical-structural approach, which emphasizes constraints on individual decisions. Although the neoclassical approach dominates research, ... the historical-structural approach offers greater opportunity for explaining language behavior and for resolving language problems facing individuals. (22)

A typology for classifying approaches to literacy that closely parallels Tollefson's neoclassical versus historical-structural paradigm features a contrast between *autonomous* and *ideological* approaches. (McKay 1996) Applied to language acquisition issues, neoclassical and autonomous approaches tend to focus on such factors as individual attitudes and motivation in seeking to explain the success and failure of language learners, while ignoring aspects of the socio-historical context of the learning situation that affect and underlie such attitudes and motivation.

Continuing study of the policy options toward African American language, specified above as acquiescence versus resistance to the Hegemony of Standard English, is informed by the ongoing discussion of scholarly orientations and approaches to language planning. Scholars of African American language, by engaging in such a dialogue, may benefit from the increased awareness of the language planning and policy implications of their work.

Wiley notes that "Approaches are influenced by *orientations* in the sense that Ruiz uses the terms. (1996: 115) The same may be said of the policy options toward African American language. The contrasting options associated with Black English and Ebonics scholars seem to correlate with Ruiz's language as a resource versus language as a right orientations, insofar as the former tend to combine a resource orientation with a policy option of acquiescence, whereas the latter evince a language as right orientation combined with a policy of resistance.

The language as a problem orientation is not alien to the study of African American language, but has been expressed mainly by non-linguists. It is prominently featured in the so-called *difference versus deficiency* debate that pitted linguists against academics from other disciplines in the 1960s. Labov (1972: 201–240) argues against a version of the "difference" view which he associates with a group of educational psychologists (Bereiter and Englemann) who characterize certain pre-school Black children as "verbally-deprived" on the basis of observations of the children producing incomplete or ungrammatical sentences such as *they mine* and *me got juice*. In general, linguists argue against the "deficiency" view by alluding to the systematic and rule-governed nature of all human language.

The verbal deprivation hypothesis of African American language is part and parcel of a vast academic tradition of applying deficit models that characterize a vast array of conditions of African American life as problems, or pathological deviations from normalcy. Ruiz's observation about orientations, in claiming that they are "largely unconscious and pre-rational" dispositions, is consistent with the foregoing account of how the policy options of scholars toward African American language are affected by their social location. The explicit use of a sociology of knowledge model, facilitates a straightforward explanation of the tendency for certain scholars to adopt a policy of acquiescence. The scholar's incumbency of an elite stratum of society in which hegemonic values are submerged below the level of consciousness adequately accounts for the tendency for crucial variables to pass beneath the radar screen of conscious and critical study and reflection and remain largely unexamined. The most crucial of all such variables, as noted above, is the stigmatization of African American language, its role in the maintenance of Standard English Hegemony, and the role of both in the exclusion of persons of African descent from full and equal participation in American society.

It may be worth repeating at this point that, while I identify myself with the camp of scholars oriented toward resistance to Standard

English Hegemony, I do not seek to advocate that position but rather consider myself a participant observer in the scholarship which is the subject of this study. I attribute my resistance to Hegemony to my social location and acknowledge that the power of hegemony is such that acquiescence to it may be a wise strategy and in the best interest of all concerned. In the short term, it is the only viable strategy. One thing that I would hope to accomplish by raising the issues presented in these pages is to demonstrate the benefits of a sociological perspective for promoting critical awareness among participating scholars of the policy implications of their work, and the untapped potential of a language planning perspective. In the remainder of the book, particular issues from the list summarized on Table I.1 are explored in detail. Two of them, *What typological category best describes African American language?* and *What should it be called?* are taken up in the next chapter.

4
What's in a Name?

Don't allow the brothers to call you out of your name.

Patricia A. Outlaw

The "star-crossed lovers" of Shakespeare's play, *Romeo and Juliet* bear the names "Montague" and "Capulet," which identify them with opposing sides of a family feud. In that context, the rhetorical question highlighted in the title of this chapter may serve as a reminder that, indeed, names matter a lot. A rose called by a different name might smell sweet right on, but the fabled flower might not appreciate what African Americans refer to as being "called out of its name."

According to Smitherman (1994) to *CALL SOMEBODY OUTA THEY NAME* means

> To insult someone; to talk about a person in a negative way, especially to call the person a name or hurl an accusation at the person.
> "She come talkin bout I stole her ring. I don't appreciate nobody callin me outa my name (i.e., implying that she's a thief)." (p. 75)

The quote at the head of this chapter is taken from a speech by Rev. Dr. Patricia A. Outlaw on the occasion of a Martin Luther King Jr. birthday panel discussion in which she is admonishing young women in the audience not to let young men address them in a certain way. Without using the words, *bitch*, and *hoe*, she gets the idea across.

Naming, whether for the purpose of insulting or merely identifying ones affiliation with a biological family or social group is of profound significance to a number of the main themes of this book including the social construction of reality; the nature of stigmatization; and two of the questions identified above as language planning issues: what should African American language be called, and what is its typological status.

A noteworthy aspect of the African American cultural revitalization movement that blossomed in the sixties involved naming, as growing numbers of African Americans, dissatisfied with their original given names and their association with European American slaveholding families, either discarded them and replaced them with an X representing a lost African name, or adopted a newly-encountered name, often of African origin.

In the West African societies from which many African Americans are descended, a person's given name is of great significance. "Among the Twi People [of Nigeria]" for instance,

[O]ne of the names a child receives is that of the day on which he was born. Of other names which he may have, there is a great variety. One name may indicate the place which he occupies among the other children of the same mother. Still another may be given from some religious motive, such as that given in honor of a god.... Still others are taken from ... animals or other objects of nature or human manufacture. (Turner 1949: 31)

Among the Gullah, two different kinds of given names are typically used. An individual will use what is called his or her "real or true name ... at school, in their correspondence, and in their dealings with strangers," and another "nickname, known also as the pet name or basket name," at home and in other in-group settings. (Turner 1949: 40) The thousands of African-derived personal names that Turner found among the Gullah include *Ajowa*, which in the Ewe language is a "name given a girl born on Monday; *Kofi*, which in several West African languages is a name given a boy born on Friday; *Kwesi*, a name given a male born on Sunday, derived from the Fula language; and *Kuta*, which in Bambara means 'water turtle.'" (43–118)

The Gullah practice of having two different personal names, one for in-group use, and one for use with strangers and public officials, is reminiscent of DuBois' concept of double-consciousness. (c.f. DeBose 2004) Another reminder of it, which highlights its role in the identity transformation experienced by African captives in their forced assimilation to American society is Alex Haley's dramatic portrayal of the resistance, and eventual surrender, of his ancestor "Kunta Kente" to repeated attempts to impose upon him the Anglicized slave name "Toby." A scene in the popular T.V. miniseries "Roots," based on Haley's novel, shows the slave being repeatedly asked, between intermittent lashes of the whip, "What's your name?" And repeatedly answering "Kunta Kente," until eventually gasping "Toby," and collapsing unconscious.

Each of the "two warring souls in one dark body," of DuBois' double-consciousness has a name, one of which became obsolete with the advent of Black Conciousness – at least in the role it once played as the Politically-Correct name for Black folk. Although the ideology of White Supremacy has been discredited, and many of its classic features have been dismantled as a consequence of the Civil Rights Movement – American society is still not colorblind. DuBois' "Negro," who for his "American" better half was an object of "amused contempt and pity," has undergone an identity transformation, resulting in – among other things – a new name.

Throughout the history of Africans on these shores, the preferred group name has changed with the changing state of the Race, and its relationship with the dominant group. It is interesting to note how some of that history is preserved in organizational names. When the African Methodist Episcopal Church emerged in 1787, the group still called itself African. By the time CME church emerged, however, the PC group name had changed to "Colored," a name also preserved in the title of the NAACP. Interestingly, the CME church, in recent times, changed the first word of its original name, "Colored Methodist Episcopal Church," to "Christian."

Political correctness and euphemism

The issue referred to above, that of a "politically-correct" name for the African American people, is a good point of departure for a more technically-oriented discussion of the subject of naming, as it pertains to the key question, *What should African American language be called?* The approach I take to the notion of politically-correct language is to view it as a special case of the more general phenomenon of *euphemism*. A common example of a euphemism is the word *expecting*, used with the meaning of "pregnant." Another is *to pass (on)*, with the sense of "to die."

Euphemisms facilitate discussion of sensitive or taboo subject matter in polite settings. Numerous euphemisms have been proliferated for taboo parts of the human anatomy; e.g., *tush, bottom, derriere*, etc. The subject of race, suffice it to say, is taboo in American society, and it is predictable that a certain part of the vocabulary of race would be taboo, in one way or another. An adequate account of such vocabulary, is organized with the understanding that members of each of the diverse American social groups has words for themselves, and for others, especially other groups with whom they are involved in an adversarial power relationship, that are reserved for in-group use.

In the following paragraphs I first discuss in-group names that Blacks use for themselves, followed by names used by Blacks among themselves in reference to Whites. I discuss both under the topic of *coded group names*. Following that, I discuss other names for Black folk that have been used by certain White Americans among themselves, and how all of the above are involved in the phenomena of taboo and euphemism. I then directly address the language planning implications of the material presented thus far.

Coded group names

The names discussed in this section are referred to as coded, because they typically serve the purpose of concealing from outsiders the focus of conversation on the sensitive subject of race. Because of the porous nature of ethnic group boundaries, the effectiveness of the coding diminishes as the meaning of words spreads outside the Black community.

When I was growing up, the word *spook* was commonly used in such a sense, as was the word *spade*. It is interesting that Smitherman (1994) characterizes both as "derogatory" references to "a black person." She characterizes a third term, *splib*, listed on the same page, simply as "a generic reference to any Black person; a fairly neutral term." (p. 213) In my thinking what distinguishes *spook* and *spade* from *splib* is not so much a "derogatory" feature, directly associated with the words in question, but the fact that they are known and used by Whites, as well as Blacks. What is derogatory is the act of a White person using such a word in reference to an African American, moreso than any intrinsic feature of the word itself.

What is distinctive about the word *splib* is contained in the feature "hip." The word first came to my attention as a young man in my twenties, whereas, *spade*, and *spook* were used for as long as I could remember by persons of my parents' generation, and are now pretty much passé. *Splib* was hip in the sense of being associated with the young generation that was up on the latest "happenings," and most crucially, because it was unknown to Whites.

Other code names for African Americans that were current in my youth are *boot*; and *mem*, which is short for *member*. Smitherman defines boot as "An African American" and continues to note that "The term is used neutrally, but may have come from a source with rather negative connotations, bootblack." Smitherman lists the full form, *member*, which she defines as "Any African American; derived from the notion of racial bonding and solidarity of Blacks." She does not list the clipped form *mem*.

One of the most widespread and fascinating coded group names is *blood*, which was current in my youth and continues with unabated resilience among today's youth. It is definitely a hip term, insofar as it is used almost exclusively by Blacks. Smitherman lists two definitions of blood. "1) A generic term for any person of African descent; a positive term, noting the genetic kinship and shared bloodlines of African people. 2) A member of the Los Angeles gang the BLOODS."

In the interest of accurately describing the semantics of coded group names, it is important to keep in mind, that even after the code is broken – and the secret meaning divulged – a word may continue to retain a neutral sense of generic reference to a black person in the context of in-group solidarity. It is necessary to emphasize the solidarity feature, because, even in an in-group context, a person skilled at "signifying" could use such a term to "call someone outa they name" rather than as a simple descriptor. Also, as noted above, when used by outsiders, or in a mixed setting, the term would ordinarily be taken as derogatory if not demeaning, offensive and highly insulting.

Several in-group terms for White people, previously unknown to Whites, became common knowledge during the sixties when the Black protest movement generated a great deal of public interests in African Americans. Whites learned through reading Black authors such as James Baldwin and Claude Brown, and from the militant rhetoric of firebrand orators like Stokeley Carmichael and H. Rapp Brown the significance of *ofay*, and *honkey*. The significance of the term *craker*, shortened from *white soda cracker*, had long been common knowledge. When Blacks use such terms, other than as authors and orators, it is usually out of the earshot of Whites.

In the community in which I was raised, the word *paddy*, was used as a code word for "White," and White guys were referred to as *paddy boys*. I did not know at the time that this sense of *paddy*, is etymologically related to the *paddy* of *paddy wagon*, and one of the current street terms for police, *rollers*. During slavery, fugitive slaves used the word *paderollers*, derived from a typical African pronunciation of patrollers, in reference to members of the slave patrols assigned to hunt down runaways and bring them back to the plantation. The word *paderoller* was eventually shortened to either *patty* or *roller*, both of which survived and shifted their reference to aspects of the urban law enforcement system.

Racial slurs

Just as some African Americans have their special terms for Whites reserved for in-group use, some White people use special terms for Blacks that are derogatory, demeaning or insulting. When used in such a way they are commonly known as racial slurs. As noted above, much of what is insulting about a racial slur is not the content of the word but its use by a member of the dominant racial group in reference to a member of the subordinate group. Some of the words listed above, like *spook* and *spade* have been used in all Black settings with generic reference. Another such word, *jig*, short for *jiggaboo*, was commonly used by some of my college peers in in-group settings. The fact that *jiggaboo* had been used in other settings by Whites as a slur was not a concern. Other words exist that are several degrees more offensive than any of the above, e.g., *coon, sambo*. I have never heard an African American use *sambo* as a genric descriptor, but the word *coon* is used in a traditional expression *ace boon coon*, meaning "best friend." (Smitherman 1994: 43) In the community in which I was raised, rhymed tributes of camaraderie like the following were commonplace. The first is based upon a shortening of the phrase, *my ace boon coon*, to *my ace*; the second contains the entire phrase.

> *You my ace in any case;*
> and
> *You my ace boon coon, You my pride and joy, You a ugly mothafucka but you still my boy.*

The discussion of group names for African Americans would be incomplete without mention of the word which is so taboo that people are hesitant to say or write it for fear of being censored. Journalists reporting on the O. J. Simpson trial were so intimidated by the word that they could not write it out in direct quotes, and settled for the oblique reference, "the N-word."

The author of a recent article in the Chronicle of Higher Education (Howard, D. L. 2004) reports of his difficulty handling passages in assigned reading material for a course on "Banned Books; Literature and Censorship" in which the taboo word frequently appears. "Should

I say the word or not," He laments. The author confesses that the ultimate irony occurred when he started thinking about censoring himself as he prepared to lecture on Mark Twain's classic *The Adventures of Huckleberry Finn*, a novel which "has been a source of controversy, especially in recent decades, for its consistent use of 'The N-word,' and for the racism that, its opponents charge, it either implicitly or explicitly endorses." It is interesting to note that the author managed to complete the article without one explicit use of the dread word.

Persons who insist that American society is colorblind can take the above-referenced author's experience as a reminder of the power the word *nigger* still has to evoke strong feelings and reactions. To understand the word in its totality, however, it is important to bear in mind that it, and other words, like the above-mentioned *coon*, may function, in different settings, as an insult, or as a term of endearment. When *nigger* is used with generic reference, or as a term or endearment, it is distinguished by r-less pronunciation, i.e., *nigga*.

In the community in which I was raised, the following expression might have been heard as a playful assertion of camaraderie in casual conversations with close friends:

> *You my nigga til I get a bigga nigga,*

In more current usage, the expression *nigga please!* might be uttered by one African American to another with no intention of insult or deprecation, but more so as an expression of incredulity or exasperation.

The generic term for "Black person" is *níga* in Gullah, and in the creole English of Guyana. In Jamaican Creole it has the similar form *níega*. (Hancock 1970) Such data supports the view that the generic sense of *nigga* predates the derogatory meaning associated with it in present day usage.

In the closing years of the twentieth century, a noticeable trend for the generic use of *nigga* to spread to non-African American youngsters has been greeted with alarm by many older Blacks who religiously observe the traditional in-group restriction. This trend is one of several instances of what is discussed further in Chapter Eight as a tendency for African American culture to "cross-over" ethnic boundaries into national and world culture.

The power dimension

One important difference between Black and White Americans in their use of "unofficial" names for themselves and others lies in the dimension of power. White racists had the power to address Blacks in derogatory and insulting ways, openly, and with impunity. In the American South, before abolishment of the Jim Crow system, Whites could and did call Black people *niggers*, *coons* and other derogatory names, the humiliation of which Blacks had little choice but to silently endure. If they resisted, they could expect serious repercussions, which did not exclude being lynched.

In the present post-Civil Rights era, all of the above group names continue to be used by all kinds of Americans. Because of the varying degrees of taboo associated with many of them, euphemisms have been available in the past, and continue to be, for persons needing to make explicit reference to a social, cultural or ethnic group in a polite and sensitive manner. In the present climate of political correctness, which some find amusing, but is a serious matter, there are serious consequences for calling someone "out of their name" anything from being sued for defamation of character, to being fired, to losing votes or customers.

African Americans have had to deal with being "called outa they name" throughout history, and there has always been a consensus in the Black community on the name that they wanted to be called. During my lifetime, I have seen the consensus change from *Colored* or *Negro*, to *Black* or *Afro-American*, to *African American*.

Implications for language planning

Given the prevalent popular conception of African American language as "bad English," the mere act of naming it is a form or recognition, and qualifies to that extent as status planning. While the scholars responsible for the names presently used for African American language do not generally consider their work language planning, the policy implications of their naming practices are clear and worthy of close examination.

Common conventions for naming language varieties typically involve choices that consciously, or unwittingly, assign to the variety in question such status features as *autonomy*, *prestige* and *stigma*. The most commonly used elements in language naming are a name associated with a group of speakers, and a word for a language type, the most common of which are *dialect*, *vernacular*, *standard* and *language*. Other such terms are *pidgin*, *creole* and *jargon*. Occasionally the word *speech* is used.

One of the most common means of naming a language variety is by extending the name of the associated group of speakers to the language variety. Following this convention the variety is given the same name as the group. The people of England, for example, are called English and so is their language. When this option is chosen, the implication is that the variety so named is autonomous, a language in its own right, as opposed to a dialect of some other language.

An interesting variation on the above case – of a language named after its speakers – is that of an independent people who speak a language that bears the name of another independent people. If such is the case, it is customary to name the variety by combining the name of a particular nation, group or geographical region, with the name of the autonomous language with which it is associated. Following that practice, the English spoken in Australia is Australian English, that of Jamaica, Jamaican English, and so forth. In such cases, there is a tendency for the variety associated with the group after which the language is named to be perceived as more prestigious than varieties spoken by other groups. The positive connotation of "The Queen's English" throughout the English-speaking world attests to this principle.

After the American Revolution, there was strong sentiment for the recognition of American English as a separate language; and had it come to pass, Americans would now be speakers, not of English, but *American*. As things stand, the language situation in the United States is a notable exception to the adage that a language is a dialect with an army and a navy.

It is interesting to note that in American society, status differences tend to be expressed through negative or adverse characterization of selected groups. This is in marked contrast to the United Kingdom, where elite status is positively marked. In the area of language, for instance, the Queen's English is held up as superior, and its presence in someone's speech marks the speaker as belonging to the upper classes. Such positive marking is consistent with the frank and open acknowledgment of class differences in British society.

Because of the egalitarian ethos of American society, Americans do not take well to the idea of a superior variety of language spoken by members of a superior social class; and are more comfortable with the idea of a standard English spoken by all who take advantage of the opportunities offered by an open and democratic society. From that perspective, the presence of stigmatized features in a person's language is viewed as evidence of their shortcomings, failure, or lack of merit.

When an autonomous language bearing the name of a nation is spoken in several different nations, there is a tendency for an alternative standard variety of the common language to develop which, within each nation, has a superior level of prestige to other varieties spoken within its borders. Such intra-national variation may be explicitly marked by modifying the name of the national variety with a typological name; e.g., *vernacular Cuban Spanish*. The use of a language name, therefore, together with a status label like *dialect* or *vernacular*, not only implies that the variety is not autonomous, but also that it has relatively low status, though not necessarily so low as to be considered stigmatized.

The terms dialect and vernacular, as used in linguistics, are considered neutral terms. Indeed, in the visionary world of linguistics, in which all language varieties are acknowledged to be systematic and rule governed, and all dialects equal, there is no difference between a dialect and a language. Outside of linguistics, however, even in academic discourse, the terms dialect and vernacular may connote low prestige as well as lack of autonomy. Autonomous languages of Africa, and other parts of the so-called "Third World," are often referred to as dialects in a sense that could only imply a sense of low prestige.

Dialects spoken in various regions of the US tend to be named by combining the name of the region in question with *English*, e.g., *Texas English*. An alternative method is to combine the name of the region with "dialect," e.g., *Louisiana dialect*. Another is to suffix *–ese*, to a place or group name, as in *Brooklynese*. In case of varieties associated with social groups, the convention is typically to combine the name of the group with either the language name, e.g., Chicano English, or the name for a typological category such as *dialect, vernacular*, or *language*; e.g., *Chicano language; Black vernacular*.

Terms that positively connote stigma are typically disclaimed by linguists as inappropriate for use in technical discourse. The term *bastardized*, for example, draws upon the stigma of illegitimacy associated with the root word *bastard*, to imply the disfranchisement of speakers of a variety so labeled to rights and privileges to which speakers of nonstigmatized varieties are entitled. Terms such as *ungrammatical, substandard, incorrect* and *broken* convey a sense of failure or deficiency on the part of speakers to attain an expected minimal level of skill. The common use of such terms by speech community members in reference to a particular language corresponds to a degree of negative evaluation of the variety and its speakers that is greater than what is implied by a more antiseptic technical term such as *nonstandard, dialect* and *vernacular*.

Because of the inappropriateness of common everyday terms for stigmatized language varieties in technical linguistic discourse, linguists

tend to employ terms which may falsely imply a social status comparable to low status nonstigmatized varieties such as regional dialects and
autonomous vernacular languages. A case in point is the fact that
although African American language is stigmatized, and subject to a
greater degree of negative evaluation than regional dialects typically
receive, it is typically labeled according to the same formula as regional
dialects such as *Texas English* – by combining the generic or politically-
correct group name with *English* notwithstanding the fact that the
speech of Black Texans might be perceived as "worse" than that of
White Texans. The above formula, is alternatively further modified
by either *dialect, vernacular,* or *nonstandard,* e.g., Negro dialect, nonstandard Negro English, vernacular Black English, African American
vernacular English.

What African American language has been called

With the exception of *Ebonics,* the names used for African American
language have conformed to the principles enumerated in the previous paragraph. At the time that African American language studies
began to coalesce as a field, Black Americans were shifting, in increasing numbers, from a preference for being called "Negro" to a preference for the term "Black." A reflection of this change can be seen in
the use of terms such as "Negro Dialect," and "Nonstandard Negro
English," in earlier works, and names such as "Black dialect," "Black
English," "Black language," and "Vernacular Black English" in later
works.

The use of the preferred group name together with "English" implies
that the variety so named is a dialect of English. Although, as a technical linguistic term, "dialect" does not denote inferiority, but only lack of
autonomy, language planners considering a name for African American
language should be mindful of the connotation of "inferiority" associated with the word in everyday usage.

Before the appearance of Ebonics, linguists generally agreed on the
characterization of Black language as a nonstandard dialect of English,
and the above typical labels reflect that consensus. The inclusion of
"English" in the name has profound symbolic meaning in the context
of the struggle of African Americans for liberation from the subordinate status imposed upon them by American society, and particularly
the demands of Nationalist and Black Power leaders for some form of
Black self-determination. Some African American scholars, highly con-

scious of such implications, are critical of the symbolism of "Black English," and other equivalent names given by others to their language. (c.f. Smith 1998)

The term "Ebonics" emerged in response to the need for an Afrocentric term that avoids the undesirable connotations of the word "English," and implies the status of a separate language. Note the definition of Ebonics which emerged from the 1973 caucus:

> Ebonics may be defined as the linguistic and paralinguistic features which on a concentric continuum represent the communicative competence of the West African, Caribbean, and United States slave descendants of African origin. It includes the various idioms, patois, argots, ideolects, and social dialects of black people. (Williams ed. 1975 vi)

One feature of the Ebonics definition of great significance, that is discussed further in the following chapters, is the implication that African American language is part of a more inclusive entity, commonly referred to as the African diaspora, in which creole languages lexified by English, French or some other European language are typically spoken. As such, it has what may be seen as a Pan African ideological orientation typical of an aspect of the African American cultural revitalization movement that emphasizes restoration of lost ties with Mother Africa.

Smitherman (2000), conscious of the Pan African scope intended for the term Ebonics, in the official definition, uses the term "US Ebonics" to refer specifically to the variety of Ebonics spoken by persons of African descent in the United States. Although not explicitly stated in the official definition, the term Ebonics implies a language variety that combines surface features of Anglo English with deep-structural influences of West African Languages. Smitherman makes this African influence explicit.

> US Ebonics refers to those language patterns and communication styles that
> 1. Are derived from Niger-Congo (African) languages; and/or
> 2. are derived from Creole languages of the Caribbean; and/or
> 3. are derived from the linguistic interaction of English and African languages, creating a language related to but not directly the same as either English or West African languages. (Smitherman 2000: 20)

The term African American Language also avoids the symbolic sense of subordination to English, and is preferred by some scholars who do not opt for the term Ebonics. A resolution approved by the Committee of Linguists of African Descent (CLAD) through intensive e-mail conversations in the wake of the Ebonics Resolution expressed the consensus of the group on a number of points regarding the nature, history and educational implications of African American language. The group was unable to reach a consensus, however, on what it should be called. "Article two. Name of the Variety" reads as follows.

> We take no position on what the variety in question should be called, whether Ebonics, Black English, Black Dialect, or African American Language. We acknowledge the ultimate right and prerogative of the African American community as a whole to decide what they want to call their language. The only labels we disapprove are inappropriate characterizations such as "bad", "incorrect", and "substandard".... .

In a recent paper (DeBose 2001b), and in chapter Seven of this book, I use the term "Variety X" as a neutral term for African American language, in recognition of the continuing variation among scholars in their preferences, and most importantly, "the right and prerogative of the African American community to decide what they want to call their language." As of this writing the term Ebonics has made great inroads as a popular name for African American language. In academic circles, with the exception of Afrocentric scholars, the term African American English, with or without "Vernacular" (Abbreviated AAVE) inserted is typically used. The use of one option or another by scholars tends to be correlated with the scholar's identification with a language as right versus language as resource orientation, or a policy option of resistance versus acquiescence to the Hegemony of Standard English. Scholars of the Black English or AAVE camp, imply by their naming preference a tendency to classify the variety typologically as a nonstandard dialect, whereas those of the Ebonics persuasion tend to classify it as a language, or at least resist the dialect classification. One other option for naming African American language, which I find appealing and use in the following pages is based on the above-mentioned formula of simply extending the group name to the language; i.e., *African American*.

Typological classification

The tendency of AAVE scholars to choose a name for the variety that includes the word "English" corresponds to a tendency to classify it typologically as a dialect of English, rather than a separate language. Generally accepted linguistic criteria for determining whether to classify a variety as a language or a dialect, e.g., speakers' attitudes, mutual intelligibility, and having "its own army and navy," have been used by such scholars to justify its classification as a social dialect of American English. The above-mentioned resolution of the Committee of Linguists of African Descent takes the position that "the variety in question is an ethnic dialect of American English."

Smitherman (2000) after reflecting on the question of whether Ebonics "is a language or a dialect" insists that it cannot

> be definitively answered by linguistics. Ultimately, this is a political, not a linguistic question.

She further notes that she

> started using the term "language" rather than "dialect"... Somewhere around the mid-1970s.

She goes on to explain her past behavior by noting that although the term dialect is

> perfectly respectable among linguists...it has gotten a bad rap among the public and is almost always used in a pejorative sense. Because of this negative public view of anything called a "dialect," many linguists started using the term "variety." (2000: 14)

Smitherman's observation is an occasion to comment on how the socially constructed nature of reality is an important factor in social scientific investigation, which, if not properly taken into account can lead to false or misleading conclusions.

A social construction of reality perspective facilitates the analysis of key issues and questions that lie outside the limited domain of linguistic theory, by treating them as social constructs. According to linguistic doctrine, all human language is cut from essentially the same mold. Regardless of what it may be called in the real world, whether vernacular, creole, dialect, "broken" or whatever; as far as linguistic theory in concerned, it is the same thing: a system made up of words, and rules for combining them into phrases, clauses and the like; and other rules describing how the words are pronounced, and sometimes built up from smaller meaningful parts called morphemes.

A resolution framed by the Linguistic Society of America at its Annual Meeting in Chicago, convened a couple of weeks after the Ebonics resolution was passed by the Oakland School Board, is true to the party line on the question of the typological status of Ebonics:

> The variety known as "Ebonics," "African American Vernacular English," (AAVE) "Vernacular Black English" and by other names is systematic and rule-governed like all natural speech varieties.

The LSA resolution explicitly plays down the difference between "languages" and "dialects," insisting that

> The distinction between "languages" and "dialects" is usually made more on social and political grounds than on purely linguistic ones... . What is important from a linguistic and educational point of view is not whether AAVE is called a "language" or a "dialect" but rather that its systematicity be recognized.

While the point that the difference between a language and a dialect is more social and political than linguistic is correct; and it underscores the value of a sociological perspective for the subject at hand, the dismissal of the "social and political grounds" on which the dialect/language distinction rests as unimportant "from a linguistic and educational point of view," is debatable, to say the least, and ultimately traceable to the linguists' abstract, idealized model of a language.

Lacking a theoretical basis for pinpointing the difference between a dialect and a language; linguists find themselves resorting to cute metaphors and trite examples when pressed for an answer. On the many occasions during the Ebonics firestorm when I witnessed linguists responding to reporter's questions about such matters, time and again, some version of the metaphorical characterization was given of a language as,

> *A dialect with an army and navy of its own.*

Linguists often elaborate on the "army and navy" metaphor with examples of different languages that are mutually intelligible as well as dialects of a single language that are not.

Certain dialects of Chinese differ so much from each other that speakers of one have difficulty understanding speakers of another, and yet they are considered dialects of the same language. On the other hand, there are varieties which are considered different languages notwithstanding a high degree of similarity in structure, and mutual intelligibility. A frequently-cited case of mutually-intelligible autonomous languages involves Norwegian, Danish and Swedish. Speakers of one of those languages are typically able to communicate with speakers of another without switching languages.

Statements such as "a language is a dialect with an army and navy;" and "Norwegian and Danish are different languages because the speakers say so" are informal ways of saying that the concepts *dialect* and *language* are social constructs. A sociological perspective helps us to formulate the policy question in terms wherein the crucial variables involved in the question of what should be done about African American language are amenable to critical discussion and analysis. Rather than lamenting about the difficulty of getting a job speaking African American language, with oblique references to the real world, we may state more precisely that the variety corresponds to the real world construct of bad English.

As a language planning issue, since language planning exists in the domain of the real world, the present typological status of African American language is "bad", i.e., stigmatized English, and it is the stigma that functions to exclude speakers of the variety from certain employment opportunities. As long as the stigma is deemed immutable, speakers of the variety have no choice but to switch to Standard English to evade the stigma. The option exists, however, for changing the stigmatized variety, to a non-stigmatized status of one type or another.

The present consensus of linguists to classify African American language as a dialect is an academic concept, the reality of which is confined to the lofty realm of academic knowledge. What is of greatest concern for me on the issue of the typological status of African American language is that even linguists are in disagreement. The focal issues are and always have been

- Whether or not African American language has the same system as other varieties of American English, and
- Whether or not it evolved historically in the same way as other varieties.

The null position on the latter issue is most commonly stated in a form known as the creolist hypothesis of the origin of African American language. Another version of the null position is known variously as an Africanist, or African continuities, hypothesis. The above-mentioned stipulation of Smitherman's definition of Ebonics that it has African-derived structural patterns and communication styles or Caribbean creole influences is stated broadly enough to include both the creolist and Africanist options. She makes an additional stipulation that the resulting system is different than English, thereby aligning herself with the null position on the former issue. The latter issue of where did African American language come from historically is taken up in the next two chapters.

5
Where did African American Language Come from?

> The lack of grammar attributed to Negro English simply means that there is a lack of English grammar – something far different, for grammar is structure, and Negro English, whether spoken in Dutch Guiana, the West Indies, or America, has as rigid rules as any language.
>
> (M. Herskovits 1930)

This chapter focuses on contested issues or the origin of African American language, beginning with the idea that has been a pivotal point of ongoing discussion of the question, the so-called creolist hypothesis. I begin the chapter by recalling the pioneering work of scholars such as Lorenzo Dow Turner, and Melville Herskovits – who stood out from their contemporaries in taking an adversarial stance to the dominant paradigm through which academic work on persons of African descent was being carried out; the notion that distinctive characteristics of African peoples are the manifestation of underlying pathologies and deficits. When focused on questions of language, the typical approach taken by scholars of the deficit orientation has been to characterize the distinctive language varieties that developed in African diaspora communities as broken or babified corruptions of the European colonial languages from which they derived much of their vocabulary and structure.

The words of Herskovits (1930) quoted at the head of the chapter, are taken from "a review of Samuel Stoney and Gertrude Shelby's Black Genesis," (cited in Gilbert 1993: 464) which Herskovits criticizes for taking the commonly-heard position that English-lexified languages of the African diaspora, which Herskovits calls "Negro English", consist of badly connected words and phrases, totally lacking in grammatical imilar fashion, Turner criticized his contemporaries for

>n that the British dialects offer a satisfactory solution to
ms presented by Gullah. They contend also that Gullah
is ... a survival of baby-talk which the white people, during the early
period of slavery, found it necessary to use in communicating with
the slaves. (1949: 5)

Turner further criticizes his adversaries lack of familiarity with the
languages spoken "in those sections of West Africa from which
the Negroes were brought to the New World as slaves," and their
failure "to study the speech of the Negroes in those parts of the
New World where English is not spoken." (1949: 5)

A key point developed in the following paragraphs – with profound
implications for the issues under study – is that the creolist hypothesis
of the origin of Black English is profoundly indebted to the scholarship
of Turner and Herskovits. One significant difference, however, of great
and far-reaching consequence, between the classical creolist position of
Turner and Herskovits, and the creolist hypothesis of the origin of
Black English, is that in the process of evolution into its present form,
the classical position was split into two separate issues, one diachronic,
the other synchronic.

Diachronic versus synchronic perspectives

Problems of historical linguistics often require the analyst to think
about two or more different times in the history of a language, and try
to explain how the system as it was at point A, became the different
system found at point B. The synchronic perspective is considered fundamental, for it is concerned with the system of elements that at a
single point in time constitute the internal structure of a language; its
phonology, morphology, syntax, semantics and lexicon. From the
diachronic perspective, interest shifts to questions of accounting for
how the language as it was spoken at earlier periods of history changed
into its present form.

Turner's Africanist position combines the synchronic claim that
Gullah has grammar – and is not incorrect or babyfied English – with
the diachronic claim that certain features of its synchronic system
qualify as Africanisms. It includes *both* the crucial point that it is *a
different system* synchronically *and* the claim that it originated

diachronically in a different way than British- American English.

The present version of the creolist hypothesis r claim about the synchronic system of African Am While the issue of whether or not Black English is a continues to be debated, it is no longer an integral co creolist argument. The evolution of the hypothesis into ent version, therefore, may be characterized as splitting of the diachronic and synchronic claims of the original version into two distinct issues. As a consequence of the separation of the issues, it is possible for a scholar to argue that African American language is not "a separate system" while conceding at the same time that it might have evolved from an earlier creole. (c.f. Labov 1972: 36–64)

Contributors to both sides of the creolist controversy are linguists. Hence the questions of whether or not it has a grammar is not an issue, only whether or not it has the same grammar as other American varieties. Furthermore, regardless of their stand on the same or different system issue, Black English scholars are of one voice in classifying the variety typologically as a nonstandard dialect. They differ on how it came to be so, however, alluding to one or the other of two opposing processes: divergence and convergence.

Divergence versus convergence

Divergent change is characterized by the splitting or separation into discrete forms what was at one time the same; and is supported by evidence that two presently distinct varieties of language were at an earlier time more alike. Convergent change, on the other hand, entails movement in the opposite direction, resulting in the merging or assimilation of previous differences into a unified whole. It is supported by evidence that two varieties were more different in the past than they presently are.

The classic approach to the study of divergent change is the so-called family-tree model of historical linguistics: sometimes referred to as *genetic linguistics*. Many of the languages of Europe and western Asia have been classified genetically as members of the Indo-European family. Similarities in Latin, Greek and Sanskrit which are greater than could be accounted for by chance suggest their descent from a Proto-Indo European language that is no longer spoken.

Genetic relationships among languages are established on the basis of similarities, known technically as *correspondences*, at all levels of

₁ure. Similarities between English and German seen in such ₁₁rrespondences and English *man, hound*; and German *mann* "man," and *hunt*, "dog," support their common membership in the Germanic sub-family or Indo-European.

Divergent change resulting in genetically-related language varieties is typically associated with two different scenarios:

- one involves the dispersal of groups of speakers of an ancestral language to new locations where the language continues to evolve in relative isolation from its parent stock;
- the other involves the spread of a language to new groups of speakers who adopt it in the place of (a) former ancestral language(s).

Language maintenance and shift

The process by which a language is transmitted from generation to generation of members of the same community of speakers, in relatively stable form, is referred to as *language maintenance*. The opposite process, in which transmission of an *ancestral language* to subsequent generations of a social group are countered by acquisition of a different language by younger generations – resulting eventually in replacement of the ancestral language by a different language – is referred to as *language shift*.

A typical scenario for language shift to be set into motion is the settling of a group of immigrants in a location already inhabited by others in which another language is already established as the community's vernacular. The most typical experience of immigrants coming to the United States has been to shift from their group's ancestral language to American English. The complete assimilation of the group to the new linguistic environment may take several generations, with the first generation consisting of monolingual speakers of the ancestral language at different stages of acquiring English as a second language, typically speaking it with an accent. The next generation tends to consist of bilinguals who acquire English as young children and also develop proficiency in the ancestral language through interaction with their parents' and grandparents' generations, while subsequent generations lose the last traces of knowledge of the old language, virtually completing the community's shift to the new host language, English.

Efforts to account for the origin of African American language have tended to focus on debate of the two following opposing positions.

- The claim that the first Africans to arrive in North America shifted to the same English that was spoken by Whites in the area where they settled, and then diverged from it in the ensuing years in developing its present distinctiveness; and
- The opposing claim that the Africans shifted to a "Plantation creole" (Dillard 1971) similar to Gullah that in the ensuing years converged with other dialects, losing all but the slightest traces of its creole ancestry.

The concepts of language maintenance and shift, together with the notions of divergence, convergence, and genetic linguistics, contribute to an analytical framework that is sufficiently broad to encompass the various positions on the origin of African American language debated by scholars, currently and in the past. One additional aspect of language change, discussed in the following section, that of *language contact* (c.f. Thomason and Kaufman 1988) directly informs the issue of whether or not African American language evolved from an earlier creole.

Language contact

Whenever a group of speakers of a language settle in a new location, unless it is uninhabited, they will encounter speakers of other languages with whom they begin to interact socially. In the process of such interaction, through trade, exchange of ideas and beliefs, intermarriage, etc., members of the diverse groups begin to acquire each others' languages and become bilingual. Weinreich (1953) alludes to such bilingual individuals in defining language contact:

> Whenever two languages are spoken by the same bilingual individuals, they are said to be "in contact."

One of the most common results of language contact is the transfer of individual sounds from the first language of a bilingual person in the process of speaking the other, commonly referred to as a foreign accent; and technically known as *interference*. It is analyzed as the substitution of phonemes of a target language with similar sounds of a speaker's native language. When native speakers of Spanish pronounce the English word *pitch* with the vowel of *peach*, it is a reflection of the fact that Spanish has a single vowel (similar to that of *peach*) corresponding to two distinct English vowels. The tendency for speakers of other languages to mispronounce the initial consonant of words like *this* and *that* as a /d/ or /z/, e.g., *dis, zat*, reflects the fact that the voiced interdental fricative consonants /θ/ and /ð/ spelled "th" in words like *thick* and *this* are rare among the language of the world in comparison to the similar sounds typically substituted for them.

Another common result of language contact is *borrowing*. When a single individual is proficient in two different languages he/she has the option of inserting words from one of them while speaking the other. Such *spontaneous borrowing* is common in conversations among bilinguals. Sometimes a bilingual speaker will insert more than a single word from one language while speaking the other, for an entire phrase or sentence, before switching back to the other language. In such cases, the phenomenon is referred to as *codeswitching*.

If a spontaneously borrowed term is for something that does not have a name in the borrowing language, it may be used so frequently in bilingual speech that it eventually spreads to monolingual speakers of the language. Often the pronunciation of a borrowed word will be assimilated to the system of the borrowing language as in the case of the English word *patio*, the first syllable of which is pronounced with the /æ/ sound of *cat*, which is foreign to the Spanish phonological system.

During the Norman conquest of England, the contact of English speakers with Norman French resulted in the incorporation of hundreds of French words into English. Many English speakers are surprised to learn that such common words as *pencil, paper, table, chair*, and *mistress* were borrowed from French, not to mention *beef, pork, salad, chef* and *government*. Prior to the Norman conquest, the population of Britain was augmented by persons of Scandinavian descent who spoke Old Norse, from which English borrowed such words as *sky, skill, skirt* and *shirt*. (Fennell 2001)

When British colonists settled in North America they encountered new types of flora and fauna, and borrowed names for them from languages of their American Indian hosts: tree names such as *hickory, pecan, sequoia* and *persimmon*; and names for unfamiliar animal types such as *chipmunk, moose, skunk* and *opposum*. (Kovecses 2000) Frequent contact between speakers of English and Spanish in North America resulted in numerous Spanish borrowings in American English, many associated with Cowboy lore and the "Wild West," *bronco, mustang, coyote, hoosegow, ranch, corral* and *vigilante*.

A substantial portion of the English vocabulary is derived from African languages. Many of them are better characterized as *retentions* than borrowings insofar as the latter typically enter a language that continues to be maintained by a community of speakers, whereas retentions are words which a community "holds on to" from a language which they are shifting away from. Such common words as *jazz*, *banjo*, *peanut*, *goober*, *yam*, *cooter* and *juke*, have been traced to various West African languages. (Holloway and Vass 1997)

In addition to interference borrowing codeswitching and retention, which are the most common outcomes of language contact, certain contact situations set a series of processes in motion that sometimes results in a new pidgin or creole language, one which derives the bulk of its vocabulary from a different language – known technically as its lexifier – but is in other ways a separate and distinct linguistic system. In the following sections, I discuss basic terms and concepts of creole studies that facilitate critical assessment of the creolist hypothesis. Following that I summarize the arguments that selected scholars have made in support of or against its key claims. I conclude by discussing some of the implications for language planning and policy of the issues discussed in this chapter.

Basic terms and concepts of creole studies

The terms *pidgin* and *creole* presently serve as technical terms, used with precisely-understood meanings in the academic literature of creole studies. Both, however, were originally folk terms (Holm 1988). The term pidgin is thought to be derived from the typical pronunciation of *business* by Chinese speakers. (c.f. DeCamp 1971) The origin of the term creole has been traced to the Portuguese word *criado* "servant." Through a series of sound changes, e.g., *criado* > *criodo*, it evolved into *Crioulo*, and originally referred to descendants of mixed unions of Portuguese colonists and Africans, forced to work on sugar plantations in Portuguese colonies on the islands of Cape Verde, Sao Tome and Anobom, in the Gulf of Guine off the West Coast of Africa. (Martinus 1988) It also became the name of language varieties that took root in those colonies consisting of elements derived from Portuguese and African languages.

The term creole continues to be used as an ethnic identity label for several different groups who claim mixed racial heritage and speak mixed languages, e.g., Haitian Creole, Louisiana Creole, Sierra Leone Krio. The term *patois* is employed in other speech communities for restructured varieties of European languages, e.g., Jamaican Patois. The term *patua* is used by Spanish speakers in the Dominican Republic in reference to Haitian Creole.

The standard definition of a creole is deceptively simple, i.e.:

> *a nativized pidgin – that is, a pidgin that has acquired a community of native speakers.*

A pidgin, however, may not be so straightforwardly defined.

Hymes (1971) defines a pidgin as:

> A contact vernacular, normally not the native language of any of its speakers. It is used in trading or in any situation requiring communication between persons who do not speak each other's native languages. It is characterized by a limited vocabulary, and elimination of many grammatical devices such as number and gender, and a drastic reduction of redundant features. (Hymes ed. 1971: 15)

Pidginization

While some pidgins have enough stability in their structure and use to be comparable to other language types, except for the fact that they are spoken only as second languages, others are markedly "reduced," "simplified" and unstable; so much so that they are accurately characterized as broken language. (c.f. Ferguson and DeBose 1977) Hymes' definition of a pidgin is sufficiently broad and general to include both types of cases. Some scholars, prefer to reserve the term pidgin, or *stable pidgin*, for the former type of situation, and refer to the latter as *pidginized language*, or *pidginization*. (Whinnom 1971)

The process of pidginization is typically analyzed into the following components, or features:

> *reduction,* (or *simplification*)
> *admixture,* and
> *instability.*

A good example of pidginized language is the pidgin French, known as Tay Boi that emerged during the occupation of Vietnam by France. The following example from Reinecke (1971) appears to be a reduced and unstable French, of the type produced by new learners, and not a different linguistic system; spoken no doubt with a Vietnamese accent, and possible admixture of Vietnamese words.

Vou pas argent, moi stop travail "If you don't pay, I won't work any longer" [literally, you not money, me stop work] (Reinecke 1971: 48)

Examples of "pidgin" English used by Australian factory workers cited in a study by Clyne (1975) are likewise fairly characterized as the English of someone at the early stages of acquiring it, e.g.:

I no understand what they mean.

Tsuzaki (1971) justifies calling Hawaiian Pidgin English a pidgin because "it meets certain linguistic and social criteria specified in current definitions of the term." Citing Hall (1966) Tsuzaki notes two conditions that a "true pidgin" must meet: that its vocabulary and structure is sharply reduced; and that it is not the native language of any of its users.

> HPE is designated an English-based pidgin because its structure is greatly simplified in comparison with English, the language on which it is based, and because it has no native speakers, since those who use it speak other languages as their native tongues – e.g., dialects of Chinese, Hawaiian, Japanese, Korean and the Philippines languages. (Tsuzaki 1971 p. 330)

Although Tsuzaki does not stipulate that a pidgin manifest the above stated feature of "admixture," a sentence that he lists containing typical pidgin features contains the word, *kaukau*, which in the Hawaiian language signifies "food."

> *My husband house kaukau no good.* "The food at my husband's house in not good."

Typically, pidginized language emerges in historical circumstances under which large numbers of persons are forced to acquire a second language and use it as a means of communication while they are still at a relatively low level of proficiency. Under such conditions, the language output of the population among whom the language is spreading is commonly referred to as "broken." Ferguson and DeBose (1977) use *broken language*, as a technical term for one of

> three types of language that are not the full, natural languages that constitute the traditional object of the linguist's study. All three are

in some sense reduced in comparison to full languages, and they are not natural in that they do not serve as the normal mother tongue of a speech community.

The other two are "simplified registers," and "the pidgin itself" of which the other two are treated as components. (Ferguson and DeBose 1977: 99, 100) Simplified registers are conventional ways in which people deliberately modify their normal speech for special purposes such as writing headlines, and talking to babies or foreigners. (Ferguson 1971; Ferguson and DeBose 1977) Broken language, and the simplified register known as *foreigner talk* are treated as components of pidginization.

Foreigner talk is activated in certain communication situations in which a language which is the "target" of non-native speakers with limited proficiency simultaneously serves as the "source" of deliberately simplified speech produced by native speakers with the aim of making it more comprehensible to the "foreigners." Such situations are analogous to the interaction of adult caretakers who produce "baby talk" in their communication with small children. The broken language component of pidginization parallels the reduction and simplification of child language, while the foreigner-talk component parallels the baby-talk responses of adult caretakers to child language.

The parallels just noted between pidginization and first and second language acquisition has inspired certain scholars to explore their implications in depth. Bickerton, for instance, develops the view that "pidginization is second-language learning with restricted input ... " (Bickerton 1977 p. 49) Schuman (1978) explicitly defines pidginization in a manner that includes the early stages of second language acquisition, regardless of whether or not it is involved in the construction of a pidgin language among a community of users. He uses the term *depidginization* in reference to the more normal process whereby the output of second language learners becomes increasingly like the target language.

Stable pidgins

While the above examples, i.e., Tai Boy, Hawaiian Pidgin English, Australian factory worker pidgin, might be adequately accounted for in terms of their reduction, instability, etc., with reference to a particular source/target language – and as such qualify as pidginized language; a *stable pidgin* has features that are more characteristic of creoles. A case in point is Nigerian pidgin, illustrated by the following example.

A ting se im go Legos "I think that he went/has gone to Lagos." (DeBose and Faraclas 1993: 377)

Although Nigerian Pidgin might be *mistakenly* identified by a naive observer as reduced, "broken," or babyfied English; upon close examination, it is systematically structured according to a complex and fully-developed different grammar than English. The above example is a complex sentence, in which the word *se* functions as a complementizer introducing the noun clause *se im go Legos*, "that she went to Lagos", which functions in turn as object of the verb *ting* "think." Although the glossed reference to past or completed time is not explicitly marked, it is the default tense-aspect interpretation for nonstative verbs such as *go* understood by speakers of Nigerian Pidgin. Speakers may overtly mark a sentence for noncompletive aspect – that is, so that the time reference is understood as ongoing – by placing the marker *de* before the verb. Without *de*, the action expressed by it is interpreted as completed action, whereas, with *de*, it is understood as referring to an incomplete or ongoing action. i.e.:

A go Legos, "I went to Lagos;"
A de go Legos "I am going/always go to Lagos;"

Other Nigerian Pidgin tense-mood-aspect markers may be placed before a verb to mark the time reference as completed action, e.g.:

A don go Legos. "I have gone to Lagos;"

anterior, that is, prior, to as specified time, e.g.:

A bin go Legos. "I had gone to Lagos;" and

future, or unreal time, e.g.:

A go go Legos. "I'm going to go to Lagos."

Nigerian Pidgin, is strikingly similar to other English lexified creoles of the African diaspora. Gullah, for instance, has the same categories of tense mood and aspect as those illustrated in the above Nigerian Pidgin examples, and uses similar particles to express them, as illustrated by the following examples from Turner (1949).

The Gullah particle *da* marks an action incomplete in a way that might be expressed by the Standard English *–ing* or *–s* suffixes, e.g.:

> *de nyung people what da work on dat place* "the young people who work on that place";
> *dat de devil what dey da give you no*w "that's the devil they are giving you now."

The particle *done* marks an action complete, and may be translated as Standard English *have* or *has*, e.g.:

> *I done tell dem nyoung one now* "I have told those young ones now."

The particle *bin* marks an action or state as anterior to an established time of reference and might translate as English *was* or *had*. The particle *gwine* marks an action as occurring in the future.

Although Nigerian Pidgin is considered a pidgin, and Gullah a creole, they have more in common than their different classification suggests. In comparison to the examples of reduced unstable pidginized language given in the previous section, both Nigerian Pidgin and Gullah are systematic and rule governed, and in every way equal to acknowledged languages, except in the status imposed on them by society. The classification of Nigerian Pidgin as a pidgin should be understood as a consequence of the way that pidgins and creoles have been defined. The important characteristics that Nigerian Pidgin shares with creoles is made explicit when analyzed in terms of the component features of *creolization*.

Creolization

Just as the process of pidginization may be analyzed into the component processes of reduction, admixture and stabilization, creolization may likewise be analyzed into components. The similarity of Nigerian Pidgin to creoles is made transparent by the fact that two of the component processes of creolization, i.e., *expansion* and *stabilization*, are common features of creoles and expanded pidgins. How they differ is in the typical existence of a community in which the creole is spoken as a native language, whereas the pidgin is typically spoken by persons who have a different native language.

Just as the study of pidginization has benefited from its similarity to "normal" second language acquisition, insight into the nature of creolization may be gleaned from consideration of its similarity to "normal" first language acquisition. When children are born into a community in which a native language is already established, the characteristically reduced and unstable output produced by children at early stages of their language, is eventually expanded and stabilized in a manner that approximates the language modeled by adult and older children. Bickerton (1977) seeks to explain the expansion component of creolization by contrasting the typical situation faced by second-language speakers of pidgins with that of children acquiring their native language from pidgin input. For the adult pidgin speaker, Bickerton contends, the "restricted" capacity of the reduced and unstable pidgin to fill all of his communication needs "matters not," to him, because he will

> usually have fellow-speakers of his own language to consort with [on topics that cannot be adequately discussed in the pidgin]. But the child creole speaker will be driven to "expand" the pidgin. (Bickerton 1977: 64)

Anderson (1983) offers an account of the nativization component of creolization, which focuses on the creative aspect of language acquisition. Such creativity is reflected in the ability of language learners to make innovative use of their target language resulting in

> the creation of form-meaning relationships which serve the creator's (learner's) communicative and expressive needs, but which cannot be explained as having been "acquired" from the input. (1983: 9)

Based on Anderson's definition, stable pidgins such as Nigerian Pidgin may qualify as "nativized," notwithstanding the fact that they are typically spoken as second languages. Nigerian Pidgin functions primarily as a lingua franca; to facilitate communication among the multilingual population of Nigeria. Another stable English-lexified pidgin, Tok Pisin, plays a similar role in Papua New Guinea. What prevents such pidgins from acquiring native speakers is the fact that their typical speakers inhabit local communities in which a single language is spoken, and only have need to speak the pidgin when traveling; or conducting business with persons from other regions of the country.

The stabilization component of creolization may be defined as a process through which the initial instability of pidgin language is decreased as innovative forms and patterns spread from individual creators throughout networks of speakers contributing to the establishment of supra-individual norms. It is no different in principle than normal processes of language change such as the creation of new words, and is seen in the increasing similarity of the internalized grammars of individual speakers.

Decreolization

A number of language situations exist in which a creole language coexists with the language which serves as its lexifier. In such situations, typically, the lexifier has higher prestige, is recognized as the standard to which creole speakers aspire, and functions as the medium of formal schooling. The upward mobility of creole speakers, and concomitant bilingualism, results in a situation of language contact in which codemixing of the kinds that commonly emerges from language contact induces change in the vernacular language of everyday communication that are adequately described as *decreolization*. According to DeBose (1984)

> Decreolization is a process of gradual language shift which operates on a creole and is targeted to the [lexifier] language of the creole. It is activated by a situation of language contact characterized by a prevalence of bilingual speakers of the creole and the [lexifier] language.

While the above definition of decreolization refers to a diachronic process, the term is sometimes used in reference to a synchronic system of variation observed in certain situations where decreolization is thought to be ongoing. The variation is conceived of as occurring between two poles of a *(post-) creole continuum*, one representing the maximal co-occurrence of creole features and referred to as the *basilect*, the opposite pole, called the *acrolect* reflects the maximal co-occurrence of standard features of the lexifier language. According to DeBose (1984), The "main components of decreolization" are

> 1. Retention of certain basilectal creole features which closely resemble corresponding acrolectal forms;
> 2. Loss of other basilectal forms which diverge markedly from corresponding acrolectal forms, and

3. Importation of acrolectal features, principally lexical items, into the creole system in a way that increases its surface similarity to the acrolect, but leaves the basic system unchanged.

Gullah texts recorded by Turner (1949: 254–89) indicate that the language situation in the Sea Islands is in the nature of a creole continuum. Speech samples extracted from informants show considerable variation between basilectal and acrolectal forms of selected features, i.e., personal pronouns, which in Gullah do not show the case distinctions maintained in Standard English between subject, object and possessive; the prepositions *to* and *for*, and preverbal markers of tense, mood and aspect.

The basilectal system of Gullah pronouns for instance has a single first person singular form *mi* for all cases: nominative, objective and possessive. In Turner's texts, however, the acrolectal first person singular form /ai/ frequently occurs. For Example, Diana Brown, in a monologue headed *hard time on Edisto*[4] is recorded saying both ...*but I ain goin go pick none there*, and *but me ain gwine there*. Turner lists *un?* as the only second person form, although the form *yu* "you" occurs frequently in the texts. Diana Brown's monologue starts out with *unə* pik *ə bascit ə bin.*, Just about all of the rest of her second person forms are *yu*, however, e.g.: *I gwine cuss em you know... I gwine tell em "you red devil! You z a red devil!"... den you da brag, but God goin pick you up*.

The variation in the prepositions *to* and *for* basically involves the use of Gullah *fa*, not only as a preposition as in *I satisfy what he done fa me*, but also as a complementizer, e.g.: *I have fa work on my hand and knee; dem bukra send feed ye fa feed we*. "those white people sent food here to feed us."

The basilectal Gullah tense/mood/aspect markers listed above occur in real speech in variation with more characteristically English forms. In the following example, we have a repetition of the same meaning, first with the verb *comin* with no preverbal marker, then with the preverbal marker *da*: *Ainty rebel time comin back?... Ainty da comin back?* "Slavery is coming back, isn't it? It's coming back, isn't it?"

Sometimes the variation among Gullah forms is of such a nature that, some speakers will exhibit a high co-occurrence of acrolectal forms. An informant from Johns Island, Sanko Singleton, exhibits

---

[4] I have taken some liberty to transliterate Turner's phonetically transcribed text into conventional orthography.

relatively acrolectal speech in a monologue on the subject of *di hag*.[5]
Much of what marks her speech as Gullah is phonological.

> de nyus to be comin in de room in yo sleep; and dark; and bear on
> you, and dey feel kinda heavy. Say de whole person is wait upon
> you in de bed. Then you caint wake. Then the person who tell say
> the hag nyus to ride em, like the two of we in the house, you'll be
> wake that time. And when the hag will ride you, you'll groan. then
> you – then de one of em who wake, dey'll take a hand full of
> mustard seed and throw em under the bed...

Further on in the same monologue we find the following dialogue
reported between the narrator and the hag: *but ain't you is a hag? Yes,*
I'm a hag, and I rides em.

The claim that African American language evolved historically from
an earlier creole implies or presupposes one or another of a variety of scenarios. The most common assumes the existence of a markedly divergent creole
variety that was at one time in widespread use among Black Americans,
which subsequently underwent a process of decreolization as a consequence
of increasing contact with varieties of English spoken by Whites.

Criteria for evaluation of creolist hypothesis

The claim that African American language was formerly a creole has
inspired seemingly endless argument and debate. What amounts to educated guesses regarding the nature of earlier African American language are
based on a variety of indirect sources: chiefly travelers' accounts and
fictional representations of the language of Black characters in written texts
of earlier times; speech attributed to fictional Black characters; the sociohistorical context of European colonialism and the African slave trade; and
similarities of selected features of Black language to acknowledged creoles
of the African diaspora. (Bailey 1965; Stewart 1968; Dillard 1972)

Much of the debate over the origin of African American language has
proceeded from the following two often unstated premises:

1. That the slave ancestors of present day African Americans arrived in
   North America speaking a number of different African languages
   which were given up in rather short order, and

---

[5] A hag is a supernatural figure of Gullah folklore, reminiscent of a ghost,
believed to visit persons in their homes at various times and various ways.

2. That African American language is presently a dialect of American English, marked by certain distinctive features that set it apart from other varieties.

Socio-historical evidence

The strongest evidence in support of the creolist hypothesis is circumstantial, that is, it consists of socio-historical conditions that are generally conducive to the emergence of pidginized and creolized varieties of European languages among the Africans, consistent with claims of the creolists. The most notable and striking of all the relevant socio-historical conditions is the multilingual nature of the areas of West and Central African from which slaves were typically taken. One noteworthy correlate of that factor is a frequently-cited practice of slave-traders of deliberately separating slaves from the same African ethnic groups, who might speak the same African languages, in order to weaken their ability to plot insurrection. Such practices heightened pressure already felt by slaves, no doubt, to resort to pidginized varieties of European languages as a means of emergency communication.

The typical multilingual composition of slave society, often cited by deficit theorists as conducive to the eradication of African cultural and linguistic traditions, also happened to have all of the prerequisite conditions for creole varieties to emerge. In the newly-created slave communities, the diversity of African languages that had served the captives as a means of everyday communication in their former lives, were frequently unknown by their new neighbors, and the only language they would have in common with other Africans was often limited knowledge of the European language of the slaveholders. Such limited knowledge of English, or other European language would serve as input to newly emerging pidgins, as those pidgins assumed ever increasing roles as the primary means of everyday communication. As knowledge of them spread to increasingly younger members of the community, they would eventually have creolized.

Structural features

In addition to the socio-historical conditions in which African American language was formed, additional evidence for prior creolization is found in the similarity of African American language to acknowledged creoles in its internal linguistic structure. Because of the established practice of using lists of isolated features to describe the grammatical structure of African American language, however, it has proven difficult to demonstrate conclusively to a skeptical audience that selected features of the variety are remnants of the grammar of a prior creole.

Three features that have been extensively discussed in connection with the synchronic claim that Black English is a separate system, as well as the diachronic claim that it evolved from an earlier creole, are the verb suffixes –s and –ed, and present tense copula/auxiliary forms *is* and *are*, all of which tend to be absent in environments where they would be expected to occur in varieties of American English spoken by whites. Evidence of the similarity of Black English to creoles, with respect to such features, is easily countered with evidence of the same or similar features in British dialects. Labov, for instance, has argued to the satisfaction of many of his peers that Black English copula absence is adequately accounted for as an extension of the copula contraction feature common to other dialects, thereby robbing the creolist of one of their most potent structural arguments. Fasold's treatment of the verb suffix and invariant *be* features as minor variations on a system common to all varieties of American English, had a similar effect, and further weakened the synchronic argument of a separate system.

Rickford (1977) examines a diverse array of phonological, syntactic/semantic, lexical and discourse features of African American language against four criteria that he considers crucial in evaluating the likelihood that there was "prior creolization in the history of Black English;" i.e.:

- Simplification,
- Admixture,
- Divergence from other dialects, and
- Similarity to creoles.

Application of those criteria to available evidence leads Rickford to conclude

> that the linguistic evidence satisfies the criteria used in this paper often enough to make the prior creolization of [Black English] very likely indeed. (215)

Rickford's conclusion, as tentative as it is, is couched in a tacit admission to his fellow creolists, that the outcome of the creolist controversy typically consisted of "standoff and stalemate." (215)

Two features of African American language that bear upon its similarity to creoles, but which Rickford does not consider in his analysis of "syntactic/semantic features that distinguish the BE verb phrase," are the completive aspect marker *done* and the future marker *gon*. DeBose 1984 – after describing the manner in which such features as the copula forms, present and past tense verb inflections, and preverbal markers such as *done* and *gon* are part and parcel of a coherent system with striking similarities to the tense-mood-aspect systems of acknowledged creoles – claims that

> The[Black English] verb system ... strongly fulfills two of the criteria proposed by Rickford ... i.e., "divergence from other dialects" and "similarity to other creoles." (p. 14)

Reflexes of English *done, been* and *going to* typically function as preverbal markers of completive aspect, anteriority, and future time, not only in the Atlantic Creoles (Hancock 1970) but in West African languages as well. (DeBose and Faraclas 1993) Such reflexes play a similar role as preverbal markers in the modern Black English verb system. (DeBose 1984; DeBose and Faraclas 1993; DeBose 1994; 2000b) Such evidence, discussed further in the following chapters, has implications not only for disputed claims about the origin of African American language, but also unresolved issues about its synchronic nature. It also has implications for several of the language planning issues summarized above.

Implications for language planning

One consequence of the removal of the synchronic claim of a separate system from the creolist hypothesis has been the reduction of the diachronic claim to "the question of whether or not there was prior creolization in the history of Black English;" (Rickford 1977) a considerably weaker claim than the classical Turner-Herskovits position that would include the question of whether or not Black English is presently a separate system which derives much of its distinctiveness from African language influences.

Inasmuch as both sides of the *weak creolist position* characterize the grammar of Black English as lists of features, and classify it as a non-standard dialect of American English, they are the same in their implications for the key language planning issues of how the grammar of African American language is best characterized and how it should be classified typologically. As such, they eliminate from consideration the alternative characterization of the grammar as an autonomous, self-contained system, and its alternative typological classification as a language.

A stronger version of the creolist hypothesis characterizes African American language synchronically as a creole continuum, the basilectal pole of which is a separate system, amenable to description by means of an autonomous grammar. (DeBose 1977, 1984) One problem with the characterization of African American language as a "post-creole," however, with respect to the language planning issues in question, is the fact that, like "dialect," the typological category, "creole" is also stigmatized.

A different approach to the origin of African American language than any of the options highlighted by the creolist controversy, builds upon the classical Africanist approach of Turner and Herskovits, and highlights the extent to which many of the same features that African American language has in common with creoles are also found in West African languages. The attention to correspondences among language varieties of the African diaspora, including African American language, inevitably bring to the forefront previously neglected questions of its genetic affiliation; and with it the option of classifying African American language typologically on the basis of its membership in a family of languages with roots on the African continent. Such questions are further explored in the next chapter.

6
Language in the African Diaspora: The Case of Samaná English

> The claim that earlier African American English ... was a
> creole, the so-called Creolist Hypothesis, has inspired seem-
> ingly endless argument and debate, pitting creolists against
> dialectologists, and both of those camps against advocates of
> ... other miscellaneous interpretations of what is distinctive
> about [African American language]. The interminable nature
> of such debate suggests that perhaps the Creolist Hypothesis is
> passé. I, for one, am convinced that it has outlived its useful-
> ness, mainly due to the fact that its principal claims cannot be
> definitively proven.
>
> (DeBose 1999)

The focus of the previous chapter on conflicting claims of Anglicist and
creolist scholars as to what best accounts for how African American
language *differs* from other varieties of American language is balanced
by a contrasting focus in this chapter on approaches to the history of
African American language that emphasize what it has in common
with other language varieties to which it is thought to be genetically
related.

The original Ebonics Resolution contained a controversial assertion
which was widely misunderstood as making the unsupportable claim
that African American children are born with Ebonics in their genes,
i.e.:

> ... WHEREAS, these studies have also demonstrated that African
> Language Systems are genetically based and not a dialect of English
> ... (Baugh 2000: 44)

In the context of the issues presently under discussion, it is rather clear that the authors of the resolution wanted to make several key points about the status of African American language, i.e.: that it is not properly treated as a dialect of English, but as a member of a family of languages known collectively as "African Language Systems." Furthermore, there is a subtle implication that the list of features used by Black English scholars to describe the variety is an inadequate account of what is in effect an autonomous, self-contained linguistic system.

A revised version of the resolution, issued January 15, 1997, changes the paragraph in question to read:

> ... WHEREAS, these studies have also demonstrated that African Language Systems have origins in West and Niger-Congo languages and are not merely dialects of English ... (Baugh 2000: 44)

As thus revised, the paragraph is clearly understood as taking a position on the genetic affiliation of African American Language.

The claim that "African Language Systems," i.e., Ebonics, belongs to the Niger-Congo family of West African languages is consistent with the fact that the African descendants of Black American slaves came primarily from areas of West Africa in which a number of different languages affiliated with the Niger-Congo family of languages are located. Niger-Congo languages are spoken throughout sub-Saharan Africa including Bantu languages such as Zulu and Xosa, spoken in South Africa, and Swahili in Eastern Africa. Kwa languages, such as Yoruba, and Igbo spoken in Nigeria, and Akan-Twi-Fante and Ewe of Ghana, constitute a distinct sub-family of Niger-Congo. West-Atlantic languages such as Wolof of Senegal; and Mande languages such as Bambara and Mende of Sierra Leone are also part of the Niger-Congo family. (Burling 1992; Comrie 1981)

The overwhelming majority of the African words found in Gullah (Turner 1949) are from Niger-Congo languages. Over a third (35.2 percent) are from languages of the Bantu group, especially Kongo/Kikongo. Another 31.1 percent are from Kwa languages, principally Yoruba, Ewe and Twi; and 23.4 percent are from languages of the Mende group, primarily from Mende, Bambara and Vai. Nearly five percent of the words are from West Atlantic languages, especially Wolof. The only language listed that is not of the Niger-Congo family is Hausa, a member of the Chadic subgroup of Afro-Asiatic, spoken in Northern Nigeria. It is identified as the source of 5.1 percent of the words in Turner's corpus. (Holloway and Vass 1997)

The claim that African American language, is an "African Language System" related genetically to the Niger Congo family, though consistent with information such as the above, is difficult to sustain without evidence to the effect that subsequent generations of slave descendants did not shift to English, as is commonly assumed, but, rather, continued speaking and *relexifying* their African languages with English words. While I would not rule out the tenability of such a hypothesis – I will concentrate my efforts, for the present, on a problem of more limited scope.

The primary focus of this chapter is on a fruitful but so far underutilized source of insight into the nature of early African American language: so-called *diaspora communities*, populated by persons of African descent in North and South America, West Africa and the Caribbean. A paper that I presented in 1999, from which the quote at the head of the chapter is taken, makes the case that the rival positions in the creolist controversy may be framed in a different manner which obviates the need for continued wrangling over what appears to be an impassible stalemate.

The approach of DeBose 1999 builds upon a wealth of evidence of the genetic relatedness of AA to the diaspora varieties in question considered in the light of certain assumptions about "factors affecting the rate of language change." Two factors of primary importance, for reasons brought out in the following discussion are *isolation*, which is said to retard the rate at which a language changes, and *superstrate influence*, which has the effect of accelerating the rate of change. A third factor, which I refer to as *functional shift*, is also assumed to have an accelerating effect. That factor is assumed to have a significant effect in the first of two stages of a *diaspora phenomenon* as explicated in the next section.

Diaspora communities

The emergence of new varieties of a parent language may gain impetus from the dispersal of subgroups of speakers to diverse locations. Such a dispersal, or *diaspora*, may result in a settlement that retains the parent language in a new environment, isolated from the main group of speakers.

This discussion focuses on a complex, two-stage, diaspora phenomenon. At the first stage, it is characterized by the settlement of Africans, on plantations in North America and elsewhere, and the extent to which they maintain their African ancestral languages, with or without varying degrees of *shift, restructuring,* or *relexification* through contact with varieties of colonial English encountered there.

At the second stage, descendants of the first African captives are dispersed to various locations, speaking what is originally a common parent language, but which continues to evolve into distinct varieties in relative isolation from each other, in various *diaspora communities.* The ones that occupy our present attention include Nova Scotia, Sierra Leone, Liberia, the Bahamas, and the Dominican Republic.

The Dominican Republic variety serves as my primary case of a diaspora variety. It is spoken by descendants of African American freedmen who migrated to the island of Hispaniola early in the nineteenth century. Following established usage of scholars, I refer to it as Samaná English (abbreviated SME), in recognition of its present location on the Samaná Peninsula, at the northeastern extreme of Hispaniola.

Expected outcomes

During the formative period of the African presence in plantation society it is predicted that the above-mentioned factor of functional shift will have the effect of accelerating the rate of language change.

> The kind of accelerated language change associated with creolization seems to be a special case of a more general set of factors subsumed under the notion of functional shift. In pidgin-creole studies, the traditional definition of a creole implies a shift in the function of a stable pidgin, or unstable pidginized variety to that of native language of a community. Prior to the migration, during the formative period of AAE, the circumstances faced by speakers of diverse African languages which no longer served their former function of local vernacular would have heightened the need for a new vernacular. Although English was the most likely candidate to fill the void, many Africans lacked both proficiency in and access to models of English, and conditions were ripe for English to undergo the accelerated change and restructuring postulated by the creolist hypothesis. (DeBose 1999 ms)

Previous discussion of the history of AA in terms of the pros and cons of the creolist hypothesis has been stifled by a paucity of direct evidence of what the variety was like at earlier times. One kind of evidence that has tended to be underutilized – and which depends on the availability of evidence from genetically-related varieties – is that which facilitates reconstruction of a common parent language for AA and the diaspora varieties, based on attested structural correspondences. The reconstructed parent serves as crucial evidence as to which of the possible outcomes of the formative period actually occurred.

Available linguistic evidence is evaluated in terms of the extent to which it supports: either the kind of shift that is typical of immigrant groups that rapidly and completely assimilate to the host culture – what Thomason and Kaufman refer to as *perfect shift* – or, the alternative outcome of *shift with restructuring*. In the former case, the first generations of Africans born in plantation society speak the same English as the British settlers and slaveholders, and it subsequently diverges. In the latter case, the English input received by the first Africans is quickly and extensively restructured – to such an extent that it no longer qualifies as genetically related to the main source of its lexicon, i.e., English. Since the contested claims of the creolist controversy, i.e., creolization versus dialect divergence, are subsumed under the options of the Thomason and Kaufman model, there is no reason to persist in efforts to resolve it one way or the other.

The Thomason and Kaufman model requires two kinds of evidence of genetic relatedness, social, and structural. Socially, there should be evidence that a set of varieties diverged from a common parent through a form of *normal transmission*; that is, either from one generation to the next of members of the same social group, or from one group to another through a process of perfect shift. Structurally, a claim of genetic relatedness should be supported by evidence of massive correspondences at all levels of structure. The historical evidence, briefly summarized in the next section strongly supports the criterion of normal transmission. The linguistic evidence in following sections calls attention to numerous correspondences among the diaspora varieties in vocabulary, pronunciation and grammar. Additional evidence to the effect that the diaspora varieties differ from British derived English in many of the same ways that they resemble each other supports the further case that their common parent came into being through rapid and massive restructuring of available English input during the formative period.

Historical background

Conditions faced by Africans in the (former) British Colonies at the time of the American Revolution were decidedly inhospitable. Free Africans, as well as those in captivity and servitude, contended with widespread opposition from white people to their acceptance in American society as equals. In such an atmosphere, proposals for migration and resettlement of African Americans in Africa, the Caribbean or elsewhere were frequently put forward. Such proposals came from Africans frustrated and discouraged in their attempts to attain acceptance and freedom, as well as whites who saw forced repatriation to Africa as a solution to the race problem.

African-led movements for repatriation generally confined their interest to *voluntary* migration, and strenuously opposed any movement that advocated some form of legislated eviction of African Americans. The founding of the colony of Sierra Leone in 1787, on the West coast of Africa, nurtured growing sentiments among Africans for voluntary repatriation. Originally settled by freed African slaves from England, Sierra Leone grew in the following years with the influx of settlers from North America and Jamaica (Holm 1987: 411). After the British outlawed the slave trade in 1803, the British navy frequently intercepted slave ships of other nations and released the freed captives in Freetown, capital of Sierra Leone.

The American Colonization Society (ACS), founded in 1816 by Robert Finley, a white Presbyterian from New Jersey, was a major proponent of the colonization movement (Campbell 1998). The A.C.S. was instrumental in the establishment of a colony in West Africa in the 1820s at what would become Liberia. In 1822, under the leadership of the Black American leader Daniel Coker, the first group of freed African Americans settled on land purchased by the A.C.S., which granted independence to Liberia in 1847 (Holm 1987: 423).

During the Revolutionary War, Canada provided refuge to British loyalists and Africans who had aligned with them. Canada also served as a magnet for Blacks fleeing slavery and persecution. About 1,100 American Blacks settled in Nova Scotia in 1792. They were joined by some 550 Maroons who were deported from Jamaica in 1800 (Holm 1987: 413). Many of the Maroon settlers were resettled in Sierra Leone after a number of them succumbed to the cold climate of Nova Scotia (Holm 1987: 414).

Fleeing British Loyalists also played a key role in the dispersal of Africans to the Bahamas. The Bahamas had maintained close ties with the colony of Carolina from the 1660s, and "these ties were strengthened in 1783 when there was a massive influx of British loyalists from the newly independent United States" (Holm 1987: 489). During that same period, events began to unfold in the United States and the Caribbean, which resulted in the diaspora community presently found in the Dominican Republic.

At the time of the migration to Hispaniola, the Republic of Haiti had just come into being through a revolutionary struggle against French colonialism (1791–1804). The African American migration to Hispaniola occurred during the second of two periods during which Haiti controlled the entire island. The first period lasted from the founding of the Republic in 1804, to 1809, when the Spanish, assisted by the English fleet, regained control of Santo Domingo, as the Spanish colony was called. The second period lasted from 1822 to 1844 when the Dominican Republic, which presently occupies the eastern part of the island, was established. During the second period, Haitian President Jean Pierre Boyer sought to solidify control over the former Spanish colony by augmenting its population with freedmen from North America. An agent by the name of Jonathan Granville was sent to New York in 1824 by the Boyer government, authorized to promise prospective settlers free passage, four months of support, and thirty-six acres of land to every twelve workers (Hoetink 1962: 6).

The first boatload of settlers, numbering approximately 6,000, arrived in Santo Domingo City on November 29, 1824 (Hoetink 1962). Some 200 of the American immigrants settled on the Samaná peninsula (Lockward 1976). Descendants of the original immigrants may be found in various locations in the Dominican Republic. Most of those who settled in other parts of the country assimilated to the dominant Spanish language and culture after a generation or two. In the town of Samaná, however, and on subsistence farms in outlying areas overlooking the Bahía de Samaná, the English of the original immigrants has been maintained to the present day.

The original settlers were reportedly from Philadelphia, or a nearby location such as Baltimore or New Jersey. Hoetink's informants "without exception" claimed Philadelphia as the place of origin of the first settlers (Hoetink 1962). Samaná residents interviewed by other researchers cite Philadelphia, as well as other nearby eastern locations such as Delaware (DeBose 1983), New York and New Jersey (Poplack and Sankoff 1987). SME may be considered representative, therefore, of earlier AAE as it was spoken in the Philadelphia area in 1824.

The fact that SME has survived for over 180 years in a predominantly Spanish-speaking nation is explained by a variety of social and physical factors which have kept the group sufficiently isolated to withstand the pressure to assimilate that immigrant groups characteristically face. The Protestant religion of the African Americans was undoubtedly an important factor in the cohesiveness which enabled them to maintain English for as long as they have.

The voyage from New York to Hispaniola organized by Granville, had the knowledge and blessings of Bishop Richard Allen, founder of the African Methodist Episcopal (AME) Church. Indeed, many of the immigrants were affiliated with the AME Church (Wilmore-Kelly p.c.). Once in Hispaniola, however, the settlers experienced difficulty securing an ordained AME minister to shepherd the local believers, and overtures were made to the Wesleyan Methodist Church in England for clergy. Those efforts were successful in getting missionaries from England assigned to Samaná, and resulted in the establishment of the first Protestant congregation in Samaná under Wesleyan Methodist auspices. The group eventually reestablished contact with the AME church which has remained involved in Samaná to the present time.

The cohesiveness of the group is reflected in, among other things, a small list of English surnames which are claimed by most members. A monograph on the history of the group by Reverend Nehmiah Wilmore (Wilmore ms) claims that there are exactly thirty three surnames which are maintained by the descendants of the African American immigrants including: Anderson, Barrett, Buck, Clark, Copeland, Dishmey, Green, Jones, Jackson, Johnson, Kelly, King, Miller, Nooney, Paul, Redmond, Rodney, Shepherd, Wilmore, and Vanderhorst. Frequently the same names were cited for both sides of an informant's family indicating that the immigrants sought to maintain group cohesiveness by marrying within the group. Conversations with group members reveal a kind of missionary zeal for imparting "culture" (Wilmore-Kelly p.c.) to the Dominicans, towards whom some immigrants seemed to harbor a condescending attitude. Some of them intermarried with Hispanics, however, as reported by L.R., a resident of Los Algorobos:

> L.R.: *My father was marry wit a Spanish woman. But then I had like the English more. He yusa tell us not to speak the Spanish, but we yusa speaks Spanish while he... twasnt in the house. But time he come we had to speak English.*

The above is one of several indications that marriage patterns were a factor in the maintenance of English. Although mixed marriages apparently inhibited the use of English, it did not stop it. L.R. explained how confusing such a situation could be:

> L.R.: *My mother didn't talks... English. But we would talk English wit her, and she yusa answer us in Spanish... so that we couldn't talk one*

clear ni the other. Because we us mixed. She talk Spanish and we talk English.

A revealing anecdote was told by a woman who had previously spoken only Spanish in conversations on the porch of a guest house where I stayed. One evening she began to speak to me in English. She indicated that she had two children: a girl of 18 who understands English, and a 20 year old son who also speaks it. Her grandfather strictly forbade the use of Spanish in his house. Until the age of fourteen, she understood English but did not speak it. She explained that although she heard English at home, Spanish was spoken at school. She said that she began to speak English after being slapped by her grandfather for responding to him in Spanish.

The language situation in Samaná

The language situation in Samaná since the time of the original settlement is an interesting case of language maintenance and language shift (Fishman 1964) incorporating the various stages of societal bilingualism specified by Haugen; i.e., a pre-bilingual period, a period of adult bilingualism, and a period of childhood bilingualism (Haugen 1969: 64, 65). The experience of the Samaná immigrants, in resisting assimilation to Dominican language and culture, is a marked exception to the usual experience of immigrant groups of quickly shifting to the host language. Upon their arrival in Samaná, the group would have entered the pre-bilingual period. Most group members were monolingual English speakers experiencing their first contact with Spanish. Some of the first Spanish they encountered consisted of place names, and they incorporated such words into their English in a manner typical of the pre-bilingual period, assimilating Spanish forms to the English system. Accordingly, *Puerto Plata* became *Port Plate*; *Hato Viejo* became *Old Hat* (Lockward 1976). They also came into contact with a local variety of Haitian creole spoken by descendants of slaves residing on the former plantation of Tesón, which had been abandoned by the owner in fleeing the advancing Haitian forces. The residents of Tesón have had limited contact with Haiti, and their Creole is archaic in comparison to modern Haitian Creole.

As the immigrants accommodated to their new environment, increasing numbers acquired proficiency in Spanish and the group embarked upon the period of adult bilingualism. During that period, the immigrants and their descendants lived within English-speaking enclaves in the town of Samaná, or in surrounding rural communities; and they restricted their use of Spanish and Creole to outside encounters with members of the other groups. They held worship services in English, and many of them attended private English-medium schools (Wilmore-Kelly p.c.). The year 1932 may serve as a benchmark for the end of the period of adult bilingualism. In that year, worship services switched to Spanish, and Spanish-medium public schools were initiated (Elías-Penso p.c.).

When I first visited Samaná in 1979, I found a community at the stage of childhood bilingualism. In fact, it seemed to have surpassed that stage, and entered a stage of incipient language shift. I was told that the younger children of the group no longer spoke English, despite efforts of the elders to teach them English at home.

Poplack and Sankoff, in assessing the extent of Spanish influence in SME assert that "the massive shift from English to Spanish ...is today almost complete" (1987: 293). Poplack and Sankoff deliberately restricted their corpus to the output of elderly speakers of SME, whom they determined to be English-dominant, if not monolingual. They hoped to maximize the extent to which their informants' English was representative of the language of the original immigrants, and minimize the extent of Spanish influence.

When I returned to Samaná in 1992 for an extended stay, I could not escape the fact that hundreds of persons of all ages continued to speak SME, although Spanish is almost always spoken in public. The apparent reason for the infrequent public use of English is that it functions primarily as an in-group language. The present generation of descendants give little public indication that they speak English at all. I observed many indications, however, that they acquire passive knowledge of English at an early age, and may or may not begin to speak it later. L.R. confirmed as much when asked if the children in her household spoke English.

> L.R.: *Naw. Them chillun don't speak English hat all... They understand, but... Ise talk wit em they understand what I tells em. If I tell em "Pick me up that," they'll go on and pick it up. But they don't talks nothin', can't speak nothin'.*

On several occasions, children were directly observed responding to English commands. In the following passage, T.A. orders her grandchildren outdoors. One of them gives a brief spoken response.

T.A.: *Go outdoors! Go outdoors! Go make noise! Outdoors chil'ren! Go!*
Raul!
R.: *What?*
T.A.: *Go outdoors! Estan loco verdad? Who got chil'ren?*
You?
Go outdoors chillun, afuera! Hey Cootchie! Outdoors!

The above example of codeswitching by T.A. is one of many examples I found of Spanish influence in my informants' speech. One subtle influence consists of literal translations of Spanish idioms in such examples as *You is takin a little walk?* based on Spanish *dar un paseo* "to go for a walk;" and *I am workin' like a bellboy* "I work as a bellboy," based on Spanish *trabajar como* "to work as" (DeBose 1983). Many SME speakers show influence of the Spanish idiom *tener años* "to be a certain age," literally "to have years," in their manner of asking for someone's age, e.g.:

How many years you got? "How old are you?"

The Spanish conjunctions *ni...ni* "neither...nor," and *pero* "but" occur frequently in SME and appear to be thoroughly assimilated loan words.

For all of the above-mentioned instances of Spanish influence, however, evidence of the overall consistency of SME with native English phonological and grammatical patterns is overwhelming. SME speakers frequently express negative attitudes toward SME, however, and use distinctive terms for what they consider better and worse types of usage. Several informants use the term *brutish*, apologetically, in reference to their nonstandard English. The terms *fine* or *fino* were often applied to their ideal of acceptable standard English. C.K. used such terms as she reluctantly fulfilled my request to tape-record her speaking SME to her sister.

C.K.: *Come on! We talks it. I say we speak it, brutish, ain't true? What they speak, it more finer than us, you know.*

The following negative evaluation of SME was offered by G.S-K. in confirming the existence of English-speaking children among the descendants of the immigrants:

G.S-K.: *... What they speaks is English, but not good English. The bad English of Samaná, cause Samaná don't speak the good... They speaks the funniest English. Yeah, they don't speak good English here.*

For all her protestations about SME being "bad," however, G.S-K.'s language exhibits complex and native-like clausal structures and includes phonemes that tend to be lost from English in contact situations. The words *they* and *the*, for instance, are pronounced with a voiced interdental fricative, and virtually all of the phonemes typically found in modern dialects of American English are found in SME, including schwa, contrasting tense and lax high and mid vowels, the low front vowel /æ/ in words like *bad*, and the morphophonemic variants of the –*s* and –*ed* suffixes corresponding to the voicing and other features of the final segment of the stem to which they attach. Several instances of particle-movement are seen in previous examples, e.g.: *pick it up*. In short, the English proficiency of bilingual SME speakers shows little evidence of externally-induced variation.

The ability of at least some bilingual SME speakers to keep their English and Spanish proficiency separate is vividly illustrated by the informant T.A.: when she refers to the town *Clará* with Spanish pronunciation in a codeswitch to Spanish, but pronounces it /klærə/ when she resumes speaking English.

Dimensions of variation

One important finding of the 1992 field work was the discovery of significant variation in the structure of SME associated with the age, geographic background, and literacy of speakers. Previous studies were based on data samples drawn primarily from older, literate, speakers, and residents of the town of Samaná. The advanced age of Poplack and Sankoff's informants may have introduced another source of bias, however, which they did not control for, i.e.: the ability of literate persons to produce more standard language in data elicitation sessions than they would otherwise. Elderly informants for the 1992 study tend to speak more standard SME than their younger counterparts, apparently because of the fact that many of them attended English-medium schools.

The 1992 field work included several excursions into the rural communities of Los Algarobos, Honduras, Noroeste, and Clará – located in the hills to the west and east of the town of Samaná – with guides who were descendants of the African-American immigrants. One of the guides, S.J., claimed that there were young children in the rural area where he grew up who speak English.

> S.J.: *Where I live in the country. In the country where I live the little babies, some of them speak English.*

DeBose: *They do. Where do you live?*
S.J.: *The country.. Los Algarobos, yeah. Baby...speak English. They don't do like, speak English well, but you can understand what they say.*

Common linguistic features of diaspora varieties

The social conditions surrounding the establishment of the diaspora communities in the Bahamas, the Dominican Republic, Canada, Liberia and Sierra Leone support the assumption that varieties of English maintained there are the result of normal transmission of the language of the first settlers. The postulated genetic relationships are further supported by the existence of numerous correspondences at all levels of linguistic structure. The diaspora varieties all differ from Standard English in as many ways as they resemble one another. The structural correspondences serve, therefore, as evidence of the restructuring that occurred with the genesis of early African American language as well as its genetic relationship to the diaspora varieties. Many of those correspondences occur more generally as common features of the Atlantic Creoles (Hancock 1970), not only those which derive their lexicon primarily from English, but also creoles based on French, Portuguese, Spanish and Dutch. Alleyne (1980) uses historical-comparative methods to argue for genetic relationships among this group of creoles, which he gives the name *Afro-American*. Some of the features that the Afro-American varieties share to the exclusion of their lexical source languages are

- Expression of tense-mood-aspect relations by particles preposed to an invariant verb stem, where the lexical source languages use inflectional suffixes;
- Occurrence of personal pronouns without reference to case categories of the lexical source language;
- Question words derived from phrasal expressions in the lexical source language, such as Gullah: *weti* "what," lit. "what thing;" *wesai* "where," lit. "what side;" Papiamentu: *kiko* "what," from Spanish *que cosa.* "what thing."
- Use of a reflex of the lexical source language word for *for* as a complementizer, e.g.: Gullah *fo* "in order to;" Papiamentu *pa*, from Spanish *para* "for; in order to" Creole *pu*, from French *pour* "for."
- Invariant word order in statements and questions where the lexical source language employs subject-verb inversion.

The subset of Afro-American varieties whose lexical source is English have many other correspondences including such phonological features as absence of post-vocalic /r/ and final consonant clusters where they appear in the English etyma, e.g.: /po/ "poor;" /lef/ "left;" and replacement of interdental fricatives of English etyma with alveolar stops, or labiodental fricatives, e.g.: /dis/ "this;" /wit/, /wif/ "with." Holm notes how this last feature is one of several features found in "The North American creoles and post-creoles," i.e., those of the diaspora communities in question, and "not found in other varieties." (1989: 488). Holm also notes that Liberian, Gullah and Bahamian all have /ʌy/ for the vowel in words such as *first,* and *work.* This feature is also attested in my Samaná data.

The claim that English was restructured in the process of being appropriated by Africans is supported by pervasive differences between diaspora varieties and standard English which correspond to striking similarities among the diaspora varieties. At the level of phonology, there is abundant evidence that Africans, in the process of acquiring English, tended to modify the phonological contours of English words to conform to phonotactic patterns of the African substrate languages, e.g., the above-mentioned change from an interdental fricative to a stop /t/ or /d/ in the pronunciation of such words as *this* and *thick,* or to a labiodental fricative /f/ or /v/ in the pronunciation of words like *mouth,* and *smooth* by some AA speakers. That change is best accounted for by noting the tendency for second language learners of English to substitute similar sounds from their native languages for English interdental fricatives, which are rare among the languages of the world. Williams (1993) shows that interdental fricatives are not found in the sound inventories of any of a sample of West African languages. Some distinctive AAE lexical items trace their origin to African languages. A good example of this is /jUg/ "to prick, poke," derived from the Efik word /juk/ "to prick, poke."

The pre-verbal tense-mood-aspect markers in the English-lexified Afro-American varieties employ reflexes of the English verbs *done, been,* and *go(ing)* within a system that differs completely from the Standard English (SE) system. While the SE system is based on the categories TENSE, MODAL, PERFECT, and PROGRESSIVE, the Afro-American English system is based on the categories COMPLETIVE, NONCOMPLETIVE, ANTERIOR, and IRREALIS. (DeBose and Faraclas 1993). Variations in the morphosyntax of AA described in the literature as isolated features, e.g.: copula absence; absence of present and past tense verb suffixes; and invariant *be*; have been shown to be manifestations of various aspects of a *Lexical Stativity Parameter* common to the languages of West Africa (Mufwene 1983; DeBose and Faraclas 1993). According to this system, the marking of tense mood and aspect is optional, and the values marked by English suffixes and inflected forms may be inferred from context, and from the value assigned to a predicate for the feature STATIVE. The past tense interpretation of sentence (1) may be derived from the nonstative feature attached to its predicate, and sentence (2) derives a present tense interpretation from the plus stative value of its predicate.

1. *I ain't see him.* "I didn't see him."
2. *He tall.* "He's tall."

In the next section, I briefly review some of the previous work on SME and note some of the linguistic features that it shares with its putative sister varieties in the diaspora.

Common Afro-American features in Samaná English

Data elicited in 1979 and 1992 from descendants of the original immigrants in Samaná, and adjacent rural communities, contains numerous correspondences with common features of the North American diaspora varieties. Such correspondences support a genetic relationship between AA, SME and other diaspora varieties.

DeBose 1983 calls attention to several features which support the view that the English spoken in Samaná is more divergent from Standard English than modern AA, consistent with what is predicted by the creolist hypothesis. While my present purpose is not to defend the creolist hypothesis, the same features that would count as creole features also qualify as *diasporic correspondences*. The distinctive SME features noted in DeBose 1983 include absence of post vocalic /r/; final consonant cluster simplification; and the non-inversion of subject and auxiliary in questions. All three features mark SME as more divergent than modern AA in that they occur variably in AAE, in alternation with acrolectal or mesolectal variants, but occur categorically, or nearly so, in SME.

The 1992 corpus, collected over a period of three weeks from over twenty informants in and around Samaná with the assistance of an in-group guide, documents many common diaspora features.

The invariant word order in questions and statements, first noted in the 1979 corpus, is confirmed in the 1992 data. The following examples are typical.

> *Since when you here?*
> *You done been up there?*
> *Why I didn't see you?*
> *Where you was?*

A number of distinctive lexical features are found in SME. They include the frequent occurrence of *plenty* and rare occurrence of *many*, or *lots of*, e.g.:

> *Plenty people here speaks English.*

Other typical SME lexical features are the use of *reach* as an intransitive verb meaning "arrive", the use of *hunt* where modern American English would use a different term such as *seek* or *look for*.

An interesting feature that SME has in common with contemporary AAE and Bahamian (Holm personal communication) is the occurrence of *I'm* as a monomorphemic variant of the first person singular personal pronoun *I* before stative predicates such as *been*, and *got* (DeBose 1983, 1988, 1992). This feature first caught my attention when one of my 1979 informants answered me, when asked if he had ever been to the United States:

> *No, I'm never been. I'm been Miami, I'm been Spain, I'm been Porto Rico...I'm got some brothers...*

It occurs many times in the 1992 corpus, e.g.:

> *I'm got eight children.*
> *I'm done been Porto Ric.*

The rural varieties of SME recorded in 1992 data contain a greater number of common diaspora features than the varieties spoken by older speakers and in the town of Samaná. One of them is the occurrence of tense, mood, aspect (TMA) markers preposed to an invariant verb. The forms *was* and *had* clearly function in the following sentence as preposed anterior markers, although they are innovative replacements for the marker *bin* found in more conservative diaspora varieties such as Gullah and Krio.

My father <u>was</u> marry wit a Spanish woman, but then I <u>had</u> like the English more.

The anterior marker *been* also occurs in the 1992 data; as in the following sentences

Where we been, in the blue house with the lady what talk to you. "Where we were, in the blue house with the lady that spoke to you."
The family Kelly they been from Atlanta. "The Kelly family was from Atlanta."

The common diasporic preverbal markers *gwine* and *done* are also attested in SME, e.g.:

I suppose you gwine sweat.
You done been up there?

The absence of pronominal case distinctions, and the use of *fo* as a complementizer, noted in the previous section as pan-diaspora features, occur frequently in rural SME data e.g.:

He want fo us fo tell him a what fambly we is? "Does he want us to tell him what family we are?"
Us mother and father die. They went away. Pero, I mean to say, us grandmother was from Philadelphia.

Some of the most striking examples of pan-diasporic features in the 1992 corpus is contained in oral testimony recorded on the dock in the town of Samaná in which a group of young men demonstrate their English competence and explain how they acquired it. They confirm, by stating their names on the tape, that they are descendants of the immigrants (DeBose 1996a). In the following excerpt from that session, J.C. explains how they "picked up" English as small children in the country from their parents.

J.C.: *Gotta' splain how we picked up the English. The English... we picked it up from we father and mother. But we small. But we don't talk the English same like we talk now, you know...we talk it different. But when come down here in the country from the city so we picked up the English little better, you know, ...talkin' to the Merican people. And so we learn it, so we learn it to talk it little better.*

J.C. elaborates on the point that the English they learned in the country is different by providing lexical examples.

> J.C.: *In the country we speak a different English. In the country we says, like,....here we picked up no fada, in de country we says papá. Here we learnt mada, and the country we says mamá. We says ...like the dock, we says muelle...We don't say dock, we say we goin to where the wharf. We says different, you know. Says wharf, muelle, dock.....We picked up dock here in the town, in the city... We say, we say awakado, we call awakado zavoká. The pigeon peas we says pwakongó.. The okras we say gombó. The country people say gombó. That's not correct.*

S.J. continues with his own lexical examples.

> S.J.: *Then like we say like gyal, a gyal. My girlfriend, we says my gyal, uh, like, ...You wanna know everything, right? When we say like "fuck a girl," you know, we say we juk a girl, you know. We juk my girl (laughter)...... You wanna know everything! Right?....*

After providing a number of lexical examples of their rural English, the young men began to act out dialogues of conversation that might take place in typical situation in the country. Typical sentences in the simulated dialogues are strikingly creole-like in appearance (DeBose 1995; 1996a). While the examples are simulations of the kinds of dialogues in which the young men typically engaged in the country, their authenticity cannot be doubted. The creole features in their English could not have been contrived, as they correspond in great detail to descriptions of other creole Englishes accessible only to specialists. Furthermore, many of the same creole features were recorded in natural conversations during the 1992 trip and are discussed in the following pages. We find *da*, for instance, functioning as a pre-verbal TMA marker in a manner similar to Gullah, and several serial verb constructions, e.g.:

> *Pick up some manyó go bring up ye fo wi da make em sell them some of them down town go eat some, you know.*

Many other examples could be given of the occurrence in SME data of common features of North American diaspora varieties. The brief account just given should be sufficient, however, to illustrate the genetic relationship of SME to the other diaspora varieties. The genetic relatedness of SME to AA is unquestionable. Not only is the normal transmission of a variety that originated among Africans in the Philadelphia area to its present location in Hispaniola fully documented, there are numerous structural correspondences between AA and SME.

The linguistic evidence in its totality shows SME as more divergent than modern AA from present day descendants of White colonial English; and that is consistent with the claim that their common parent came into being through rapid and massive restructuring of colonial English input. In the intervening years, by all indications, AA changed at a relatively accelerated rate in response to pressure from the hegomonic superstrate, adopting many of its surface features in the process; while SME, in relative isolation, changed little since the time of the migration to Hispaniola.

The popular claim that there was prior creolization in the history of AA (Rickford 1977) remains tenable. Without direct evidence of an earlier stage in which pidgin-creole varieties were widely spoken by persons of African descent in North America, however, it is hypothetical and speculative. Furthermore, the key issues of the creolist controversy, i.e., dialect divergence versus prior creolization, may be framed, without reference to the pidgin-creole life cycle, within a language maintenance versus language shift paradigm; by contrasting the equivalent options of *language shift with and without restructuring*.

Implications for language planning

Approaches to the history of AA that place a premium on questions of its genetic relatedness to African and diasporic language varieties are congruent with a number of the language planning issues heretofore identified. The most basic is the opening of new options for naming AA after the family of languages to which it is proven to be genetically related. A suggested technical name for the family of diaspora languages discussed in this chapter is North American African-Derived, English-lexified Languages (NAADEL). Future research may confirm the membership of that family is a more inclusive group of languages.

SME shows many indications of being an endangered language, on the verge of extinction. Although it was still alive at the time of my 1992 visit, in the hills surrounding the town of Samaná, it appears to be constantly losing ground to the national vernacular Spanish, as well as to modern varieties of American English that SME speakers "pick up" through contact with tourists and other visitors. Conscious and deliberate efforts to document the language as it survives today, as fully as possible, and preserve surviving historical landmarks and cultural artifacts, would be a valuable and welcome contribution to African American history in general as well as the history of African American language. If adequately planned, such efforts could also be addressed to current educational and economic needs of the descendants of the original settlers.

7

The Language Situation in the African American Speech Community: The Status of Variety X

> When the term Ebonics was coined, it was not as a mere synonym for the more commonly used appellation *Black English*.
> (Ernie Smith 1998: 49)

The language situation in the African American speech community, which is the focus of this chapter, is in many ways a microcosm of the language situation in the United States. To the extent that such is an accurate premise, one overwhelming generalization, of far-reaching significance is the acknowledgment that it is a virtually monolingual English-speaking community. Although other languages are spoken, English is – with few exceptions – the language normally spoken in everyday public interaction. Major exceptions are places like Miami, Florida, where one is as likely to hear Spanish spoken in certain areas of the city.

Results of the 2000 census provide clear statistical evidence of the extent of English monolingualism in the US. Of over 262 million persons who responded to a census question regarding their English-speaking ability and languages spoken in the home, over eighty percent responded that they only speak English. Most of the remaining 18 percent indicate that they speak Spanish in the home, about 11 percent. The results are not broken down by race, but I would strongly suspect that African Americans responded in a similar manner to the overall population.

In the summer of 2001, I had the occasion to collect a small sample of data on how members of the American speech community assign status to varieties in their linguistic repertoire. It consists of responses given by students in my Introduction to Language class to the essay question "How accurate is the statement, 'The United States is an English-speaking country?' Explain." Of 24 students who responded to the question, 8 indicated that the statement is "very accurate." Nine answered "somewhat accurate," and the remaining seven responded "Not very accurate."

Fourteen students, including 4 of the ones who answered "not very accurate," attributed the status of "Dominant" or "Official Language" to English. Five of the students who responded "very accurate" also mentioned that English is predominantly used in mass communication, and 5 stated that it is the language of government and business. Three of the 8 students in the "very accurate" category specifically mentioned that English is the language expected in everyday communication, or needed for survival. Of 6 responses in the very accurate category which acknowledged that other languages are spoken, 4 did so with the caveat that other languages are not accommodated, or that they are "looked down on."

Five of the students who responded "somewhat accurate, " and all of the ones who answered "not very accurate" mentioned the fact that other languages are spoken as well in their explanation. Six responses in the "somewhat accurate" category explicitly mention the function of English as the language of everyday communication, or the idea that it is needed for survival, in their explanations.

Insofar as my students' responses are typical of current attitudes toward language in the United States, they reveal the ideological basis of the frequently-heard assertion that the United States is "an English-speaking country." What it means is that although languages other than English are spoken, English is the language that everyone is expected to use in everyday communication. It is also the dominant language of business, government, education, and mass communication.

One of several approaches taken in the following pages to the language situation in the African American speech community is to examine the extent to which it may be fairly characterized as a microcosm of the language situation in the United States. Within that context several issues that have recently come to the forefront in academic discussions of African American language, are brought into focus. One such issue, which I have previously alluded to as a language planning issue, is the question of the typological status of African American language, and the controversy surrounding its typical classification as a nonstandard dialect. Some of the scholars who take issue with that classification take the position that AA is not English. Ernie Smith, for instance, quoted at the head of the chapter, argues that Ebonics is not a dialect of English but rather

> an African Language System that has adopted European words. (1998: 56)

An adequate account of the language situation in the African American speech community can clarify the issue just alluded to, and others raised below, through a detailed description of the specific number and types of varieties that constitute the African American linguistic repertoire.

Language situation

For the sake of the present discussion, the term *language situation* is defined as

> a comprehensive account of the overall pattern of language use characteristic of a given speech community in terms of relevant demographic, historical, political and economic factors; as well as the manner in which social meaning is constructed and expressed through available means of verbal communication.

The language situation in the African American speech community is the focus of a paper (DeBose 2001b) in which "I examine how meaning is constructed by speech community members in the course of their everyday experience; as well as how established meaning affects the selection of expressive means from the linguistic repertoire of the community."

The linguistic repertoire was defined above informally by analogy to a wardrobe, making reference, among other things, to the incongruity of wearing a tuxedo to a barbecue. In more formal terms the linguistic repertoire may be defined as the totality of linguistic means available to members of a speech community. Such "linguistic means" may consist of

1. Several different languages; in which case analysis may focus on the conditions under which one or another language may or should be used; or
2. Several different dialects, or stylistic options, of a single language in which case analysis is focused on such parameters as the social con-

ditions under which using one or another particular variety is deemed acceptable.

In the former case, in which several different language varieties are salient features of the language situation under study, a useful tool for systematically describing them in terms that highlight distinctive aspects of their status in the speech community is a "Sociolinguistic typology for describing national multilingualism" proposed by Stewart (1968) and elaborated by Ferguson (1971) which specifies such language types, as *Standard, Vernacular, Classical, Creole*, etc., and such language functions as *official, group, religious, medium of instruction, literary*, and *school subject*, that may be used to describe various aspects of the status of language varieties in the linguistic repertoire of a community under study. In a situation such as the US, where the bulk of the functional load for various communicative needs is carried by a single language, other useful tools may be applied toward the end of analyzing variation among different styles and levels of usage of the common language.

A frequently used tool for the analysis of stylistic variation in English is Martin Joos' *Five Clocks* model which specifies a *Frozen Style* typical of written literature; a *Formal Style* associated with speeches and lectures; a *Consultative Style*, in which differences in power and status among the participants contribute to an uneven distribution of turns in the conversation – rendering it more relaxed than the formal style; a *Casual Style* – in which turns of conversational participants may overlap to such an extent that several people, are talking at the same time; and the *Intimate Style*, in which a great deal can be communicated through few if any words, due to the exceptional amount of shared experience of the participants. Yet another useful tool for analysis of status differences among different varieties of a single language is the concept of stigmatization, especially as it informs the hegemony of Standard English. Systematic study of the allocation of language varieties to the linguistic repertoire of a given speech community may be framed within the general topic of social meaning.

Social meaning

Two distinct but related approaches to the subject of social meaning are found in sociolinguistic literature. One is the study of how members of speech communities convey, through their choice among available expressive means, something beyond the literal meaning of utterances. The choice between "Serena totally dominated her opponent" and "Serena kicked the girl's ass" is such a choice. Both literally mean the same thing, but involve different presuppositions about the social situation in which they would be appropriately uttered. The other approach to social meaning concerns the study of how members of a social group construct and maintain a particular ideology.

I use the term ideology here in a sense that is synonymous with "world view" and "perspective." More specifically, I mean the taken for granted, or self-evident, aspects of the everyday experience of a people. It includes constructs such as race, class and gender. It also includes the statuses assigned to language varieties. The status of a linguistic system may be defined as a composite assessment of its prestige, utility, type and function from the –*emic* perspective of speech community members. For present purposes, the fundamental difference between –emic, and –etic, approaches to data collection and analysis is that the former approach attempts to *get inside the heads*, so to speak, of a social group under study. What one strives *not* to do is to impose one's own world view upon the data. An "–etic" approach – which describes a situation from the perspective of the investigator, using descriptive and analytical categories of an abstract or universal framework, one that the investigator imposes upon the subject matter – is not necessarily bad, and in some cases may be necessary at a preliminary stage of study.

An illustration of the difference between –etic and –emic data that is directly relevant to the issues at hand is the evidence cited in the previous chapter of the prevalence of negative attitudes among speakers of Samaná English seen in a tendency to describe it by such terms as "bad" and "brutish." Such evidence is interpreted from an –emic perspective as documenting the reality of the construct of "bad" English as a salient aspect of the status of SME in the community's linguistic repertoire. From an –etic perspective, a linguist could take the position that the speech community members are ill-informed, or ignorant, of the fact that all human language, including SME is systematic and rule-governed. That would not alter the fact, however, that in the real world of their everyday experience it is the embodiment of the social construct, "The Bad English of Samaná."

In the ensuing discussion, I devote considerable attention to clarifying the status, in the linguistic repertoire of the African American community, of what I refer to as "Variety X". As noted in Chapter Four, I began using the term "Variety X" in a course unit on "What should [African American language] be called? The letter X, in addition to evoking associations with the Black Nationalist leader Malcolm X and the practice of using an X to stand for a lost African name, is an expression of my belief that it is the prerogative of the Black community, in the final analysis, to decide what their language should be called. Hence I suggested using Variety X "as a neutral label for what is variously called BE, AA(V)E, AAL, (US) Ebonics, as well as other terms," including "Nation Language," a name not mentioned in Chapter Four, but increasingly used in literature of the language of Hip Hop. (c.f. Spady, Lee and Alim 1999)

My use of "Variety X" in the title of DeBose 2001 is for the expressed purpose of avoiding "get[ting] into a hassle over terminology" – while raising, at the same time "some substantive issues that involve terminology." One such issue is the above-mentioned tendency for some Black English scholars to use the term Ebonics as a synonym for AAVE, in spite of the insistence of certain scholars that Ebonics is not Nonstandard English.

Typical of the view that Ebonics is not a synonym for Black English is an article by Robert L. Williams and Mary Brantley (1975) dedicated to "Disentangling the confusion surrounding slang, nonstandard English, Black English and Ebonics." The following quote summarizes their position:

> Ebonics is unique in both its stylistic and linguistic dimensions. The stylistic dimension includes features such as rhyming, signifying, playing the dozens, jiving, capping, rapping, etc. (133, 34).

From this perspective, Black slang tends to be included, rather than excluded from the domain of relevant discourse, and the classification of the variety as a nonstandard dialect of English is rejected.

Williams and Brantley make a clear distinction between Ebonics and nonstandard English which are represented by two different types of sentences on a list presented to research subjects. Their finding that black subjects tend to identify certain sentences as "uniquely black" e.g.: "Joe lost his gig and had to give up his crib;" and others as "typically spoken by Blacks and whites" e.g.: "I been trying to call you all day;" support their approach of treating Black language and culture as a seamless whole characterized by the co-occurrence of Variety X structural features, with slang expressions and nonverbal behavior.

Smitherman (2000) addresses the issue of Nonstandard English versus Ebonics, insisting that "Nonstandard American English refers to those language patterns and communication styles that are non-African in origin and which are used by the working class." She goes on to give the following examples "the pronunciation of 'ask' as 'axe,' the use of double negatives... and the use of 'ain't.'" "Such features of American English," she continues, "are often erroneously characterized as Ebonics. They are not" (p. 10).

After careful thought and consideration, I find myself basically in agreement with the latter view, i.e.: that there are two distinct linguistic phenomena that tend to be confused. The definitions presented above raise as many questions, however, as they answer. One is the need for clarification of the "stylistic dimension" referred to by Williams and Brantley. What other forms and genres of the African American tradition are included, besides those explicitly named by Williams and Brantley, i.e., "signifying, playing the dozens ... rapping, etc."? What about spirituals? Blues and other secular music? What about the African American National Anthem "Lift every voice and sing"? What about Langston Hughes' Simple stories, and Paul Lawrence Dunbar's dialect poetry.

Another type of question, raised by Smitherman's discussion of dialect features as criteria for classifying an instance of language as Nonstandard English versus Ebonics, concerns how the presence (or absence) of non-standard dialect features in traditional African American genres is to be regarded. Is it the feature, or the use to which it is put, that determines its inclusion in, or exclusion from the uniquely black linguistic corpus? A case in point is a conversational exchange reported by Claudia Mitchell-Kernan, where a male interlocutor opens a conversation with her with the words

Mamma you sho is fine.

The utterance has features associated with nonstandard English, i.e., the pronunciation of <u>sure</u> as /šo/, and the use of <u>is</u> with a second person subject. It is not perceived as "nonstandard English" in African American cultural settings such as the one under discussion, however, but rather as an instance of talking trash.

While Smitherman's point about the tendency to confuse instances of general nonstandard English with African American language is well taken, the above example is one of many that might be cited of the *ambiguity of dialect features*. That is, a single particular linguistic feature may serve, in various contexts, to identify a speaker as lower class, to identify a situation of use as casual, or – to mark the discourse context of a particular speech event as an instance of signifying, talking trash, or some other distinctively-black mode of communication.

The issue of Ebonics versus nonstandard English is further explored in the following paragraphs, within the general framework of alternative accounts of the language situation in the African American speech community, including the strategy alluded to above of treating the situation in Black America as a microcosm of the language situation in the United States.

A microcosm of the US language situation

In this section I look closely at several generalizations commonly made by linguists that are supposed to apply to all varieties of American English in terms of their implications for the status of Variety X in the AA linguistic repertoire. The first is what I call *the doctrine of the equality and inequality of dialects*. That is, the above-noted tendency for linguists to affirm that *everybody speaks a dialect and all dialects are equal*, followed – however – with the caveat that *some dialects are more equal than others*. The first part of the doctrine, that affirms the equality of all varieties is an *–etic* claim, derived from the application of linguistic theory to the facts. The caveat of recognizing a degree of *inequality*, represents what members of the speech community feel in their guts, which leads them to consistently favor certain varieties over others. The observation that certain varieties, such as Southern, Appalachian, and African American tend to be *disfavored* when measured by the reactions of speech community members, is –emic in nature, and attributed to their experience of everyday reality.

Building on the above observation, it may be concluded that one component of the AA linguistic repertoire is the variety of American English that everybody speaks, in the particular form that it is typically spoken by African Americans. A likely candidate for that status is the variety commonly known as Black English, or AAVE. Another component, undoubtedly, is Standard English. A good part of the above-noted controversy may be seen as a question of whether or not a *third variety*, corresponding to the name, *Ebonics*, coexists in the AA linguistic repertoire with SE and AAVE.

The key question, i.e., of whether or not AAVE and Ebonics are different words for the same language variety, is approached indirectly in the following paragraphs by closely examining the implications of several alternative accounts of the AA language situation that shed light on the issue in various ways. The first is the frequently heard claim that the situation is adequately accounted for by a model of class stratification.

Class stratification

The class-stratification model claims that the linguistic repertoire of the African American speech community is adequately described as the coexistence of two varieties Black English and Standard English, which are spoken by two different sub-groups of the community. The former is said to be spoken mainly by poor and uneducated persons, whereas the latter is spoken by middle and upper class persons. What is often overlooked by those who make such a claim is that it is not just Black English, but all varieties of American English that are stratified by class. To that extent the situation in the African American speech community is indeed a microcosm of the national language situation. Another aspect of the language situation that is frequently overlooked is the fact that both Black and Standard English may be spoken by the same *bilingual* individuals.

Bilingualism

The term bilingualism, as used here, is not meant to imply that the two varieties postulated as components of a bilingual linguistic repertoire are separate languages, but only that they qualify as separate linguistic systems according to agreed upon criteria. One version of a bilingual model, which I have defended in the past (DeBose 1992; VanKeulen et al. 1998) uses evidence of codeswitching, and structural differences that are tantamount to two different linguistic systems, to support the assertion that the typical member of the African American speech community is proficient in Standard English and African American language. In DeBose 1992, I treat African American language and Standard English

> as two different closely – related linguistic systems which co-exist in the African American linguistic repertoire. Each system is defined as an autonomous grammar, and the interaction between them is considered to be governed by the same principles as those that govern languages in contact ... generally. (DeBose 1992: 159)

The speech of one of the informants for the above-mentioned Oakland pilot study, identified as *P.*, is "a college graduate who works for a government agency" and who

> in my estimation is a balanced bilingual speaker of BE and SE... . P. switches effortlessly from one variety to another according to cues that become apparent in the course of the analysis. (161)

From listening to the first few minutes of the recording, one might be led to the false conclusion that P. is a monolingual speaker of Standard English (SE). The choice of SE in the first example cited is associated with the outsider status of my research partner, N. to whom she addresses the following comment

> *I just can't stay in bed late. I can't do it.*

One feature of that segment, besides the grammar that identifies it as SE, is the pronunciation of *can't* with the low front vowel /æ/, which contrasts markedly with her pronunciation of it as *cain't* at points in the conversation in which she switches to BE. P. continues to speak SE, still talking to N. after introducing him to her daughter, M. who is attending college. "The topic of the conversation is the experience of being a university student."

> *I mean there's no talking to them, you know, when, I mean, you're just part of the statistics. That's what, her cousin D went there. He said, I'm just a number up here, boy.*

P. first switches to BE as a member of the audience of her husband F. as he tells humorous stories from the rural Louisiana folk culture in which he was raised. P.'s contributions to the conversation at this point are in the form of feed-back to the narrator at breaks in the ongoing narrative. A response to a humorous line in a story about F.'s "Uncle Zeke's first trip to California," is typical of such feed-back.

> F: ... *a guy came by there from the, comin down the interstate, and stopped. He asked him where was he goin, he say "I'm goin up to Mr. Billy-Bob's to get me a box of snuff."*
> P: *He done lost his poor mind out there, huh?*

As F. continues to tell stories, P. continues to inject feed-back responses in BE:

> *What about some more of them stories?*
> *Is that y'all church?*
> *What about the time they was in the church prayin?*
> *Oh! I done forgot it.*

Another mode of codeswitching in which P., engages on several occa-sions is to directly quote, herself or other family members in personal narratives. One such narrative relates an instance in which P. "fusses" at her daughter L. "who is late coming home from a music rehearsal, and admits having spent time at a local shopping mall "looking around." (segments of the narrative identified as in Black English are underscored)

> P. *So at about, uh, two o'clock they <u>wasn't</u> back, you know, one o'clock they weren't back. They <u>was</u> supposed to take the bus. Two o'clock they weren't back, you know, till a round four or five, I was sitting here at this counter, and I <u>seen</u>, saw 'em, seen 'em come, you know, slippin by here. I said "L! <u>Bring yo ass</u> (laughter)! She slip ..., she's goin' over to my sister's house." I said "Where have you been all day! Where have you been!"* "We just went up to the Mall. <u>We was, we just walkin' around. We just lookin at the Mall</u>," I said, "<u>Lookin' at the Mall? Thugs and hoods hang out at the Mall! I ain't raise no thug and hood, here!</u>" You know. So then she "<u>Well, we didn't, we wasn't, we just lookin' around and we got us sumpm to eat and stuff.</u>" Oh I fussed and I cussed. I said "<u>You on punishment now for six months. You cain't look at no TV. You cain't do nothin!</u>" So then, uh, a few nights ago me and F went up to the Mall (laughter) ... (163–4)

The article concludes with the observation that the codeswitching data just considered

> is striking counter evidence to the claim that BE is spoken mainly by poor and uneducated persons. We must await the results of future research for a definitive assessment of the prevalence of BE/SE codeswitching among African-Americans, but my impression as a member of the speech community is that BE is frequently spoken by middle-class persons. (165)

The informant, P. is typical of educated middle-class Americans, many of whom experience a marked degree of mobility, upward and outward from predominantly black urban enclaves, and rural communities in the South where African American language is the normal medium of everyday communication. Her bilingualism, and codeswitching behavior is striking counterevidence to the class-stratification model of the language situation in the African American speech community.

Although the evidence of codeswitching just presented tends to refute the class-stratification model, it tends to support the characterization of the African American linguistic repertoire as consisting of just two varieties, Black English/Ebonics, and Standard English. In my more recent work, I have begun to explore a diglossia model, which has the potential of clarifying the issue of two varieties or three. In the following discussion of the diglossia model, I restrict the term Black English to distinctively-black language which functions as the vernacular of everyday communication in predominantly-Black neighborhoods. I reserve the term Ebonics for language that serves to situate certain acts of speaking within a Black tradition of oral performance that has existed in various forms since slavery; (c.f. Hughes and Bontemps 1958; Gates 1988; Goss and Barnes 1989) the most recent form of which is currently being fashioned by younger Blacks born in the post-civil era, under the general rubric of Hip-Hop culture.

Diglossia

The concept of diglossia, introduced by Ferguson (1959) calls attention to the existence of a pattern found in various parts of the world where two very divergent varieties of the same language, designated H and L, coexist in a complementary functional relationship in which H functions mainly for formal and written purposes and L for everyday interaction. The H variety has the typological classification, Classical, and the L variety that of Vernacular.

Applied to the language situation in the African American community, the L variety is the variety of English that speakers use in everyday public encounters, AAVE for some, General American English, for others. African Americans like the above-mentioned informant, P., born in the rural South and raised in predominantly Black urban enclaves in the North or West, speak a distinctively Black variety as their native language, and acquire bilingual proficiency in Standard English through education and upward mobility. The children of such persons are frequently raised in integrated neighborhoods and attend schools with predominantly White student bodies. Many such children grow up as native speakers of a variety of General American English that has few, if any, of the features typically listed as characteristic of Black English.

The H variety of the proposed Diglossia model, is difficult to conceptualize, partly because of the way that it often uses vernacular forms and features, but for different functions than those fulfilled by the local vernacular. It is the language of the Negro Spirituals highlighted in lyrics such as "Josh'a fit de battle ob Jericho" and "Steal away to Jesus, I ain't got long to stay here;" of Blues lyrics like "The eagle flies on Friday; Rhythm and Blues lines like "Lawdy, Lawdy, Lawdy Miss Claudie, you sho look good to me;" of memorable Jazz songs like "Is you is or is you ain't my baby."

In general, the functions fulfilled by the H variety have to do with the performance of rituals associated with the Black Experience. For the sake of this discussion, African American Culture, the Black Experience, and The African American Tradition are equivalent terms for a system of meaning consisting of both verbal and nonverbal symbols, which exists in several variants including Church life, Street Life, and Political Activism. The language of certain aspects of the Black tradition, such as the Negro Spiritual, is clearly Classical, and qualifies unquestionably as a diglossic H. It is not spoken by any sector of the community as a native language, and its use is strictly limited to performance. Other aspects of the Black Experience involve language that is not as divergent from everyday language as the Spirituals, however. Such language may, nevertheless, be treated as *Classical African American* language because of its use as a medium of *performance*; with the understanding that the performance of Black culture takes place on a continuum ranging from mundane everyday settings, to the more formal settings of the stage, the pulpit and podium, to the street corner.

It may be surprising to an outsider the extent to which mundane aspects of the everyday experience of African Americans involve performance. An indication of the high value that African Americans place on verbal skill is the preponderance of highly-stylized patterns of communication characterized by indirection and artful use of language, known by such names as signifying, marking, rapping, talking trash, and playing the dozens. (Mitchell-Kernan 1971, Morgan 2002) Gates Jr. provides a succinct summary of the mundane character of what he calls "traditions of the race". It is amazing he observes, "how much black people, in ritual settings such as barbershops and pool halls, street corners and family reunions, talk about talking." (1998, xi)

The diglossia model of the African American language situation, offers a useful way of studying African American discourse patterns within a more comprehensive framework which facilitates its interaction with other significant aspects of the language situation. One thing that is highlighted by such a perspective is a growing prevalence of younger members of the speech community, who speak a variety of General American English as their everyday vernacular, but find occasion to use a markedly African American variety in the performance of such genres as Rap and Hip Hop.

The original idea for DeBose 2001 was inspired by evidence discussed by Alim (2001) of variation in the frequency of typical Black English features in performances by Hip-Hop artists. The features in question are shown to occur in a pattern that is the opposite of what would be expected in the speech of persons whose everyday vernacular is marked by such features, that is, they occur more frequently on stage, when greater attention is focused on their language; and decrease in frequency when the speakers pay minimal attention to their speech.

Alim's evidence is consistent with an emerging diglossia in the African American speech community, in which the vernacular of everyday communication of former generations is threatened with extinction. Because of an established tradition, however, of artful use of language based on traditional Black vernacular forms, continues to evolve into new forms, the most recent of which is Hip-Hop.

Ferguson lists several definitional criteria for diglossia which may be applied to the African American situation. One is that it is the vehicle of a large and respected body of literature. What I am calling Classical African American satisfies that criterion well. Although much of it is of the nature of an oral tradition, it is generally recognized as the source of the greatest contributions of American culture to world culture.

The range of language usage found in African American literature is sufficient to satisfy Ferguson's definitional criterion of being "highly codified" and "(often grammatically more complex)." In addition to slang, profanity and vernacular features, of the kind found in some of the above-mentioned genres, we have the distinctive syntax of lines such as "Stony the road we trod, Bitter the chastening rod" and "We have come over a way that with tears have been watered" found in the second verse of the "Negro National Anthem" "Lift Every Voice and Sing."

Ferguson's claim that the diglossic H "is learned largely by formal education and is used for most written and formal spoken purposes but is not used by any sector of the community of ordinary conversation" does not strictly fit the African American situation in all respects, although it shows signs of becoming increasingly so. Because of the subtle ways in which performance is embedded in mundane everyday experiences of African Americans, the whole notion of "ordinary conversation" is problematical. It is interesting to note, however, that long before the debate over whether Ebonics should be allowed in the classroom, Americans of every background have learned about and performed Negro Spirituals in school settings. When one considers the amazing cross-over appeal of African American Culture, which is the focus of the next chapter, and how it continues to be seen in the international appeal of Hip Hop culture it would seem that the teaching of Classical AA in formal settings is likely to increase in the future.

A conversation that I recently heard on the radio, between two actors who played leading roles in a performance of the Zora Neale

Hurston play, *Polk County*, was a striking reminder the extent to which what was once the everyday vernacular of a large segment of the Black community has become a classic language of performance. One of the actors, in response to a question of the radio program host about the challenge of learning the dialect of Hurston's characters, indicated that it had been very stressful, adding that she had majored in English. She referred to the dialect of the play as both "bad" English, and "Ebonics." The other actor said that learning the dialect was not so bad for him. He noted that he was from the South, and had ongoing relations with relatives who still live there; adding, however, that no one in his family spoke a dialect anywhere near as "broad" as the language of the characters in the play. One interesting thing that the first actor's remark corroborates, is the extent to which the name Ebonics has caught on as an everyday word, which overlaps, in meaning at least, with the traditional notion of "bad English."

The variety of Black language preserved in Zora Neale Hurston's play, and in her ethnographic collections of stories and other folk traditions upon which she draws for her artistic creations is undoubtedly now a classic in the sense of no longer being spoken as the native language of a community.

The diglosssic model of the language situation in the African American speech community has clear implications for the issue of whether or not there are two different language varieties corresponding to the names Black English and Ebonics. According to the account just given, two different varieties are alluded to characterized as the vernacular of everyday interaction, and a classical language of performance. A subtly different way of accounting for the same facts, however, that I find appealing, is the idea of a speech continuum, of the same kind frequently alluded to in accounts of the language situation in creole-speaking communities such as Jamaica, Guyana, and the Sea Islands. Rather than call AA a creole, however, and apply the label of post-creole continuum to the African American situation, I simply assert that the linguistic performance of African Americans occurs at different points of a continuum of variation between two different idealized systems that are never consistently spoken by anyone in a pure form. I would further hypothesize that members of the speech community learn to draw from the traditional *lect* in skillful ways as a resource for artistic performance, not only on the stage or in the pulpit, but on street corners, in barber shops, and other venues of everyday interaction. I build upon the speech continuum model in Chapter Ten, which focuses on recent efforts of linguists who are native speakers of African

American language to describe the Grammar of the traditional lect using their intuitive knowledge of the language as a primary source of data.

Implications for language planning

The strategy utilized in the foregoing discussion, of characterizing the language situation in Black America as a microcosm of the language situation in the United States suggests that the general U S language situation cannot be adequately accounted for without reference to the special status of African American language in literature and the performing arts. To the extent that the situation involves conscious and deliberate decision-making about the forms and uses of this language of performance, it may be considered a form of language planning. Such decision-making may sometimes be motivated by an interest in, or have the effect of, preserving, honoring or revitalizing the traditions from which the current activity is derived. As such it may be seen as yet another instance of a theme of language planning for the sake of cultural revitalization that seems to permeate the topics and issues addressed thus far.

The focal issue of this chapter of whether or not there are two different language varieties corresponding to the names Ebonics and Black English is a reminder of another recurring theme, that of DuBois' concept of double consciousness. It is interesting to note how much the notion of dual consciousness directly informs the idea of cultural revitalization. In DeBose 2003, I define cultural revitalization as

> a response of being pulled toward one of two conflicting identities, while resisting being pushed by the other; the latter serving as the repository of hegemonic values, the former serving as a manifestation of one's most basic, authentic and deeply-felt identity.

The insistence of scholars such as Ernie Smith that Ebonics has a distinct identity from that of Black English might be best seen as just such a response. Furthermore, it is consistent with the policy orientation characterized above as resistance to the hegemony of Standard English – and, alternately, Cultural Revitalization.

In the specific case of the African American speech community, there is the additional contested issue as to whether or not Ebonics is a different language than English. It is clear from the use of the phrase, "both in their primary language and in English," by the authors of the

Ebonics resolution, in the above-cited excerpt, that they consider the two names to correspond to two different language varieties. Baugh (2000) attributes that aspect of the wording of the resolution to the influence of

> ... Ernie Smith (1992, 1998) who staunchly advocated Ebonics as something other than English ... It is on this fundamental point, Baugh continues, that most linguists strongly disagree ... Any suggestion that American slave descendants speak a language other than English is overstated, linguistically uninformed, and – frankly – wrong. (Baugh 2000: 41)

While I agree with Baugh and other linguists that African American language is a variety of English, I do not claim the authority as a linguist to determine the "correct" typological status of the variety. Inasmuch as "Ebonics," "English," and language varieties in general are social constructs, the status they occupy in the hierarchy of language types and functions is grounded in the reality of everyday experience. Without having the definitive data that would be revealed by a poll of the African American speech community, I am confident that such a poll, if taken, would show overwhelmingly that African Americans consider their language English. I also acknowledge that social constructs such as dialect and language are not immutable, but are subject to change. Furthermore, when viewed from a language planning perspective, the option exists for partisans to the *Ebonics as a separate language* view to campaign and lobby for acceptance of their position. If successful, the status of Ebonics as a different language than English would not be a hypothesis, but a social reality.

8
Cross-Over: From African American to National and World Culture

> Independence of judgment, refusal to blindly accept the
> prevalent stereotypes about blacks and whites, marked many
> black songs ... The tension was inherent in the black situ-
> ation: a need to role-play – to use the stereotypes of the
> larger society to one's own advantage – and a need to make
> sure the role was not internalized, that the stereotype did
> not become real.
>
> (Levine, 1977: 254, 5)

Throughout American history, the language of African Americans has had a special place in the performing arts and is featured in the lyrics of Negro spirituals, Jazz, Rhythm and Blues, Hip Hop and Gospel songs, as well as the salacious banter of stand-up comedians. It has been used not only by African American performers, but also by minstrels performing in blackface, and the white creators of the Amos n' Andy radio hit.

The term *cross-over*, in the title of this chapter, calls attention to a notable historical tendency for the influence of forms originating in Black culture to appear in contexts external to the Black community. An article in *The Encyclopedia of Black America* (Lowe and Clift 1981) calls attention to the historical depth of the phenomenon.

> The contributions of Afro-Americans to the history of music in the
> United States began with the arrival of the first blacks on the main-
> land in 1619. (Lowe and Clift 1981: 585)

The importance of music in the life of African captives imported to the US is attributed to "their memories of the rich music and dance traditions of the land of their ancestors," traditions in which "music appropriate to the occasion" permeated all aspects of daily life in the African societies that the slaves left behind. The continuation of such traditions is seen in "huge slave festivals that took place in northern colonies" documented in records from the colonial period. One such event of special note due to the participation of white spectators is

> the Pinkster festivals, held in various cities of New York state, in which Afro-Americans danced traditional dances to the music of drums and singing , while large crowds of white spectators watched the "exotic" scenes.

A similar type of event that occurred *in* England, referred to as "'lection Day" celebrations apparently attracted

> crowds of whites to watch slaves and free blacks parade, dance, and sing to the accompaniment of drums, woodwinds and string instruments.

Evidence tracing the role of music in African American life to traditional African societies in which performance of song and dance is embedded in everyday life provides a historical basis for the observation made in the previous chapter regarding "the extent to which mundane aspects of the everyday experience of African Americans involve performance."

In the section of the Lowe and Clift article focused on the Negro Spiritual, the authors remark, after noting a number of ways in which spirituals "form a vital part of the great musical heritage of Afro-Americans, suggest that "the element of performance" may be "the single most important factor in spirituals."

> This is largely due to the importance of improvisation in the African tradition. The song as written down represented only one performance ... All else could change from performance to performance. (596)

One noteworthy aspect of African American performance that makes it exceptional in the context of European traditions, in which performer and audience play distinct roles is the blurring of such distinctions in the fact that in the performance of spirituals "there was no audience.

There were only singers and nonsingers." The introduction of white onlookers, however, changed the "audience" dynamics.

> The whites who came by to listen might sit quietly, showing their appreciation of a performance by facial expressions and by applause ... But the Afro-Americans actively participated in the performance, not only by clapping and tapping, but also by constantly interjecting spoken or chanted words.

The characteristic call-and-response pattern alluded to above permeates the African American experience, from the Amen Corner of Black worship to the engaged onlookers to a bout of the Dozens on a street corner in urban America, from the performance of a spiritual like "Mary had a Baby (Yes, Lord)" to Ray Charles' memorable, "Baby What I say (What I say)".

The topic of cross-over, as it involves the genre of the Negro Spiritual would be incomplete without mention of the career of Marian Anderson. An acclaimed contralto, nurtured in the incubator of the Black Church before "receiving her early training and inspiration in church choirs," (104–5) she made history as the first African American artist admitted to the New York Metropolitan Opera. She was at the center of a civil-rights issue, in 1939, when the "Daughters of the American Revolution" barred her, because of her race from singing at Constitution Hall; an incident which led to an alternative performance, arranged by Eleanor Roosevelt, in an Easter Concert at the Lincoln Memorial before an estimated audience of 75,000. (105) Anderson's performances typically included Negro Spirituals. Spirituals, more than any other genre of traditional music has attained universal recognition as a classical genre. The fact that the lyrics of spirituals are typically in African American language enhances the case for treating the language of Black performance as a diglossic H variety.

A noteworthy incidence of musical lyrics inspired or influenced by AA language, although stereotypical in ways is the folk opera, Porgy and Bess, by George Gershwin and DuBose Heyward. Typical example of the kind of language in question are the song titles "Bess, You Is my Woman Now," and "I got Plenty of Nuttin." Porgy and Bess, whatever might be said about the authenticity of the language attributed to its characters, should be included in any comprehensive study of the cross-over phenomenon. Two features that clearly qualify it for such treatment is its European American authorship, and its attempted use of African American language to embellish a romanticized Black folk culture.

Another dimension of the cross-over phenomenon, that co ments its historical depth, is emphasized in Levine (1977). The pas cited at the head of the chapter, calls attention to the situation which Black people perpetually find themselves of trying to "keep it real," so to speak. What Levine characterizes as "a need to role-play," using "the stereotypes of the larger society to one's own advantage," a need constantly fed by a dynamic tension "inherent in the black situation," may be seen as tantamount to a *culture of resistance*. Such a culture is a natural outgrowth of the predicament constantly faced by African Americans of having to resist the unrelenting assault of hegemonic ideas bent on maintaining and reinforcing the stigmatization of Black identity.

The idea of a *culture of resistance* is supported by a plethora of documented examples of how African Americans constantly resort to wit, humor, sarcasm and numerous other clever and ingenious ways of "speaking truth to power." Some of the in-group naming practices of African Americans, discussed in Chapter Four, and the tendency they include of using names for themselves as terms of endearment that would be insulting if used by outsiders may be explained as such – as a means of defusing the words of their destructive power.

Culture of resistance

In spite of pervasive and continuing efforts to construct African American identity in negative terms, there has always existed, side by side with such efforts, a spirit of fighting back and struggling with all the energy and resources at one's disposal, to retain the sense of intrinsic dignity and worth that lies at the heart of a healthy sense of self. One of the most frequently exploited resources that Blacks have availed themselves of is that of using language in creative and critical ways to encode wisdom and serve as a source of inspiration to continue fighting.

An old folk expression artfully sums up the stratification of American society by degrees of skin lightness. It encodes a not too subtle criticism of the existing social order.

If you white you all right, if you're yellow you're mellow, if you brown you can stick around, but if you black, get back!

of Black resistance allows a dark-skinned
r intrinsic worth – notwithstanding society's
ʰly-endowed pigmentation, i.e.:

weeter the juice.

ₐnd pervasive examples of a traditional
...ₙce involves the extension of meanings associ-
... adjective "bad" to include a sense of markedly positive
...uation, or emphatic approval of the kind normally expressed by
its opposite, i.e., "good." (Smitherman 1977: 59–60, 1994: 52) One
widely-diffused example of this special appreciative sense of *bad* is the
opening line of soul-singer James Brown's hit record, "I'm black and
I'm proud," in which he salutes his audience, the Black community:

Wit' yo' bad self – Say it loud, I'm black and I'm proud.

Another is in the title of a prize-winning movie of the Blaxploitation
genre created by Melvin Van Peebles entitled

Sweet Sweetback's Bad Ass Song.

Morgan (1993) develops the notion of "counterlanguage," which she
defines as "a conscious attempt on the part of U.S. slaves and their
descendants to represent an alternative reality through a communication system based on ambiguity, irony, and satire," which was in large
part "inherited from Africa." (423)

Acknowledgment of a culture of resistance that has flourished
throughout the Black experience, from slavery to the present, facilitates the analysis of Black identity in dynamic terms that underscore
the relentless struggle for freedom, as one form of systematic racial
oppression gave way to another; and highlight the complexity of the
language component. For the purpose at hand of informing issues at
hand, it contributes significantly to an adequate account of the origin
of the creative energy behind the diverse genres of African American
performance that contribute to its amazing potential to cross-over the
boundaries of the group of origin and into the mainstream of
American and international culture. The other side of the phenomenon accounts for the interest shown by outsider audience in the creative products of the in-group. A convenient term for that dimension
of the cross-over phenomenon is the ethnicity factor.

The ethnicity factor

DuBois' characterization of "double-consciousness" as the experience of "looking at one's self through the eyes of others," offers insights into the embryonic state of cross-over in which one of the two selves of the ethnic group member, has on out-of-body experience of sorts assuming the persona of "the others." Inasmuch as such an experience is acted out within the personality of a single individual, it may be thought of as a kind of *intra-personal cross-over*: and the object of the others' gaze seems to be adequately subsumed under the notion of *ethnicity*. For the sake of the present discussion ethnicity may be be defined simply as the perception of culture (X) from the perspective of culture (Y). (Van Keulen, Weddington and DeBose 1998) Much of the attraction of outsiders to the art of a given cultural group may be accounted for as predictable reactions to ethnicity.

One of the most common reactions to ethnicity is the formation of stereotypes. Closely related to that is the reaction of humor. The popular 1950's radio show *Amos n' Andy* is a classic example of the use of stereotypes of Black people in general, and Black language in particular, to evoke reactions of laughter. Complimentary stereotypes that endow Blacks with "a natural sense of rhythm" coexist with negative images which portray all Blacks as "lazy."

Many examples could be given of the way that ethnicity sometimes elicits a reaction of fascination with the ethnic culture. African Americans probably don't mind being stereotyped as good dancers, superb athletes, or gifted musicians, as much as they do negative stereotypes of themselves; and it is such complimentary stereotypes that often evoke reactions of fascination. Van Keulen et al. provides an interesting example of how such predictable fascination has been consciously exploited.

> When historically-black colleges utilize their marching bands and choruses in effective fund-raising efforts, their success may be seen as a predictable fascination with African-American music.

A good example of the fear that black ethnicity sometimes elicits is the effectiveness of the notorious "Willie Horton" commercials utilized during the 1988 Presidential campaign. The underlying stereotype is clearly that of the violent street criminal who will commit merciless acts of rape, mugging and aggravated assault on his victims. Television dramas often portray crime and violence, and they frequently employ

African American male actors to play street hoodlum and violent criminal roles. Such casting decisions are probably influenced partly, consciously or unconsciously, by the fear that tends to be evoked by the perception of certain forms of African American ethnicity. In addition to stereotypes, humor, fascination and fear; another note-worthy predictable reactions to ethnicity is *cultural appropriation*, detailed discussion of which is taken up further below.

In the following pages I attempt a preliminary characterization of the cross-over phenomenon which builds upon the two dimensions introduced above – historical and ethnographic – and a third economic dimension discussed in the context of the sound recording industry, which is apparently the etymological source of the term *cross-over*. I draw liberally from my own life experience, which includes an early phase in which I sang and composed for a Rhythm and Blues group of the Doo-Wop genre. From such sources, I develop several descriptive categories that may prove insightful for continuing inquiry into the general phenomenon of cultural cross-over.

Etymology of the term cross-over

The term *cross-over* is of rather recent vintage, and is traceable to the jargon of the recording industry where it refers to artistic products identified with a particular ethnic or cultural group, such as Rhythm and Blues or Country and Western music, which attract interest and generate sales beyond the boundaries of the associated group. Some of the first Rhythm and Blues artists to successfully cross-over to the Pop music market were Little Richard, Chuck Berry and the Platters.

Little Richard's mega hit *Tutti Frutti* is one of several R&B tunes that were redone by White artists whose imitations sold better than the original. One noteworthy feature of Little Richard's version of *Tutti Frutti* is its performance in African American language. Because several key lines are in the third person singular, there are repeated instances of the distinctively African American absence of the –s suffix on verbs, e.g.:

> Got a gal name Daisy
> She almost *drive* me crazy
> She *know* how to love me yes indeed,
> Boy, you don't know what she *do* to me ...

When picked up by the Pop artist, Pat Boone, the tune and lyrics of the song remain unchanged, except for slight changes in the verb morphology: *drives me crazy; knows how to love me*, etc. Boone's achievement is a prime example of the type of cross-over which consists essentially of the replication in the American Popular music market of a production that had formerly been successful in the R&B market.

Another phenomenon that was referred to as cross-over in the recording industry involves the successful packaging of a typical African American genre, such as R&B, performed by Black performers, to enhance its appeal to Pop audiences. Two examples of this kind of crossing are the Platters singing group, and the Motown Sound.

In the late fifties, an African American quintet consisting of four men and a woman, The Platters, were catapulted to fame with their record, *The Great Pretender*. Some features of The Platters' hit, that might have contributed to its cross-over success are substitution of certain classic features of ballads of the Doo Wop genre with features more familiar to Pop audiences.

Doo Wop is a sub-genre of Rhythm and Blues music that flourished in the fifties. It was typically performed by a male quintet, of which one member, usually a tenor, would sing lead, and the other members would sing background harmonies, simultaneously with, or in call-and-response patterns with the lyrics sung by the lead.

Doo Wop ballads typically featured dissonant harmonies and an unhurried pace, overlaid with a falsetto male voice singing in counterpart with the lead singer. Amateur doo wop groups often performed *a capella*, and the background singers typically contributed the kinds of accompaniment that an instrumental ensemble would provide a solo vocalist. Doo Wop recordings typically had minimal instrumental accompaniment, such as a piano or guitar, drums and a saxaphone.

The Platters' cross-over hits maintained many of the classic features of the Doo Wop ballad. Their mega-hit, *The Great Pretender*, was elaborated, however, by such innovative features as a strict, majestic tempo, reminiscent of J. S. Bach, glorious major chords, with no funky notes, and a female singing the high part.

During the fifties, Doo Wop was the dominant contemporary form of R&B music and was typically referred to simply as Rhythm and Blues. The up-tempo pieces were often referred to as Rock and Roll, and the traditional, "Down Home" kind of Blues performed by the likes of B. B. King was known as "Blues" proper. The emergence of a distinctive genre of popular music known as Rock and Roll, or simply Rock, is an instance of cross-over on a massive scale, and may serve as one of several case studies of the phenomenon on a societal scale.

A major progenitor of the Rock phenomenon, without reference to which any study of it would be incomplete, is Elvis Presley, often referred to as the King of Rock and Roll. That title itself is an instance of cross-over, insofar as it was first claimed by Chuck Berry. One of Elvis' biggest hits, *Shake, Rattle and Roll*, was first recorded by the R&B artist, Big Joe Turner. The song has the classic twelve-bar blues pattern, and a typical Black pattern of versification structured on repetition of key lines. The lyrics contain sufficient words with distinctive Black pronunciation such as *get* /git/, *your* /yo/ and *with* /wit/ to create the sense of being in African American, as opposed to General American English, e.g.:

> Git outta that bed and wash yo face and hands.
> You git in that kitchen makin noise wit the pots and pans
> Shake, rattle and roll (repeated four times)
> Well you never feel nothin to save yo doggone soul.

Elvis was as a Southerner, born and raised in Mississippi. Because of the similarity of African American language to Southern dialect, Elvis was able to perform music borrowed from the Black tradition in a reasonably authentic manner, which accounts largely for his success.

Next to Elvis, the most important progenitor of Rock and Roll is the Beatles. Their introduction to African American music was by way of exposure to African American musicians who performed in England, such as B. B. King and Little Richard. One clear influence of Little Richard in the Beatles' recording of *She Loves Me*, is the insertion of a falsetto whoop just like the one that Richard gives in the refrain, of *Tutti Frutti*. Another British group, the Rolling Stones, served as a conduit for the song *I Can't Get no Satisfaction* – originally recorded by its African American author Otis Redding – to cross the Atlantic and back atop the rising tide of Rock and Roll.

Types and categories of cross-over

Of the various types of cross-over summarized above, Rock and Roll may be seen as a representative case of outsiders to the culture in which a particular art form resides successfully copying, imitating or being influenced by the work of selected insider artists in performances to outsider audiences. For convenience, I refer to that type of cross-over as *transfer*. A different type of cross-over, which might be termed *assimilation*, is represented by the Platters. It is the case in which insiders of the culture to which the art form in question belongs successfully package their product to appeal to outsider audiences. The above-mentioned features of the Platters work that contributed to its cross-over appeal might be summarized as embellishing it with familiar features of the outsider culture while removing or modifying features that are strange, unusual or unfamiliar to cross-over audiences. One of the most successful cross-over phenomena of this type is that of the "Motown sound."

Motown Records, organized by Detroit entrepreneur Berry Gordy Jr. on a virtual shoestring, served as the launching pad for the phenomenally successful careers of such big name performers as Stevie Wonder, Diana Ross, Marvin Gaye, and the self-styled King of Pop, Michael Jackson. It was an achievement which consisted of repackaging Rhythm and Blues music from the typical ways in which it was produced in the Doo Wop era and embellishing it with familiar features of Popular American music.

One such feature that clearly set the Motown sound apart from R&B music of the fifties is more elaborate instrumentation. At the same time that Doo Wop records were being produced with the sparse accompaniment of a guitar, piano and drums, popular music produced by major recording labels was typically backed up by a full orchestra and chorus. The Motown sound retained the syncopated rhythms and heavy beat of traditional R&B music but embellished each downbeat with the sound of violins, brass, tympani and other orchestral pieces.

In the particular cases of Diana Ross, and Michael Jackson, the transformation of each from the role of lead singer of a Motown group to Pop superstardom are striking examples of assimilation. As the lead singer of the Supremes, Diana maintained the aura of an inner-city teenager, dressed the part, and wore her hair in a short unassuming style. When she ascended the throne of Pop Divadom, her dress became comparably regal, and her hair quickly lengthened to her lower back. Michael not only experienced cosmetic narrowing of his nose and lightening of his skin, but also had his hair transformed from the blooming natural he wore as lead singer of the Jackson Five to the long, straight tresses of his present Pop persona.

A closer examination of the Motown phenomenon would hopefully reveal other features that contribute to the end of making Rhythm and Blues music appealing to outsider audiences. The observations made thus far may be sufficient, however, to support a first attempt at a systematic account of the nature of cross-over and its significance for African American language studies.

The foregoing discussion of the economic dimension of cross-over, as represented by the sound recording industry lays the groundwork for completing the survey of predictable reactions to ethnicity.

Cultural appropriation

Most of the above predictable reactions to ethnicity, may also involve cultural appropriation. In order to qualify as such, however, there should be an additional ingredient of economic exploitation. A considerable element of tourism involves the promotion of excursions to exotic places where one may witness anything from ceremonial pagentry to strange religious rites for the price of an admission ticket.

At the height of the Harlem Renaissance, when racial segregation characterized many aspects of everyday life, even in New York City, it was customary for members of the social elite to go the Harlem night clubs and be entertained by the great Jazz artists of the day. African American musicians who would not be allowed to sit down and be served a drink as a patron performed to white audiences who had come to the Black part of town to engage in some cultural voyeurism.

The emergence of Rock music, exemplified by white artists such as Elvis Presley, Pat Boone, and the Beattles, effectively exploited the predictable response of fascination with African American music of the Rhythm and Blues genre. The "Amos and Andy" show might also be seen as cultural appropriation insofar as its white creators Freeman Gosden and Charles Correl relied upon their ability to manipulate dialectal English in such a way as to produce convincing voice representations of comic black characters. The fact that the Amos n' Andy script was written and acted out by two white men, Freeman Godsen and Charles Correll, as well as its popularity with white audiences are both important features of cross-over, as well.

Sub-types of cross-over

Although all of the above examples involve European-American performers, it is by no means necessary that the performers be non-African American for a given case to qualify as cultural appropriation. A very important ingredient is that the case involve a conscious effort to capitalize on the money-making prospects of performing a genre appropriated from a given culture.

For a given case to qualify as cross-over, it should flow from the decision of a performer to either

a) perform material of genre (A) for an audience typically performed to in genre (B); e.g., R&B material for a Pop audience,

b) create a new genre, or sub-genre inspired or influenced by an existing model; e.g., Rock on the model of R&B, or

c) cease working in genre (A) primarily for intrinsic (i.e., non-economic) motives in order to take advantage of opportunities for financial gain; e.g., cease doing Gospel music in the church to initiate a new career as an R&B artist.

If the above patterns (a–c) are taken as ideal types, they may be fruitfully applied to the analysis of real cases which may contains elements of several ideal cases. Some specific sub-types of cross-over are suggested by those patterns to which I apply the labels: *genre cross-over*; *market cross over*; *sacred to secular crossover*; *generational cross-over* and *academic cross-over*. I discuss each sub-type in detail in the following paragraphs.

The above mentioned cases of established Pop artists such as Pat Boone successfully appropriating R&B material qualify as genre cross-over, as does the performance of Country and Western music by an acknowledged R&B star such as Ray Charles. The above mentioned cases of the Platters and the Motown Sound qualify as market cross-over. One of the best known cases of sacred to secular cross-over is that of the late Sam Cook who, long before attaining stardom with his R&B hit *You Send Me*, was the lead singer for a male Gospel quintet, *The Soul Stirrers*. The distinctive genre of Black religious music represented by the Soul Stirrers, and other famous groups who continue to perform it, e.g., the *Mighty Clouds of Joy*, and the *Five Blind Boys of Alabama*, served as a prototype for the secular Doo Wop genre.

A prime example of generational cross-over is emergence of Hip Hop.

Generational cross-over and Hip Hop

The Hip Hop genre, as a case of cross-over, may exceed any other mode of artistic performance associated with African American culture in the extent to which it has crossed barriers of race, class and culture in the United States and spread throughout the world. As a form of artistic expression, Hip Hop may be fruitfully analyzed as the expression of a youth culture that has assumed the dimensions of a veritable movement; one that originated in a generation of African Americans born and socialized in the Post-Civil Rights era. As a movement, a primary motivating factor seems to be that of cultural revitalization.

As a phenomenon of cross-over, the primary locus of the crossing associated with the Hip Hop movement is in the realm of ideology. Of the three main ideological components of Black culture, those that concern Street Life, and Black Nationalism are especially prominent in Hip Hop culture. From the former comes the fascination with the world of Pimps and Gangsters, a world about which many members of the Hip Hop generation born and raised in middle class environments fantacize, but have never experienced directly. Unlike many of their parents, who like myself , have first hand experience of a world in which pimping and hustling was a way of life engaged in by friends, neighbors and relatives as a means of survival, young middle-class hip hoppers fantacize about Ghetto life while watching Rap stars dressed as pimps and hoes enact video performances in flashy settings, wearing outlandish hustler attire, getting in and out of shiny Benzes, Bentlys and vintage Cadillacs.

Implications for language planning

The role of African American language in the stigmatization of Black identity informs a number of key decisions of Black English scholars, in the area of language planning and policy. One is the typological classification of the variety as a nonstandard dialect. Closely related to that is the decision to name it in a way that combines the pre-ferred group name with "English," "vernacular," or "dialect;" e.g., "Negro Dialect," "African American Vernacular English;" etc. What they have in common is *the characterization of a central component of African American identity in negative terms.*

Ebonics scholars tend to resent the pejorative connotations of "dialect" and "vernacular," and prefer to name the variety in a manner that does not imply its subordination to English. The contro-versy generated by the decisions of linguists on the above issues sug-gests that the scholars who made them would have benefited from paying more conscious attention to their policy implications, in the context of sustained and critical dialogue.

It was suggested above that the social location of Black English schol-ars can account for the scarcity of evidence of their having engaged in any such reflection and dialogue; largely due to the fact that the crucial variables are part of the taken-for-granted commonsense world of their everyday reality, and as such pass uncritically, as it were, "below the radar screen" of conscious thought.

9
Ebonics and Black School Achievement: The Language Difference Hypothesis

> What we are all witnessing here is the latest chapter in a story that made big news in December 1996 and the first half of 1997, and then subsided. Hopefully it is the last. The greatest accomplishment of this research team without a doubt has been to carry out the research without the barest mention of the E word.
>
> (DeBose 2001a)

The subject matter of this chapter connects with the Ebonics phenomenon on two different levels. At the most concrete level, it is about a research project that grew out of the politics surrounding the Ebonics controversy. At a deeper level it is a fascinating case study of the current state of national policy toward the education of African American children, and the contributions of the various academic disciplines represented by the research team to the ongoing debate. At the concrete level, the only way of making sense of how the project came to be structured in the particular manner that eventually emerged, and involve the particular personalities that it brought together, is with reference to its highly-charged political context.

The words quoted at the head of the chapter are extracted from comments that I made in the role of discussant of contributions of my project colleagues to a panel discussion at the National Education Association Meeting in New Orleans, in April of 2000. The compliment extended to the research team for successfully avoiding "the barest mention of the E word" was spoken in serious jest.

The appropriations bill for the research grant was a direct outgrowth of hearings conducted by a joint committee of the Senate and House of Representatives called in response to the Ebonics Resolution.

Pennsylvania Senator Arlen Specter was a member of the committee; which heard testimony from a variety of School District officials and expert scholars, including University of Pennsylvania Professor, William Labov. The bill stipulated that the money was to be spent through a noncompetitive grant to a consortium of educational institutions *that included the University of Pennsylvania*. The consortium eventually funded included the University of Pennsylvania, the Oakland Unified School District and my home institution, California State University, Hayward.

The African American Literacy and Culture Project, or AALCP, as the project came to be known – although it was funded through a congressional appropriation of a million dollars to study the issues of Black school achievement raised by the School Board Resolution – amazingly managed to avoid publicity of the kind that attended the Ebonics firestorm. The low-key execution of the project was by no means unintentional.

One lesson that the School District and its allies clearly learned from the experience of the Ebonics firestorm was the lethal consequences of challenging the Hegemony of Standard English with an upstart dialect called Ebonics. The backlash was so intense, and seemingly endless, that the initial response of toning the resolution down, and backing off of some of its more controversial assertions and demands, was insufficient to calm the rising tempest. The Superintendent of the School District eventually resigned, and School Board members who voted for the resolution became political "lame ducks." Ultimately, it required the assistance of public relations experts and other outside consultants to adequately control the damage.

An unwritten ground rule of the AALCP was the understanding that it was *not an Ebonics research project*, strictly speaking. To avoid the false impression that it might have some relationship to Ebonics, every effort was made to minimize discussion or commentary on the grant that associated it with the firestorm, especially within the earshot of journalists.

As I sat through the presentations of my AALCP colleagues, thankful that only eight minutes were set aside for my remarks, I took notes of, among other things, how many times the word Ebonics was uttered. Although I understood the context, I found it difficult to imagine how a project that literally grew out of the politics of the Ebonics controversy could be the focus of an hour long series of presentations without a single mention of the "E word." But it did happen, and I truly was impressed.

The practice of avoiding the word Ebonics, did
New Orleans panel discussion presentations. It goes
the wording of the original call for proposals which
research on how *the language usage patterns of African*
might affect their learning to read and write Stand.
research proposal eventually funded had developed
foci corresponding not only to the academic interests a
affiliations of the research partners, but also concerns   .. School
District that the research serve the needs of students, and not interfere
with the educational process. What were in effect four different loosely
related studies proceeded.

Had it not been for the political circumstances that gave birth to the
project it is unlikely that the particular group of scholars and practi-
tioners who comprised the AALCP research team, and the diverse academic traditions they represented, would have come together in such a
collaborative effort as the AALCP. As things turned out, the project
came to have an organizational structure in which scholars aligned
with two different bodies of knowledge with implications for the educational achievement of African American children were brought
together.

Organizational structure of the research project

The project was organized into two major units, known as *the Linguistic
Component* and *the Cultural Component*. The former was located in
Philadelphia, and headed by linguist, William Labov, who served as co-
principal investigator with educational researcher Etta Hollins. She
headed the cultural component, located in Hayward, and was directly
involved in one of the three studies carried out under it – which investigated the efficacy of teacher study groups. The other two efforts of
the cultural component were a parent advocacy study under the direction of linguist, John Baugh, and a study of ongoing in-service teacher
development efforts of the school district headed by practitioner-
scholar Nabeehah Shakir.

The scope and specific dimensions of the research is summarized on
a five page handout distributed at the above-mentioned meeting in
New Orleans as

> to develop and field test teacher development, reading instruction
> and parent advocacy approaches that take into account culture and
> language when seeking to improve and advance the performance

...d achievement of African American students enrolled in the elementary grades.

Following that brief general description, the brochure comments on "The national significance of the project" which is characterized as "enormous," having the potential for

> providing much needed insight in the development of effective in-service and pre-service teacher education and reading strategies/practices ... designed to improve the achievement and performance of African American students in literacy acquisition and development;

and

> Advancing a more effective parent/caregiver advocacy strategy to strengthen the ties that must exist between the home, school and community when seeking to improve student performance and achievement.

Hollins' study-group research was motivated in part by findings to the effect that "existing approaches to in-service teacher education do not tend to have long term effects." Her research was structured to generate insights into a working hypothesis "that enduring changes in teaching practices require changes in teachers' habits of mind." Such changes, the research predicted, are "more likely to occur when teachers engage in a structured study group problem-solving process."

Two different study group models were designed and field-tested: an *external input model*, and an *internal input model*. Both models featured a process in which teachers identify and discuss challenges encountered in their classroom practice, eventually settling on particular challenges to study in-depth, with the goal of coming up with workable solutions.

The external input model relies on the use of facilitators with expertise in particular areas of knowledge who expose teachers to what research has revealed about effective teaching for African American students. Teachers discuss those findings in their study groups, reflect on how they relate to their own classroom practices, make attempts to implement specific strategies and behaviors, and discuss their experiences with the study group. The internal input model utilizes a similar approach to the above except that instead of relying on an expert facil-

itator for input, the teachers select the issues to be investigate
acquire relevant data on their own.

The teacher development effort investigated by Shakir is also described as using an "external input model." It is more structured than either of the study group approaches, however, and features ways of facilitating the literacy development of speakers of African American language in ways that are informed by linguistic knowledge of the surface features of the language as well as specific characteristics of African American culture.

The parent advocacy study, focused on finding effective strategies for strengthening ties between home and school, and the hypothesis "that parental or adult monitoring of a child's progress through home record keeping and regular dialogue with teachers is likely to improve academic achievement and performance." One particular way in which parents are supported in the role of monitoring their children's school work is through a website, maintained in collaboration with the Oakland School District.

I was also assigned to the Cultural Component, with the title of "Research Faculty." I was not directly involved, however, for the first few months of the project, in either of the studies described above. One task that I was frequently asked to perform was to interpret fellow linguist Labov's research to my colleagues in the cultural component.

During the second project year, I served as a study-group facilitator for Hollins' research of the internal input model on an emergency basis. When the project was continued in a scaled down form for a third year of operation, only the cultural component survived. I continued to serve as a study-group facilitator, becoming acclimated, in the process, to a new area of academic research. I had an opportunity to observe first hand the reality of the conditions addressed by the model and the power of the processes of reflection and decision-making in which participating teachers engage. A recently published article on the teacher study-group approach notes a number of specific indications "that the teachers' participation in the internal model has potential for supporting positive learning outcomes." (Hollins, E.; McIntyre; DeBose; Hollins K. and Towner 2005)

Labov and his associates in the linguistic component studied the frequency of reading errors made by African American students enrolled in after-school remedial reading programs in selected schools in Philadelphia, before and after the intervention of instruction with reading material designed to improve students' ability to decode words

:ir spelling that do not correspond to the typical
ie words in African American language.
the linguistic component are outlined in a section of
handout dedicated specifically to elaboration of its
s.

.ocused on the question of how knowledge of the language a... ulture of children in the inner city can be applied to
improve the reading and writing of standard English. For a number
of years, we have been working in the elementary schools of West
Philadelphia towards that end. In the first year of the project, we
have analyzed the reading errors of children in the 2nd to 5th grades,
developed methods of instruction to correct those errors ...

The linguistic component sought to draw upon the culture of the children in the study by utilizing culturally-relevant reading material. A
progress report of the linguistic component for the period from August
1998 to July 1999 cites evidence of "a profound and persistent interest
in the hip-hop culture and lyrics of rap songs" that served as a guiding
principle in the development of such material.

> Without exception, children have been more strongly motivated by
> the desire to read materials associated with this cultural complex
> than any other type of reading. Many of them have memorized the
> most popular lyrics, and have persistently requested from tutors
> copies of lyrics to read.

In addition to using culturally-relevant reading material with high
motivational value, the material used in the tutorial sessions was
informed by linguistic knowledge of phonological features of African
American language that pose potential difficulties for children in the
process of learning to decode words.

National significance of AALCP

The manner in which the AALCP came to be organized – with its two
major components corresponding to two different academic disciplines
– is fortuitous, in that it tends to highlight its national significance.
Corresponding to each discipline are distinctive ways of responding to
the established national policy toward the education of Black children.
The deficit-pathology orientation noted above as a dominant theme of

academic study of peoples of African descent throughout the twentieth century continues to influence state and federal policies, in ways that are explicated below.

Challenges to the deficit-pathology policy orientation

The seventh paragraph of original Ebonics resolution combines one of its most controversial assertions – that African Americans speak a different language than English – with the sobering reminder that the school achievement of African American children is too often disappointingly low, and disturbingly indicative of failed policies and misdirected practice.

> ... the standardized tests and grade scores of African-American students in reading and language arts skills measuring their application of English skills are substantially below state and national norms and ... such deficiencies will be remedied by application of a program featuring African Language Systems principles in instructing African-American children both in their primary language and in English ...

A number of governmental programs addressed to one category or another of so-called *special needs students* are relevant to key issues raised by the Ebonics resolution. One such *categorical program* is the federal bilingual education act, which sets aside funds for students with special needs that flow from their *limited English proficiency*. Two other categories of special needs students which – though not directly mentioned in the Ebonics resolution – are of central relevance to the academic achievement of African American children are:

- students whose low academic achievement is presumed to be a consequence of their low socioeconomic status; and
- students with certified disabilities which entitle them to one form or another of *special education*.

Statistics reported by the Oakland school district at the time of the Ebonics controversy feed the suspicion that African American students were often mistakenly or inappropriately placed in special education classes. Although 53 percent of the students in the Oakland district were African American, they accounted for 71 percent of all student enrolled in special education. Other statistical indicators of low achievement of Black students in the Oakland schools at the time of the Ebonics controversy involve grade point averages, rates of retention at the same grade level, and rates of suspension and graduation. While the grade point average for all students in the Oakland district was 2.4, the average for African American students was only 1.8. African American students comprised 64 percent of all students who repeated the same grade, and 80 percent of all student suspensions. Finally, of those Oakland students who made it to the twelfth grade, "only 81 percent ... actually graduated." (Gethridge 1996)

A similar cluster of complaints of educational malpractice regarding African American children is seen in the issues raised by the plaintiffs in the 1978 case of Martin Luther King Jr. Elementary School Children vs. the School Board of Ann Arbor Michigan. (Baugh 1998; Chambers 1983) According to Geneva Smitherman, who served as "chief consultant and expert witness for the plaintiff children in the King case,"

> The allegation was that the defendants had failed to properly educate the children, who were thus in danger of becoming functionally illiterate. Specifically, the plaintiffs charged that school officials had improperly placed the children in learning disability and speech pathology classes; that they had suspended, disciplined, and repeatedly retained the children at grade level without taking into account their social, economic and cultural differences; and that they had failed to overcome language barriers preventing them from learning standard English and learning to read. (Smitherman 2000: 133).

The tendency to treat African American students as affected by speech pathologies and learning disorders that inhibit their academic performance may be viewed as microcosmic consequences of the reigning deficit-pathology policy orientation.

A challenge to established policies for the education of Black children based on deficit models, and a parallel claim that such children would be better served by policies reserved for students who speak a different language than English, is implicit in the reference in the above excerpt from the Ebonics resolution to a

> program featuring African Language Systems principles in instructing African-American children both in their primary language and in English.

By characterizing African American language as a different language than English, the authors of the resolution, appear intent on legitimizing a claim of eligibility for bilingual education funding. There is more, however, to the Ebonics resolution, than a thinly-veiled attempt to secure badly needed funds for a financially-challenged school district. Upon closer examination, it is clearly one piece of the emerging picture of an ongoing challenge to the established orientation of national policies toward the education of African American children based on deficit models. Before directly examining the nature of that challenge, I return in the next section to the continuing saga of avoidance of the E-word in my public presentations on the AALCP.

The language difference hypothesis

In January of 2001, I presented at a Para-session on "Reading and Dialect" organized for the Annual Meeting of the Linguistic Society of America. The problem of the E-word surfaced again – this time as a consequence of the fact that my contribution had been given the tentative title "The Oakland Collaboration on Ebonics" by one of the panel organizers, which I had to correct by substituting the less-sexy, but more accurate, title "The African American Literacy and Culture Project." As I explained in the opening paragraph of my presentation

> the two-year, federally-funded study in which my institution collaborated with the University of Pennsylvania and the Oakland Unified School District (OUSD) was not strictly-speaking on the subject of Ebonics; although the Ebonics controversy did provide the political context in which the funds were allocated.

The main point of that presentation was a critique of the idea that surface differences between African American language and Standard English are of sufficient magnitude to constitute a barrier to teaching and learning, an idea that I had begun to call *The Language Difference Hypothesis*. Citing generally accepted linguistic principles, as well as common knowledge, that speak against the notion that surface features of Black language are a significant source of reading difficulties faced by African American learners, I argue against the language difference hypothesis.

It is common knowledge that during slavery it was deemed necessary to pass laws to forbid teaching slaves to read. (c.f. McPhail 2005: 12) If there had been a barrier to slave literacy presented by differences between the English typically spoken by slaves and Standard Written English, there would have been no need to pass such laws. It is also common knowledge that African Americans as a group have never raised the issue of language difference as a barrier to the goal of quality education.

A centerpiece of my argument against the language difference hypothesis is what I call the *dialect neutrality* of Standard Written English. (Van Keulen; Weddington and DeBose 1998) The main idea is that, although all spoken varieties of American English differ from Standard Written English; (SWE) as a general rule, the difference is not sufficient, in principle, to constitute a barrier to the acquisition of literacy. This is especially true at the early stages of learning to read when the emphasis is on the ability to decode visual symbols corresponding to forms and elements of spoken language. Most of the basic vocabulary of beginning reading materials is common to all varieties of American English including African American language.

Speakers of various spoken varieties, in the process of learning to read, form associations between the written form of a word, and the particular way that it is pronounced in the person's spoken language. The word *house*, for instance, has a variety of dialectal pronunciations, represented by the phonetic transcriptions [haws], [hæws] and [hʌ ws]. The written word is equally accessible to speakers of the various pronunciations, who simply learn to match their particular dialectal pronunciation to a dialectally neutral visual form. Many other basic words such as *mouse, brown, loud* and *clown*, share the dialectal variability of the word *house*.

Some dialectal differences are marked by their association with a stigmatized group such as African Americans; e.g., the tendency of words like *mouth*, which, end in an interdental fricative /θ/ or /ð/ in Standard English, to be pronounced by African Americans with a final labiodental fricative /f/ or /v/, resulting in words such as *death* and *deaf* being pronounced as homonyms. The only difference between the various dialectal pronunciations of the final consonant of *mouth,* and its vowel nucleus, is that one variant of the former is stigmatized. In principal, however, the written symbol <u>mouth</u> is neutral with respect to the various dialectal pronunciations of it, and it is equally easy or difficult for speakers of either dialect to learn.

The language difference hypothesis in the form in which it is typically stated considers AAVE a nonstandard dialect of American English which is equal in status to varieties spoken by other Americans but may constitute a barrier to effective teaching and learning either because of differences in phonology, morphology and syntax between AAVE and standard English, or because of negative societal attitudes toward AAVE maintained by some educators, or a combination of both.

Contrasting hypotheses of Black school achievement

My 2001 presentation was organized around comparison and contrast of the two major components of AALCP and the opportunity presented by their organizational juxtaposition to critically assess the relative merits of two different hypotheses regarding the academic failure of African American children, informed by two different fields of academic inquiry – linguistics, and educational research. I talk candidly of the political nature of the project, how it had contributed to my being involved in it, and how I had used the situation as an opportunity to informally pursue a research agenda of my own.

> My primary research interests are neither in educational research nor the design of reading material. They include Language Planning and Policy, and the questions that have most engaged me all along have centered on the project itself. That is, AALCP became the main focus of my interest, which I came to see as a case study in Language Planning, and pursued informally from the perspective of a participant observer. Two issues have been clarified for me through the lens of a Language Planning focus. The first is the fact that, although I am a linguist, I find myself in the non-linguists' camp; not only organizationally, but also intellectually and ideologically. The second is the issue of how the focus of the research shifted from "the language usage patterns of African American students" called for by the RFP, to the present focus on the diverse issues of teacher education, parent advocacy, and reading material.

A good part of my intellectual disagreement with my colleagues in the linguistic component is summarized above as opposition to the fundamental premise of the language difference hypothesis that structural differences between AA and Standard English constitute a significant barrier to the acquisition of literacy by African American children. I was critical of Labov, in particular, because of his seeming ambivalence on the issue. My first public expression of concern about the contribution of the linguistic component of AALCP was expressed at the above-mentioned New Orleans meeting, at which I quipped about the participants' avoidance of the "E word." In the ensuing remarks, after using up some time talking about my interest in language planning and policy, I offer reasons for my colleagues' avoidance of the "E word."

> I think the main reason for the lack of attention to Ebonics, is the growing realization among members of the research team that Ebonics is an educational non-issue. What I mean by this primarily is that whenever attention is called to the language of African Americans, there is a tendency to treat it as a "problem-in-need-of-fixing."

I proceeded to explain my support for a policy of full recognition of African American language based on the linguistically-sound premise that there is nothing wrong with it; the premise that

> If it ain't broke don't fix it.

I remark on how my colleagues in the AALCP are all contributing in their own way to the quiet, low-key recognition of AAL that comes from leaving it alone. I then proceed to comment on the work of the various research studies on which my colleagues had just reported; beginning with the Cultural Component, which "does not need to make an issue of the language that many African American children bring to the classroom because of the conviction that if there is a problem in need of fixing, it is the 'habits-of-mind' that teachers bring to the classroom."

When I get to the Linguistic Component, I find occasion to insert a slight note of criticism. The preoccupation of the Linguistic Component with the analysis of "reading errors" of African American remedial students, in a manner that subtly smacked of a deficit orientation, was a major source of my concern. The implication of that approach, that surface features of African American language are a barrier to the acquisition of literacy by Black learners seemed to contradict findings of a 1965 study, that Labov headed, which concluded that structural differences between African American language and classroom English are slight, and insufficient to account for typical adverse indicators of Black school achievement. (Labov, Cohen and Robbins 1965) The findings of that study are consistent with my own view, that, as a general rule, there is no barrier to the acquisition of literacy posed by the difference between any spoken dialect of American

English and Standard English. The current focus of the linguistic component, however, struck me as contradictory to that view.

Educational programs based on the language difference hypothesis vary in the extent to which they may focus on the oral language of AAVE speakers, or their proficiency in reading and writing. Those which focus on oral proficiency often rationalize their program by claiming that the students will never be able to succeed in the world of work speaking AAVE. Some advocates of this focus proceed from the premise that teaching standard English as a second dialect to AAVE speakers can be enhanced by using quasi foreign language teaching methods.

Versions of the language difference hypothesis which focus on the acquisition of reading proficiency proceed from the premise that the teaching of reading skills to AAVE speakers can be enhanced by taking such differences into account in the design of instructional material. Labov has long argued that, because of the tendency for phonological segments at the ends of words such as *test*; to be simplified, resulting in homophonous pronunciation of words such as *told* and *toll* and *toe*; it could be extremely difficult for AAVE-speaking students to learn the sound to letter correspondences which underlie English spelling.

The study conducted in the sixties by Labov and his associates, however, (Labov, Cohen and Robbins 1965) concludes, as noted above, that the surface differences between what was then called Black English Vernacular, and Standard English, are not sufficient to account for the reading failure of African American students. Labov makes reference to that study in the first chapter of *Language in the Inner City* where he states:

> We do not believe that these structural differences are major causes of the problem. (Labov 1972: 35)

Notwithstanding the findings of the 1965 study, however, Labov decided to organize his part of the AALCP research around the question of how knowledge of structural differences between African American and Standard English informs the design of reading material for African American students. When one considers the paucity of support for the Language Difference Hypothesis, however, in linguistic knowledge, and common knowledge, together with the slight mention of language difference as a causal factor in the educational research literature alluded to above, we should be extremely wary of claims that posit structural differences between African American and Standard English as the cause of academic failure of African American children.

The difference versus deficiency issue

From an historical perspective, the language difference hypothesis may be traced to the position typically taken by linguists on what is known as the difference versus deficiency controversy, i.e., the insistence that, contrary to popular belief, distinctive characteristics of African American language do not constitute mistakes or failure to speak English correctly, but, rather, are consistent with the rules of a different grammar than that of Standard English. The primary argument given in support of the "difference" position is the systematic and rule-governed nature of all human language. Within the context of that controversy, the postulated language barrier does not consist so much of structural differences as it does of attitudinal barriers erected by traditional fallacies about African American language that lead teachers to conclude that students who exhibit its characteristics in their speech are in need of speech therapy.

The practice of treating African American language patterns as speech disorders is totally incompatible with the current state of linguistic knowledge which shows it to be a systematic and rule-governed instance of normal language. Such misinformed practice can and should be eliminated by policies of teacher preparation and licensing that insure that teachers are abreast of current linguistic research, especially as it informs issues of teaching and learning.

A classic example of using linguistic knowledge to argue against the deficit-pathology orientation is an article by Labov entitled *The Logic of Nonstandard English* (Labov 1972: 201–40) in which he makes an important observation about the danger of using deficit models of Black behavior as bases for intervention programs aimed at solving "problems" and correcting "pathological" conditions identified with Black communities and individuals.

> The notion of verbal deprivation is a part of the modern mythology of educational psychology [which is] particularly dangerous, because it diverts attention from real defects of our educational system to imaginary defects of the child... . it leads its sponsors inevitably to the hypothesis of the genetic inferiority of black children that it was originally intended to avoid. (1972: 201–2)

Labov bases his concern about the danger of deficit theories on the fact that historically they have been used to refute alternative accounts of

Black behavior which attribute distinctive characteristics of Black people to their basic genetic make up.

In fashioning his argument, Labov calls attention to a number of fallacious claims and methodological errors associated with a particular version of the verbal deficit position advanced by educational psychologists.

> The most extreme view which proceeds from this orientation – and one that is now being widely accepted – is that lower-class black children have no language at all. (Labov 1972: 204)

One noteworthy feature of Labov's argument against the verbal deprivation hypothesis is that in making his case, he characterizes African American language as completely adequate for teaching and learning, and cites the attitudes of teachers – conditioned by their acceptance of deficit theory – as a key factor in the children's failure.

> It is widely recognized that the teacher's attitude toward the child is an important factor in his success or failure.

Citing the "work of Rosenthal and Jacobson (1968) on self-fulfilling prophecies" and the effects of labeling children on their subsequent achievement, Labov cautions that

> When the everyday language of black children is stigmatized as "not a language at all" and " not possessing the means for logical thought," the effect of such a labeling is repeated many times during each day of the school year ... When teachers hear [them] say *I don't want none* or *They mine*, they will be hearing through the bias provided by the verbal deprivation theory ... (Labov 1972: 230, 31)

Labov's rebuttal of the verbal deprivation hypothesis is one with which all linguists concur. For all linguists agree that the stigmatization of African American language is incompatible with the current state of linguistic knowledge. The desirability of teachers being able to teach in a way that is informed by the current state of linguistic knowledge of African American Language is a recurring theme of Black English literature. In the words of Dillard:

> It is my feeling, and that of my colleagues, that lack of adequate structural and historical information about Black English (also called

Negro Non-Standard or Merican) has been a major handicap to educational programs for Black children. (1972: ix)

The issue of teachers' having adequate linguistic knowledge to provide
competent instruction to speakers of African American language came
to be a key element on which the Ann Arbor-King -Black English case
was decided. The judge found for the plaintiffs on the allegation that
their teachers had failed to teach them to read Standard English due
to their inability to teach in a way that takes the students' home language into account. He ordered in-service teacher training as a
remedy. Although the case was eventually decided on the single issue
of a "language barrier," it was clearly part of a more general pattern of
educational malpractice to which the children had been subjected.

Baugh (2000) calls attention to a connection between the Ann Arbor-
King decision and the Ebonics Resolution in the fact that it provided
impetus for creation of the Standard English Proficiency Program, (SEP)
a California State program established in response to the needs of
speakers of African American language for special help in acquiring
proficiency in Standard English.

> California state educators who followed the black English trial
> observed the ruling in favor of the plaintiffs and consequently
> developed the SEP program to ward off the prospect of similar liti-
> gation from African Americans in California, who – prior to the
> establishment of the SEP program – could have easily brought
> similar suits against school districts throughout the state. (Baugh
> 2000: 66)

Adopted in 1981 by the California State Board of Education, SEP estab-
lishes formal procedures for promoting equal educational opportunities for "California students who are speakers of Black language"
(Baugh 2000: 67)

The Oakland school district had an ongoing SEP program providing
in-service teacher development on a voluntary basis of more than ten
years standing at the time of the Ebonics Resolution, one provision of
which was to expand participation in the program making it manda-
tory for all teachers to avail themselves of the opportunities it provided for increasing their skills in teaching in a manner that is
informed by current and accurate linguistic and cultural knowledge
upon which to base approaches to teaching African American children
that are effective in improving their proficiency in Standard English.

Analogies to foreign language teaching and bilingual education

The implication of Labov's argument that African American language is a factor in school achievement *only to the extent that it is misperceived by teachers as a deficiency* is not as strong a position as some linguists and Ebonics scholars have taken, claiming that structural differences between African American language and Standard English are sufficient – in and of themselves – to account for the chronic academic underachievement of Black children.

Several proposals advanced by Black English scholars are framed in terms of an explicit or implicit analogy between literacy issues that affect Black children and similar issues associated with speakers of acknowledged different languages such as Spanish and Chinese. One obvious area where the analogy breaks down is that African American children, unlike children for whom English is a second language, begin their schooling with a language that is strictly speaking English, and, furthermore, has a high degree of similarity with classroom English, so much so that they can understand most of what is said to them by teachers. Likewise, teachers can understand most, if not all, of what AAE-speaking children say to them. A key finding of the Ann Arbor Black English decision is that whatever language barrier might exist consists mainly of teacher attitudes. Although teachers can understand the Black English of the children, and the children can understand the teachers' Standard English, the teachers lack of knowledge of the linguistic nature of Black English causes them to react to it in the speech of students in ways that are detrimental to the learning process.

An experimental proposal that parallels many aspects of bilingual education programs for children of limited English proficiency calls for the use of initial reading material in African American language as a means of bridging the gap between AAL and SE. In bilingual education, children who speak languages other than English are taught to read in their native language, and have access to initial reading material written in that language. The similar idea of using *dialect readers* to teach African American children to read is enthusiastically endorsed by a group linguists who contributed to a volume on the proposal (Baratz and Shuy 1969).

Another noteworthy application of Black language to literacy development is a reading program called *Bridge*. (Simpkins and Simpkins 1981; Simpkins, Holt and Simpkins 1977) Unlike the dialect reader proposal which focuses on initial reading material, the Bridge program uses printed material and accompanying audiotapes to promote reading achievement for children at the secondary level who were not reading at grade level. It consists of a series of narratives incorporating various degrees of African American language in such a way as to facilitate reading development of Black students. Experimental field testing of the Bridge program on seventh to twelfth graders, reported in Simpkins and Simpkins (1981) suggest that it is more effective than traditional ways of teaching remedial reading. Rickford and Rickford (1995) recently tested a version of the Bridge program in East Palo Alto California and found that many students, especially boys, preferred the reading material in African American language.

The dialect readers proposal and the Bridge program were no doubt significant influences in the planning of the reading materials strand of AALCP associated with the linguistic component. The AALCP reading materials program share with Bridge, not only a target population of remedial students, but also the use of narratives enhanced by the prevalence of slang terms from youth culture which enhance their potential for motivating students to engage in planned instructional sessions.

My declaration to fellow linguists in the audience of my 2001 LSA presentation of being in the non-linguists camp "ideologically," is in recognition of the fact that I share with my fellow Ebonicists an interest in recognition of African American language, not only as a means of enhancing the prospects for successful outcomes for African American students in the classroom, but also as a means of cultural revitalization. The other focal point of my LSA presentation, "the issue of how the focus of the research shifted" from what was called for by the original request for proposals, to a multi-faceted investigation of "diverse issues of teacher education, parent-advocacy and reading material" was made without the benefit of being several years removed from the action, and thereby able to better discern the "emerging picture," alluded to above, of an ongoing challenge to the still dominant deficit-pathology policy orientation, one piece of which is the Ebonics Resolution. The primary source of the challenge is what I call a different-culture policy orientation, a succinct summary of which is offered by Janice Hale (1982) who cites a number of reasons for the ineffectiveness of American education with respect to the needs of African American children

[the American Educational System] is not working because of the disproportionate number of Black children who are labeled hyperactive ... given drugs and tranquilizers ... labeled mentally retarded and placed in "special classes.".... [and] because of the disproportionate number of Black children who are being suspended, expelled, and "pushed out" ... (Hale 1982: 1)

Hale proceeds to characterize "the aim of [her] research perspective" as

... to describe the influence of African American culture on child rearing. The hypothesis is that certain characteristics, peculiar to Black culture, have their roots in West Africa and have implications for the way in which Black children learn and think. (4)

The definition of "culture" in the above-mentioned AALCP document distributed at the New Orleans meeting clearly aligns the Cultural Component of the project with the different-culture orientation.

In this project, culture refers to cognition, a way of understanding and responding to the world that is shared by members of a particular group of people. These understandings and responses are passed from one generation to the next through cultural practices and values, including the peculiar use of language characteristic of the particular culture. Children are socialized within the culture of their immediate family and community. The habits of cognition and discourse that support formal school learning are developed within the context of the child's home-culture and immediate community. Difference between practices in school and those in the home can interfere with learning. This includes the surface features of language as well as the meaning transmitted.

It is interesting to note that Hale (1982) in her book-length discussion of academic research in support of the general thesis of cultural difference as a key factor in Black school achievement, pays scant attention to linguistic research on Black English. The few studies of Black language that are mentioned, are those that focus on African American verbal culture, and distinctively Black ways of speaking such as signifying and playing the dozens. The primary focus is on describing typical ways in which language is used by Black children in African American cultural contexts – interacting with parents, siblings, peers and church members – as a basis for capitalizing on the strengths revealed in such contexts in the planning and delivery of classroom interaction.

The explicit inclusion of "surface feature of language" in the AALCP list of cultural differences that "can interfere with learning" may be seen as a concession to the perspective of the linguistic component, and of particular persons in the cultural component who attach special significance to surface features of African American language, either as a barrier to the acquisition of Standard English literacy, or as a resource for materials development, and the planning and delivery of instruction. The surface details of African American language were a significant part of the content of ongoing efforts of the School District aimed at introducing teachers to successful strategies for teaching African American children in ways that involve specific characteristics of Black culture and language.

The AALCP, for all its effort to avoid the appearance of being an "Oakland collaboration of Ebonics," included, nonetheless, in its complement of research efforts, the above-mentioned study headed by Nabeehah Shakir of teacher development efforts of the Oakland District's Standard English Proficiency Program (SEP) based on Ebonics principles. No direct reference to "Ebonics," or "Standard English Proficiency" is to be found, however, anywhere in the proposals, reports, and other project documents. In the project description distributed at the New Orleans meeting, the study of that phase of the research is described as

> ... an external input model in which teachers are provided information about the role of culture and language in the literacy acquisition and development process. In this approach teachers are guided through carefully designed professional development which enables them to identify and critically analyze successful strategies. As teachers study the research on the role and responsibility of culture and language in teaching and learning, they are given exemplars of these strategies. Teachers are expected to apply the concepts as they develop their unique individual style and creativity in their respective classrooms. Through a process of peer and cognitive coaching, teachers become increasingly cognizant of their implementation of these effective strategies and make a commitment of attaining mastery of implementation.

A frequently cited case of exemplary classroom practice based on Ebonics principles is Carrie Secret, an elementary teacher in the Oakland School District, who credits positive distinctive features of Oakland's SEP program to "the inspirational directorship of Nabeehah

Shakir." Secret underscores what she sees as most distinctive about the Oakland program, in comparison to other SEP programs in California,

> we ... dared to honor and respect Ebonics as the home language that stands on its own rather than as a dialectal form of English. (Miner 1998: 79, 80)

Secret also acknowledges the influence of "Professor Ernie Smith" stating that

> Before I met [him], my approach was different. I used the "fix-something-that-was-wrong" approach.

Noteworthy features of Secret's approach to the development of Standard English proficiency in her students include the characterization of what would traditionally be considered correction of faulty or ungrammatical English usage as "translation into English." She emphasizes that she does not like to think of herself as requiring, but rather, encouraging students to speak English in situations in which it is appropriate and in their best interest. She also indicates that her students "read literature that has Ebonics language patterns in it," citing examples of "Joyce Hansen's *Yellow Bird and Me*, and *The Gift Giver*."

In view of the recognition given to Ebonics as a different language than English in the Oakland SEP program, one might be misled to classify it as based on a version of the language difference hypothesis. A crucial difference, however, is the honor and recognition it affords the home and community language of many African American students. As such it belies a policy orientation toward African American language shared by its primary backers of full recognition of Ebonics. Efforts to promote Standard English proficiency are implemented in a spirit of resistance to the Hegemony of Standard English while acknowledging the intrinsic dignity and worth of African American language. The pull of the African component of DuBois' double-consciousness is sufficient to counteract any pressure to acquiesce to Standard English hegemony with a stronger motivation to resist it.

Implications for language planning

The Ebonics resolution raises a crucially important point about the current state of national educational policy that is frequently overlooked, or from which observers tend to be distracted by the controversy it ignited. It concerns the inequity of responding to the presence of students with comparable special needs in unequal ways depending on whether or not they speak a different language than English at home. School districts with a critical mass of students of limited English proficiency may qualify for bilingual education funding, while districts with predominantly African American student bodies can only qualify for federal funding to the extent that their students qualify as disadvantaged, low achieving, learning disabled or afflicted with pathological speech. In the paragraph of the Resolution prior to the one cited above, the Oakland School District cites a compelling interest in

> providing equal opportunities for all of its students

as a rationale for

> recognizing [that] the language acquisition and improvement skills of African American students are as fundamental as is application of bilingual education for others whose primary languages are other than English.

In committing itself to such a policy, the Oakland District may be seen as correcting a blatant inequity in the current structure of federal categorical programs, by recognizing the parallel nature of the language needs of students who speak a stigmatized variety of English and students of limited English proficiency.

10
The Grammar: We Be Following Rules

> My mamma, your mamma, hangin out clothes; my mamma
> hit your mamma in the nose. Did it hurt?

The grammar of African American language, is approached in this chapter in a manner that is commonly reserved for recognized languages. Since one of the language planning issues identified in the introduction, is the question of how its grammar should be described, I take the occasion in the following pages to offer a succinct overview of what an *autonomous grammar* of AA would look like, as contrasted to the list of features commonly used by Black English scholars. The approach that I follow could alternatively be referred to as a paradigmatic grammar, because of the manner in which sets of words or sounds or other elements of the language that alternate with one another in grammatical sequences are displayed in a manner that makes their systematicity clear and explicit.

Many people continue to be influenced by the stigmatized status of African American language, and the erroneous belief that persons speaking it are attempting, but failing, to speak Standard English. In such a climate, the point that AA is systematic and rule-governed can hardly be overstated. A paradigmatic approach tends to make a more striking impression on audiences of the systematic and rule-governed nature of the variety being described, especially if it is a stigmatized variety such as African American.

The subtitle of this chapter, *We be followin rules*, is a succinct rebuttal to that commonsense view that it is Bad English. I often dramatize the point under discussion in presentations to lay audiences, switching from Standard English, to African American language,

> When we talk that way, we dont be messin up. . We be followin rules.

177

The line at the head of the chapter is one of a variety of rhymed jingles that my playmates and I used to chant in the course of playing *hide and go seek*. The child designated "It" would give the others time to hide by counting to a hundred by five, and when finished calling, "All hid?"

If anyone responded, "no," it meant that they needed more time, so the caller might recite the above jingle.

When I have the attention of my audience, I call attention to the possessive pronouns *my* and *your* in the jingle to illustrate the entire paradigm of AAL possessive pronouns, shown in Table 10.1.

As I discuss the set of possessive pronouns, I emphasize the typical AA pronunciation of *my* with a monophthong /a/ instead of the diphthong /ay/ of its standard pronunciation; and the r-less manner in which *your* is often pronounced, i.e., as /yo/.

Once attention is focused on distinctive aspects of AA pronunciation, it is an ideal point at which to introduce another paradigm such as the following chart of English phonemes (Table 10.2) to indicate that there is a system to our distinctive pronunciation. We don't be messing up the way other people pronounce the words, we just be following a different set of rules.

The phoneme chart is one of several concrete illustrations of a pervasive theme of the following discussion, which I call *the uniformity of American English*. One of the main points that I develop is that, although African American language participates considerably in that uniformity, it has, nevertheless, a distinctiveness that cannot be fully described by lists of features representing points at which it diverges from what would be expected in Standard English.

The uniformity of American English at the level of phonology is seen in the fact that, although there are numerous instances of differences in pronunciation that characterize the speech of different regions or social strata, the differences are largely a consequence of combining the same set of basic sounds, or phonemes in different

Table 10.1 AA Possessive Pronouns

	Singular	Plural
FIRST	my /ma/	Our
SECOND	your /yo/	Y'all
THIRD	his, her, it's	They

Table 10.2   English Phonemes by Place and Manner of Articulation

CONSONANTS

	Bilabial	Labio-Dental	Dental	Alveolar	Alveo-Palatal	Velar	Glottal
Stops							
Voiceless	pit /p/			tip /t/		cap /k/	
Voiced	bit /b/			dip /d/		gap /g/	
Fricatives							
Voiceless		fan /f/	thin /θ/		cash /š/		
Voiced		van /v/	then /ð/	sip /s/	beige /ž/		
				zip /z/			
Affricates							
Voiceless					choke/č/		
Voiced					joke /ǰ/		
Nasals	map /m/	nap /n/				song /ŋ/	
Approximants	well /w/			lip /l/	yell /y/		help /h/
				rip /r/			

VOWELS

	Front		Back
High			
Tense	beet /i/		Luke /u/
Lax	bit /I/		look /U/
Mid			
Tense	bait /e/		boat /o/
Lax	bet /ɛ/	cup /ʌ/	
Low			
ı round			caught /ɔ/
– round	cat /æ/	sofa /ə/	cot /a/

DIPHTHONGS

mice /ay/	mouse /aw/	boy /oy/

ways. All varieties of American English, including AA share a common phonemic inventory that consists of thirty-nine distinct sounds.

Pronunciation differences among the various regional and social varieties of American English are accounted for by differences in the particular sounds that are selected from the common inventory of phonemes; to account for different pronunciations of particular words.

Different dialectal pronunciations of *syrup*, for instance, are the conse-quence of selecting different vowels, either /i/, /e/, or /ʌ/, for the segment represented by "y" in the word's spelling, i.e., /sirəp/, /sɛrəp/ or /sʌrəp/. A similar selection between the vowels /I/ and /U/ accounts for the different pronunciation of *sister*, either in the standard form, /sIst?r/, or the distinctive African American form, /sUst?/.

The last of the above examples calls attention to another aspect of the uniformity of American English, which manifests itself at the level of vocabulary. The distinctively AA pronunciation of *sister* is a particu-lar instance of the general point that, although African American shares the bulk of its lexicon with other varieties of American English, there are a number of forms that have distinctively African American pronunciations, special meanings, or both, which tend to co-occur in segments of speech produced in African American language. AA also has some closed lexical categories that have no exact counterpart in Standard American English. A cursory overview of distinctive aspects of the AA lexicon is undertaken in the following sections.

The uniformity of all varieties of American English in the area of basic vocabulary is uncontroversial. Efforts to identify significant vocabulary differences for African American tend to focus on slang terms, and other areas of special vocabulary such as the in-group names for African Americans and other groups discussed in Chapter Four. The area of general vocabulary that is most salient for bringing out distinctive aspects of the grammar of African American, however, consists of so-called closed classes, or function words, such as pro-nouns, determiners, auxiliaries, qualifiers and the like. There *are* distinctively African American content words too, however. A few common examples of them are given in the next section.

Distinctively African American content words

A distinctive quality that may be noted in certain basic AA vocabulary items in the open classes of nouns, verbs and adjectives is derived – not so much from their absolute difference from their General American English counterparts – as from the extension of the range of meaning of a common English word to include a distinctive African American sense. Some are pronounced in a distinctive African American manner; and others exhibit some combination of the above qualities. Two examples of the first type are the word *fine*, used in the sense of "attrac-tive," or "good-looking," and *yellow*, in the expression *high-yellow*, used to describe a notably "light-skinned" Black person.

Noteworthy examples of content words with distinctive AA pronunciations are the above-mentioned noun *sister* pronounced with the vowel of *look*, in its first syllable, and with the final "r" of its spelling not pronounced, i.e., /sʊstə/, and *hungry*, pronounced as /hongri/. Additionally, the African American noun *sister* includes in its range of meaning, in addition to the general English "female sibling," the sense of "African American woman."

Some distinctively African American content words have been traced to African source languages. One that is part of my dialect, but appears to be dying out, does not even have a standard spelling. It is transcribed phonemically /j Ug/, and spelled inventively, *joog*, by analogy with words like *good*, and *look*, which have the same vowel nucleus. It means "to stick, prick or poke," and is derived from a word in the African language Efik /juk/ meaning "to prick or poke." A number of words that have entered the general English lexicon from African language sources are not considered here because they are not distinctively African American. A word, the origin of which I am unsure, but may be of African origin in *saditty* (c.f. Mitchell-Kernan 1971) meaning "conceited" or "stuck up."

In addition to the above mentioned content words that contribute to the lexical distinctiveness of African American language, quite a few others might be added which would be analyzed from a list of features approach as deriving their distinctiveness from the phonological feature of r-lessness. A case can be made, however, for treating them as instances of lexical alternation, due to the manner in which they are often used by the same persons in a pattern of codeswitching. One particular word that I remember being used by older aunties to describe me is the word *poor*, pronounced /po/, which has extended its range of meaning to include "skinny," "emaciated." As a child, I was very skinny, and fit the description quite well. A number of other content words that rhyme with *poor*, alternate in African American usage between standard r-full pronunciation and a markedly African American r-less variant, e.g., *store*, *floor*, etc. Several other single-syllable words pronounced in a similar way, are categorized as closed-class or function words.

Closed word classes, and function words

The classes of African American language discussed in the following sections consist mainly of function words, also known as grammatical morphemes, but includes pronouns. The main point I develop is that, while African American – with a few important exceptions noted below – has the same sets of pronouns and function words as other varieties, there are special features of pronunciation which lend to the distinctiveness of the variety and its effectiveness as a marker of discourse for such purposes as signifying. There is at least one set of such words that have distinctively African American syntactic properties, and function as markers of tense-mood and aspect. Some of them are noted in passing in the present discussion of vocabulary, and discussed further below with a focus on their syntactic properties.

Auxiliaries and other tense-mood-aspect markers

In the discussion of African American codeswitching in Chapter Seven, a pattern of alternation was noted in the usage of one informant between the standard pronunciation of *can't*, and a markedly African American pronunciation, underscored by the dialect spelling, *cain't*. Similar alternation is frequently observed between the markedly Black/Southern form *gon*, pronounced /gõ/, except with the subject pronoun *I'm*, in which case the initial /g/ is suppressed, resulting in /ʌmõ/, and the more general American form *gona*, in patterns of codeswitching (DeBose 1992; Van Keulen et al. 1998)

The form *cain't* is uncontrovertibly classified as a modal auxiliary, a category common to African American and other American varieties. It is the negated form of the auxiliary *can*, which also has a distinctive African American pronunciation, *kin*. Other words of this type, which have corresponding positive and negated forms are *is* and *ain't*, *do* and *don't*, *will* and *won't*, *was* and *wasn't*. The form *wasn't* has a distinctively AA pronunciation, /wʌdn/. Two of the AA negation markers, *ain't* and *didn't* are sometimes used interchangeably in a manner that is discussed further below under the topic of syntactic patterns.

Pronouns and determiners

Other closed word classes that are grammatically the same as other varieties of American English, but have distinctively African American forms among their members include personal and possessive pronouns, demonstratives and other determiners. Markedly African American personal pronoun forms include, in addition to the second person plural form *y'all*, and the monopthongal pronunciation of *I*, as /a/; special forms of *I*, *it*, *that* and *what*, pronounced /ʌm/, /Is/, /ðæs/

and /hwʌs/, and derived from the pronoun plus copula contractions, *I'm*, *it's*, *that's* and *what's*. Their classification as mono-morphemic variants of the basic pronouns is justified by syntactic evidence presented further below.

The class of possessive pronouns, includes the markedly Black forms *my*, pronounced /ma/, and *your*, pronounced /yo/, referred to above. The demonstratives include the frequently lampooned pronunciation of *this*, *that*, *these* and *them*, with the initial stop consonant, /d/. As such, they are very similar to equivalent aspects of other American varieties. The definite article in African American is subject to the same alternative pronunciation with an initial stop, /d/, as other varieties. Otherwise it is the same. The indefinite article likewise differs little from other varieties. One slight difference is that it is categorically realized as *a*, and does not alternate with *an*, e.g. as is typically the case in Standard English, e.g., *I ate a apple and a orange*.

Adverbs and qualifiers

A number of words traditionally classified as adverbs have distinctive African American characteristics. A noteworthy case in point is the form *sure*, frequently pronounced /ˢo/, and sometimes used in combination with *nuff*, i.e., *sho nuff*. While it is etymologically related to *sure enough*, which typically is used in other varieties with the sense of reporting that something has turned out in an expected manner; it is commonly used in AA either as an intensifier similar to "really," e.g., *You sho nuff is a fast walker*, "You certainly are a fast walker." *It sho nuff is heavy!* "It really is heavy." Another qualifier with a distinctively African American pronunciation is the word *kinda*, derived from the coalescence of *kind of*, and typically pronounced /kana/, e.g., *She kana tall*, "She is sort of tall."

Most of the closed word classes presently under discussion are very similar, if not identical, in African American language, to equivalent aspects of Standard English. There are, however, some closed classes of African American words that, although etymologically related to cognates in other varieties of American English, occur in grammatical patterns that are unique to African American. The most important such category for the points presently under consideration is that of tense-mood-aspect markers. They include not only the future marker *gon*, and the completive aspect marker *done*, but also the habitual aspect marker *be*. They are discussed further below under syntax.

The paradigmatic approach to the elements of AA grammar discussed thus far has served to highlight certain distinctive characteristics of AA that would not be brought out by the list of features approach. An unstated premise of the more common approach of using feature lists is that AA participates in the overall uniformity of American English in such a manner, and to such an extent, that it is adequately accounted for by the features listed. It should be clear, however, that although AA does indeed participate, to a very high degree, in the uniformity of American English, it is endowed with a distinctiveness that is not fully and adequately described without resort to an autonomous grammar that concentrates on accounting for the elements and rules of which the variety is constructed, without reference to some other known system from which the system under study deviates in listed ways.

From features to systems

When I was a graduate student in the early seventies, taking courses in which I was introduced the work of transformational – generative grammarians, I was simultaneously becoming familiar with sociolinguistics, creole studies, and the rapidly-growing field of Black English studies. As a native speaker, I was fascinated by the fact that I have very clear intuitions of a Black English linguistic system. I began at that time, using what was then considered the *Standard Theory* of transformational-generative grammar, to write an intuition-based account of an autonomous linguistic system underlying the diversity of speech patterns produced by members of the African American speech community.

An adequate description of AA as an autonomous system can be of great value in clarifying the issue of the uniformity of American English, and the extent to which AA participates in it. Evidence considered thus far indicates that, at the levels of vocabulary and phonology, AA participates to a very high degree in the overall uniformity of American English, while at the same time exhibiting a distinctiveness that pervades the basic vocabulary with respect to the pronunciation of certain words, and the range of meanings associated with them. It is shown in the following pages, that at the levels of morphology and syntax, it manifests a similar pattern of distinctive elements that pervade an overall high level of similarity to other varieties of American English. The distinctiveness of AA is most profound and pervasive in the system of marking tense, mood and aspect.

Grammatical uniformity of American English

At the highest level of generality the grammatical uniformity of American English may be seen in

- the structure of noun phrases,
- the patterning of syntactic predicates in the environment following the main verb, and
- the patterning of auxiliaries before the main verb.

Using the notation of the standard theory of transformational-generative grammar, the above generalization may be summarized in the following phrase structure rules:

1. S → NP VP
2. VP → AUX V (X)
3. AUX → T (M) (have+EN) (be+ing)
4. T → past or present

Rule one is a shorthand way of stating that

> a "sentence" (S) may be realized as a noun phrase (NP) followed by a verb phrase (VP)

Rule (2) indicates that

> the verb phrase may be realized as a main verb (V) preceded by an auxiliary component and followed by a pattern (X) determined by the sub-categorization of the verb.

Rule (3) stipulates that

> the auxiliary component consists of "tense," (T) optionally followed by one or more of the following elements – a modal, have, and be. The symbol +EN specifies that whatever follows have is in the past participle form. The notation +ing specifies that whatever follows be is in the present participle form.

Rule (4) simply states that

> the options for "tense" are "present", "past."

Other rules specify the form that X may assume under various conditions, e.g., indirect object and/or direct object following a transitive verb; adjective phrase following a linking verb; etc. Of special interest for the issue of the extent to which AA participates in the overall uniformity of American English is the possibility that such rules offer for pinpointing specific conditions under which AA differs from what other varieties have in common.

Although AA participates to a very high degree in the above patterning as it pertains to noun phrases; and what comes after the main verb; it contrasts markedly with Standard English and other varieties in the kinds of grammatical patterns that occur in the auxiliary component.

The distinctiveness of African American sentence structure

In noting what is distinctive about AA, I do not wish to imply that AA speakers lack knowledge of the General American English patterns noted above. African Americans who are literate and/or bilingual have intuitive knowledge of Standard English and AA patterns, as well as appropriateness conditions for drawing upon one area or another of their vast linguistic competence.

The emerging description of AA as an autonomous system, at the level of syntax, support the generalization that, while AA shares the overwhelming majority of its elements and rules with other varieties of American English, it differs markedly in a number of noteworthy ways. At the highest level of generality, at which the two major constituents of sentence structure are specified, AA sentences do not conform strictly to the generalization expressed formulaically in the above phrase-structure rules 1–4.

Sentence constituents

Although AA is the same as other varieties of American English in having a primary division of its basic sentence pattern into a subject and a predicate, the AA predicate differs from the general pattern in that it does not always consist of a verb phrase. Previous accounts based on the list of features approach have attempted to force it to fit the overall pattern by postulating copula deletion and other low level rules. Without resorting to such explanations, however, the complete range of patterns that actually occur in AA syntactic predicates may be accounted for by means of a different system of expressing tense-mood and aspect (TMA) than that of the General American English

AUX. The distinctive African American TMA system is similar in many ways to a system typically found in West African languages and Caribbean creoles. (DeBose and Faraclas 1993) Before looking at that aspect of the grammar, however, I briefly focus on the structure of noun phrases in the next section, in order to call attention to a few distinctive characteristics Some of them pertain specifically to noun phrases in the function of subject of a sentence.

Noun phrases

At the highest level of sentence structure, a noun phrase functioning as a subject is typically followed by a predicate phrase. One important distinction of AA noun phrases when functioning as the subject, is the existence of special variants of subject pronouns (DeBose and Faraclas 1993) derived from contractions of the forms *I*, *it*, *that* and *what*. Whenever certain types of nominal subject complements are directly juxtaposed to either of those forms, they are realized as /ʌm/ "I'm", /Is/ "it's", /ðæs/ "that's," and /hwʌs/ "what's". They are discussed in greater detail below.

Another distinctive aspect of African American noun phrases is the existence of a special means of referring to a plurality of persons typically associated with a particular named individual, by suffixing *nim* to the name of the individual in question. The expression *Big Mama nim*, was adopted by a member of my extended family to name a web-site dedicated to family genealogical records and information, with reference to the way she and her siblings addressed their grandmother. The *nim* suffix extends the reference to all of the other members of Big Mama's generation with whom she is associated.

The use of *nim* as a proper noun pluralizer is similar to the more extensive use of a reflex of *them*, rather than the suffix *-s* to mark nouns plural, in Gullah and other diaspora varieties, e.g., *bwai-dem* "boys," *Kuta-dem*, "Kuta and the others." A similar pattern of noun pluralization is found in a number of West African languages. West African languages have also, as noted above, exerted a major influence on the distinctively AA tense-mood-aspect system.

Tense-Mood-Aspect system

A distinctive system of marking tense-mood and aspect, commonly found in West African and diaspora languages, is described in detail in DeBose and Faraclas (1993) and referred to as the Lexical Stativity

Parameter. It is a system that assigns TMA values to syntactic predicates based on their value for the feature "stative," which is an expression whether the event predicated by the verb of a given sentence is interpreted semantically as an action or as a state. In the West African languages in which this system is typically found, many words classified in English as adjectives are classified as stative verbs. In Nigerian Pidgin, (NP) for example, *sik*, "sick," is classified as a stative verb, whereas *go*, "to go," is classified as a nonstative verb. If a verb is classified [+stative] a predicate in which it occurs has a default TMA interpretation as non-completive aspect and present tense. A predicates headed by a non-stative verb, on the other hand, has a default TMA interpretation of completive aspect and past tense.

The Nigerian Pidgin sentence, *A go Legos*, "I went to Lagos," derives a completive aspect/past tense interpretation from the unmarked form of the active verb *go*, whereas the sentence, *A sik*, "I am sick," is interpreted as non-completive aspect/present tense because of the classification of the verb *sik* as [+stative]. Speakers of NP and other similarly structured languages have the option of overtly marking a predicate for a different TMA interpretation than the default value according to the lexical stativity parameter, or indeed, of reinforcing or emphasizing its default value.

Although the NP form *sik* is derived from the English adjective *sick*, its classification as a stative verb in Nigerian Pidgin is justified by the fact that it patterns like verbs, in relation to preverbal markers such as *don*, which overtly marks a predicated event "completive," e.g., *A don go Legos* "I went/have gone to Lagos;" *A don sik* "I got/have gotten sick;" and *de*, which marks an action or state as "incomplete," e.g., *A de go Legos* "I go/am going to Lagos, *A de sik*," "I get/am getting sick."

DeBose and Faraclas (1993) note the similarity of the AA verb system to such systems as that of NP, and examine evidence of the extent to which a similar system is retained in African American. While making the case that the lexical stativity parameter is "alive and well" so to speak in the grammar of AA, the form that it assumes in AA is masked, by its surface similarity to the General American English system. DeBose and Faraclas 1993, capture this subtlety by characterizing the AA system, as one in which

> Verb forms similar to the English infinitive, simple present, simple past and past participle frequently occur.., but .. [do] not play a primary role in the tense-mood-aspect interpretation of BE sentences... (p. 368)

A good example of the kinds of verb forms alluded to by DeBose and Faraclas as "similar to the English infinitive, simple present, simple past," etc., is the verb <u>jumps</u> uttered by an Oakland informant when describing an incident in which his car broke down on the San Mateo Bridge, saying:

> My car had stopped. The fuel pump had went out on me, you know. The car had stopped, and I seen this car. The headlights was about two miles behind me. Because it was straight, you could see. And I sit there and I watch. I hit my brakes, you know, see this cat bearin' down on me, you know. Hit my brakes again. He ain't slowin' up, you know. So I jumps out my car.

The DeBose and Faraclas model would account for this instance of *jumps*, in the last sentence by showing that the verb suffix –s does not function in the AA system as a marker of present tense with third-person-singular subjects, but as a marker of non-completive aspect, without regard for the person of the subject.

The similarity of the AA system to the West African/creole system is highlighted in Table 10.3, which compares the preverbal markers used in NP and Gullah to relevant features of the AA system, which are discussed in greater detail in the next section. One striking similarity that the comparison underscores is the manner in which reflexes of the English forms *done*, *do/does*, *been*, and *go/going* function as optional overt markers of completive, noncompletive, anterior and future/irrealis, aspect-tense, respectively, in Nigerian Pidgin, Gullah and African American.

While the marking of completive aspect and future time is very similar in AA, NP and Gullah, the AA system has evolved into a system

Table 10.3 Common Features of Nigerian Pidgin, Gullah and African American Tense-mood-aspect Systems

	Nigerian Pidgin	Gullah	African American
Completive	don	done	done
Noncompletive	de	də	do –s –in
Anterior	bin	been	was had
Future	go	gwine	gó

in which the tense/aspect interpretation of predicates is an automatic consequence of their classification into one of three basic types. Predicates of the first type corresponds closely to the [+stative] category of the NP system, and have a default noncompletive aspect/ present tense interpretation, consistent with what would be predicted for a system organized around the lexical stativity parameter (LSP).

The hypothesis that the LSP continues to operate in AA – although supported by a great deal of evidence presented in the next section – must be qualified to account for innovations in the AA system, that increase its divergence from the prototypical West African-creole model, and surface similarity to Standard American English and other spoken varieties. One clear instance of such a change involves the reclassification of many words classified as stative verbs in the proto-typical system as adjectives in the AA system. A similarity of patterning may still be seen, notwithstanding the reclassification, however. Compare, for example, the similarity of the AA unmarked predicate adjective construction, e.g., *she sick*, to Nigerian Pidgin, unmarked stative verb construction, e.g., *i sik*, "She's sick."

Since *sick* is not a verb in AA, it must complement the verb *get* to express the meaning equivalent to marked NP predicates such as *don sik*, "has gotten sick," "*go sik*," "will get sick," *de sik*, "is getting sick," etc. In the next section, I provide a step by step analysis of AA syntactic predicates supported by native speaker intuitions as well as empirical data, resulting in a comprehensive account of the patterns of grammat-ical structure that characterize the AA syntactic predicate. The account culminates in the identification of three basic types of predicates, two of which, when unmarked, have an aspect/tense interpretation that is consistent with the operation of a lexical stativity parameter.

The syntactic predicate

Since DeBose 1977, I have continued to work on the description of AA as an autonomous grammar following an approach that uses native speaker intuitions, as well as empirical data. (DeBose 1984; DeBose and Faraclas 1993; DeBose 1994a, 2001c) DeBose 1977 provides a detailed list of basic AA "verb phrase constructions" beginning with certain constructions that are markedly similar to particular Standard English constructions such as to indicate a high level of participation in the uniformity of American English, i.e. Simple present,

1. *John work in Los Angeles;*

Future time, marked by *will* or *gon,*

   2a. *John will work in Los Angeles.*
   2b. *John gon work in Los Angeles*; and

Present, past or future progressive:

   3. *They fightin.*
   4. *They was fightin.*
   5. *They gon be fightin.*

A key point in the description of the above constructions is the fact that although they "differ little" from equivalent constructions in other varieties, they do, as a matter of fact differ – and an adequate account of the grammar should account for the difference however subtle or slight. Two of the sentences, 2a and 4, conform fully to the traditional constructions with which they are grouped. Two others, 1, and 3 are amenable to explanation in terms of minor or superficial changes in what is common to other varieties, i.e., deletion of the verb suffix, –s, to get *work* in example 1, and deletion of the contracted copula form, –re from *They're* to get *They* in example 3. The form *gon*, in 2b and 5, may be accounted for in a similar manner, although it involves more that a single deletion.

Assuming that *gon* is a casual variant of the *be going to* construction, realized in other varieties as *gonna* following a contracted form of the auxiliary *be*, e.g., *she's gonna, we're gonna*, the same deletion rule used to account for the "absence" of the contraction '*re* in sentences like 3 can account for its "absence" before *gon* in 5, as well as the "absence of the contraction '*s*, in 2b. One problem with that analysis, however, is that contracted forms of *is* and *are* rarely occur before *gon*; and con trived examples such as (6, 7) in which they occur, do not fully satisfy my native speaker intuitions of grammaticality.

   6. *? John's gon work in Los Angeles,*
   7. ** They're gon be fightin.*

The question mark before example 6, indicates my reluctance to accept it; the asterisk before example (7) marks the fact that it does not "sound" like AA language, to me at all.

The fact that sentences 1–5 are grammatical, in the sense that they sounds right to AA speakers, notwithstanding the absence of certain features expected in other varieties, indicates that the rules of AA verb phrase structure differ in certain ways from those common to other varieties. Upon close examination, many of the differences in question are difficult to reconcile with the idea that all differences between AA and other varieties of American English are superficial variations in a common system. The above mentioned use of *gon* as a marker of future time, is a case in point.

Although *gon* is similar to *will* in its reference to future time, and in the occurrence of both forms in the same position in declarative sentences, before a stem form of the verb, the two forms behave very differently under conditions of sentence negation, and yes-no question formation. The negative particle *not* may follow *will*, but not *gon*, in a grammatical sequence, e.g.;

> 8a. *He will not arrive on time.*
> 8b. * *He gon not arrive on time.*

In the formation of yes-no questions, *will* may switch positions with the subject

> 9a. *Will you arrive on time?*

The position of *gon* immediately preceding the verb is unchangeable, however, as indicated by the ungrammaticality of (7b).

> 9b. * *Gon you arrive on time?*

The grammaticality judgments or native speakers are crucial to efforts to describe the grammar of a language variety as the internalized knowledge of native speakers. My intuitions, and those of other native speaker linguists (c.f. Green 2002) accept sentences based on all of the patterns represented by (1–5) and others discussed below as grammatical instances of African American language. Linguists striving to account for the grammar of AA internalized by its speakers, i.e., their linguistic competence, are challenged to account for the differences they represent from other varieties of American English as differences in the rules that speakers *sho nuf do be followin*.

Other aspects of the distinctiveness of AA syntactic predicates are illustrated by the next set of examples (10–14). They are not as easy to dismiss as the ones just considered as superficial variation in a system common to all varieties of American English. Sentences 10 and 11 represent a typical Black English verb phrase pattern which I refer to in the 1977 article as "a *perfect* construction marked by the particle *done.*" I note that, in that construction, *done* is followed by a form of the main verb similar to the standard English past tense or past participle form; explaining that "[t]his construction takes the place of both the simple past and present perfect of acrolectal English. The particle *done* may sometimes be omitted" (468)

10. (with *done*) *John done broke his leg.*
11. (without *done*) *They gone home.*

The *done* construction is amply attested in data samples collected by Black English scholars, and is commonly included in the basic list of syntactic features. Explanations of its relationship to Standard English vary considerably, however. Fasold and Wolfram (1975) describe it as a completive aspect marker.

> The completive aspect is formed from the verb *done* plus a past form of the [main] verb. Because of the uncertain status of the past participle in the grammar of the dialect, it is difficult to determine whether this form is the past participle or not. (66)

Labov expresses a different take on the form.

> *Done* has for all intents and purposes become an adverb, functioning sometimes like *already* or *really*, and lost its status as a verb. (Labov 1972: 56)

Labov's analysis of *done* is consistent with his position on the same versus different system issue to the effect that Black English and Standard English "do indeed form a single system." (Labov 1972: 63)

Another distinctive AA verb phrase construction, which DeBose 1977 calls "a *habitual progressive* construction ... is marked by the infinitive form of *be*" directly following the subject," and "contrasts with the present progressive marked by "zero" copula." The contrast is illustrated in the following examples, 12 and 13.

12. *They be fightin all the time.*
13. *They fightin right now.*

I also note a "habitual perfect construction" marked by the sequential occurrence of *be* and *done*, as in 14.

14. He always be done lost his cool.

After discussion of the constructions represented by the above examples (1–14) I proceed to discuss, under the heading "Copula constructions," the AA equivalent to so called predicate nominal constructions, which typically occur in the environment following a linking verb; noting however that in AA

> Predicate noun phrases adjectives and locatives directly follow the subject noun phrase in present tense declarative sentences. (DeBose 1977: 469)

Such adjectival, nominal and locative complements of the subject are instances of a high level of participation of AA in the uniformity of American English in terms of what may come after the main verb. AA differs from other varieties in this aspect of predicate phrase structure to the extent that such complements may "directly follow the subject." Some examples of such zero-copula constructions were provided in the introduction, and others are provided further below in this chapter. They are accounted for in the list of features approach in the same way as predicates in which *gon*, or a present participle such as *fightin* occur directly following the subject, as in 2b, 3 and 5, above; i.e., by postulating a low-level rule of copula deletion. which applies, "wherever Standard English can contract the copula." (Labov 1969)

A noteworthy generalization about the grammar of AA that tends to be obscured by its similarity to other varieties of American English is the possibility for a number of predicate types to occur directly after the subject: not only the kinds of "copula constructions" just noted, but also present participles, past participles and the markers *gon*, *done* and *be*. One implication of that generalization is that the distinctiveness of AA extends beyond superficial differences that may be described by postulating phonological deletion rules, and affects the fundamental structure of the syntactic predicate; so much so that it does not fit the generalization that holds for Standard English and other varieties that a sentence consists of a subject noun phrase, followed by a predicate in the form of a verb phrase. While the first part of the rule holds, the second part must be modified to account for the fact that AA predicates frequently do not take the form of a verb phrase.

A major reason for the difference just noted between AA syntactic predicate and that of General American English is the fact that the element (T), which, in other varieties, obligatorily attaches to the first verbal element, has optional status in the grammar of AA, *if it has any status at all*. One kind of evidence of the obligatory status of tense marking in General American English is the typical manner in which at least a trace of tense marking – such as the contracted copula in the following example (15a) occurs – even in clipped or casual speech.

15a. *You're gonna be on time, aren't you?*

The following sentence (15b) is a direct translation of (15a) into AA. Note the lack of any trace of tense-marking:

15b. *You gon be on time, ain't you?*

A second generalization supported by examples (1–5) is that AA has lexical items that function as markers of tense-mood-aspect (TMA) which have no exact counterpart in General American English. They include the form *gon*, which functions to mark a predicated event as occurring in the future, as well as the completive aspect marker, *done*, and habitual aspect marker, *be*. As has already been noted with respect to *gon*, these markers occupy a fixed position in the sentences in which they occur. Unlike typical auxiliaries, they do not have the option of "moving" to the beginning of the sentence in yes-no questions. Nor do they have special negated forms such as *isn't*, *don't* and *can't*; or serve as pivotal elements in sentence negation with *not*. Finally, unlike pro totypical auxiliaries, AA TMA markers frequently occur directly after the subject of a sentence without any trace of being marked for present or past tense.

Green includes both *done* and *be* in a category she calls "aspect markers." (2002: 45–62). She cites them as specific examples of "ways in which the verbal paradigms of AAE differ from those in General American English." (74) She further notes that

Aspectual markers differ from auxiliaries, as shown in processes such as emphatic affirmation, negation, yes-no question formation and tag question formation. (Green 2002: 74).

Another generalization about the distinctiveness of AA syntactic predicates, suggested by sentence (3) is that participles such as *workin* frequently occur in AA in the position directly following the subject. The AA construction represented by (3), while similar to the present progressive construction in other varieties, differs in a manner that suggests another AA syntactic category that has no exact counterpart in other varieties – participles derived from verbs, but which function as complements of the subject in a similar manner to predicate noun phrase, adjective phrase and locative phrase complements.

Unlike the typical case in other varieties, in which the selection of a verb (or auxiliary) in the present participle form is dictated by its position directly after the AUX element, (be+ing), there is no trace of any such auxiliary in AA sentences like (3). Such evidence supports the working hypothesis that in AA grammar, the suffix –*in* is a derivational morpheme, used to form a distinctive AA lexical category. Similar evidence represented by examples 10 and 11 above, regarding the unclear status of past tense and past participles in AA grammar, suggests a possible unified analysis of both issues, that is, one that treats both present and past participles as distinctive AA syntactic categories, rather than as inflected forms of the verb. DeBose and Faraclas (1993) use the term "derived verbal predicate" in accounting for the different types of phrasal patterns that may directly follow the subject of an AA sentence

> either a nonverbal predicate (examples 1 a–c), a derived verbal predicate (examples 1d and 1e) or a verbal predicate ... (368).

The examples given of nonverbal predicates are of predicate adjective, noun and locative phrases, respectively. Derived verbal predicates, exemplified by *She walkin home*, and *She done walk home*, are defined as

> those in which the main verb is delimited in some way, such as by the suffix –*in* or the preverbal marker *done*.

One question that DeBose and Faraclas leave open in the above definition of derived verbal predicates is the question of how to classify a predicate in which a cognate of the Standard English past participle occurs directly following the subject. They do so by not commenting – at the definitional stage of the discussion – on the various suffixes commonly associated with past tense and past participle forms, and the extent to which they tend to overlap or coalesce in General American English as well as AA.

The verb forms in examples (10, 11) are typical of the manner in which the categories past tense and past participle tend to be conflated in all varieties of American English. With regular verbs, the distinction is obliterated by the fact that both are formed in the same way by addition of the –ed suffix to the verb stem. With irregular verbs, usage varies so much that teachers and other guardians of correct English rely on lists of *principle parts of verbs* such as those shown on the following Table (10.4) to aid students in their speaking and writing in a grammatically acceptable manner.

The above excerpt from an informant's story about a car breakdown is typical of the manner in which the distinction between past tense and past participles observed in Standard English tends to be condensed in AA into a single category. The standard past form *went* in the second sentence, i.e., *The fuel pump had went out on me*, occurring as it does after *had*, seems to be functioning as a past participle. On the other hand, the form *seen* in the third sentence, *and I seen this car*; although it is the standard past participle of *see*, is apparently functioning in this instance as the simple past tense construction. DeBose 2001 builds upon the perspective of DeBose and Faraclas, focusing on the notion of patterns of complementation as a more adequate way of accounting for frequently-observed patterns of variation in AA data than previous accounts based on isolated features.

At the most general level, DeBose 2001 shows that the sentence constituents: subject, and predicate, pattern in a way that reveals the basic workings of the system. Within that general analysis, I show how predicates may be subcategorized on the basis of intuitive tests, and how the classification of predicates crucially affect the tense-mood-aspect interpretation of sentences.

Table 10.4 Sample List of Principle Parts of Verbs

Base form	Past tense	Past participle
eat	ate	eaten
drink	drank	drunk
see	saw	seen
think	thought	thought
teach	taught	taught
drive	drove	driven

Patterns of complementation

For the sake of the issues raised in DeBose 2001, I define *complementation*, as

> *completion* of syntactic structures in a manner that satisfies native speakers' intuitive sense of grammaticality. Expressions of the form X takes Y are used to formulate, in an informal manner, patterns purported to hold in the system under study.

Applied to the study of syntactic predicates in General American English, relevant examples are

- the rule that whatever follows the auxiliary *have* must be in the form of a past participle, alternatively stated as, the auxiliary *have* takes a past participle, or –EN, complement, e.g., *has eaten*.
- the auxiliary *be* takes a present participle, or *–ing*, complement, e.g., *is eating*, and
- modal auxiliaries take a bare verb stem complement, e.g., *will eat*.

The patterns just alluded to differ in an important manner from other patterns of complementation that specify what may follow the main verb of a sentence – dictated by the general principle noted above that verbs are subcategorized on the basis of the kinds of complements they take.

The basic subcategories of verbs in General American English are transitive, intransitive and linking. A transitive verb is said to take an object – either direct, e.g., *Mary sent the package*; or both direct and indirect, e.g., *Mary sent Paul the package*; as well as other patterns. Intransitive verbs do not take an object, as in the acknowledged shortest verse in the Bible, *Jesus wept*. Linking verbs take either noun phrase, adjective phrase or locative phrase complements.

An important distinction between auxiliary verbs and main verbs is that the latter (with the exception of the main verb *be*) not only select syntactic complements (known technically as c-selection), they also assign semantic roles, also known in the literature as theta roles; that is, they function as semantic predicates in assigning semantic roles. (technically known as s-selection) (c.f. Chomsky 1995: 31)

The difference between c-selection and s-selection is illustrated by the following example. In the sentence *Mother baked the children some cookies*, the transitive verb *baked* c-selects an indirect object, *the chil-*

dren, and a direct object *some cookies*. It also s-selects, by assigning the semantic role of "agent" to *mother*, the role of "result," to *some cookies*, and the role of "beneficiary" to *the children*. Hence it s-selects as well as c-selects. Auxiliaries, and the main verb *be* functioning as a copula, typically c-select, but do not s-select.

In copula constructions, the semantic predicate may be expressed by a non-verb such as the noun phrase *my best friend* in example 16 below, which predicates the identity of the speaker's best friend of the person referred to by the subject *Paul*. Similarly, the adjective phrase *mad*, in sentence 17, predicates of the subject the state of being "angry", and the prepositional phrase *at home* in example 18 predicates the location "at home" of the subject.

16. *Paul is my best friend.*
17. *Paul is mad.*
18. *Paul is at home.*

Following traditional grammar, we may use the terms nominal, adjectival and locative *subject complements*, for the portions of examples (16–18) that follow the verb .When the same kinds of structures occur in the positions they occupy in examples (19–21) they may be referred to as *object complements*.

19. *I consider Paul <u>my best friend</u>.*
20. *I made Paul <u>mad</u>.*
21. *I left Paul <u>at home</u>.*

It is interesting to note that SE subject complements may be *linked* to the subject by the copula, whereas object complements may be *directly juxtaposed* to the object. Some object complements, of course, may also be linked to the object as in 22.

22. *I consider Paul to be <u>my best friend</u>.*

Examples 19 and 22 illustrate two options that SE presents for nominal object complements: they may be directly juxtaposed to the object, or linked to it by *to be*. One distinctive characteristic of the AA system, discussed further in the following sections is that speakers have the option of directly juxtaposing nominal, adjectival and locative subject complements to the subject, as well as the option of linking them to the subject by means of a copula.

What is most distinctive about AA syntactic predicates is that, as noted above, *all types of predicates* may be directly juxtaposed to the subject. Not only nominal, adjectival and locative subject complements, as illustrated by examples 23–25, respectively.

23. *Paula my friend.*
24. *She mad.*
25. *Paul at home*

Participles derived from verbs by addition of the suffix, *–in*; (example 26) and predicates marked for future time by the form *gon*, (27) also may occur directly after the subject.

26. *I'm takin' my time.*
27. *We gon' take our time.*

Derived participles of the form V+EN also occur directly after the subject. The verb *lost*, in example 28, is typical of many English verbs that have the same form for past tense and past participle. The verb *stop*, in 29 further illustrates the fact that the *–ed*, suffix is frequently not attached to regular AA verbs with past time, or completive aspectual reference.

28. *I lost my wallet*
29. *We stop yesterday at six*

The AA completive aspect marker *done* also may directly follow the subject, as in example (30). Furthermore, The standard past tense form, *went* in (30) alternates freely with the standard past participle form *gone*, in the same environment, as in example (31).

30. *They done went home*
31. *They done gone home.*

Examples (32, 33) represent AA predicates in which a verb stem with an optional suffix, *–s*, directly follows the subject, and which – for want of a better name – may be called the V(+s) construction. With the suffix, it resembles the Standard English present tense form, although unlike standard English, the suffix may attach to a verb with a non-third person singular subject.

32. *She cook fish everyday.*
33. I takes the train often.

Examples (34, 35) represent the case in which the habitual aspect marker *be* directly follows the subject. It is interesting to note the parallels between the habitual *be* and the general V(+s) constructions. Not only do they have the same morphological structure, they also share a typical habitual aspect interpretation.

34. *He be drivin the truck.*
35. *It bees that way sometime.*

Intuitive tests for sub-classification of predicates

The various AA constructions represented by the above examples may be grouped into two major classes based on their grammatical acceptability when negated with either *aint* or *dont*. The ones that accept *aint* may be further divided into those that are also grammatical when *aint* is replaced by *not*. The constructions that accept both *aint* and *not* are labeled Type I predicates. They include nominal, adjective and locative complements, V+in derived verbal predicates, and the future marker, *gon*, e.g.:

36. *She aint mad | She not mad*
37. *She aint cookin | She not cookin*
38. *He gon take the train | He not gon take the train*

Predicates that take *ain't*, but are ungrammatical when *not* substitutes for *aint*, are classified Type IIa, e.g.:

39. *I aint see her | *I not see her*
40. *They aint done went home | *They not done went home*

Predicates that accept negation by *dont*, are classified as typed IIb, e.g.:

41. *She dont cook fish everyday*
42. *He dont be playin*

An interesting property of Type IIa predicates is that they typically accept negation by *havent* (or *didnt*) as well as <u>*aint*</u>, as examples 43–45 show.

43. *We aint stop yesterday at six | We didn't stop yesterday at six*
44. *We aint been studyin | We havent been studying*
45. *I aint see her | I didnt see her*

A noteworthy advantage of the above analysis of basic AA syntactic constructions over the alternative of listing features is that what is commonly treated as copula absence or copula deletion, are accounted for in a straightforward manner as instances of Type I predicates. Likewise, the so-called habitual *be* feature is accounted for as an instance of the Type IIb construction. There is no need to postulate a copula deletion feature which operates on the output of SE copula contraction. The zero-copula is a consequence of the generalization that all types of predicates, including nominal, adjectival and locative complements may occur directly after the AA subject. Likewise there is no need to posit the existence of an invariant *be*, or *be2* in AA in addition to the inflected be of SE, since the present analysis allows all types of verb forms, including the stem form, to occur directly after the subject.

Tense-mood-aspect interpretation

The types of AA predicates that may occur directly following the subject are listed on Table 10.5, grouped into types I, IIa and IIb according to the intuitive tests introduced above.

The claim of DeBose and Faraclas 1993 that type I predicates are assigned a value of [+stative] by the lexical stativity parameter is consistent with the fact that AA speakers, intuitively assign to them a present

Table 10.5   Types of African American Predicates

Type I	Examples
Noun Phrase	She my sister
Predicate Adjective	He tall
Locative Phrase	We at the office
Verb+in Phrase	I'm takin' my time
Future marker *gon'*	We gon' take our time
Type IIa	Examples
Verb (+EN)	I lost my wallet
	We stop yesterday at six
Completive marker *done*	They done went home
Perfective marker *been*	We been studyin'
Type IIb	Examples
Verb (+s)	I takes my time
	She take her time
Habitual marker *be* (+s)	We be takin our time
	It bees that way sometime

tense interpretation, and speakers of others dialects perceive an absent or deleted present tense copula/auxiliary. Likewise, the fact that type IIa predicates are perceived/interpreted as past tense or completive aspect is consistent with the claim that they are assigned a value of [–stative] by the LSP.

The multiple marking of type IIb predicates – by selection of the bare verb stem and optional attachment of the –*s* suffix has the same effect of overriding the default completive aspect past tense assigned to such constructions by the LSP with a present tense/habitual aspect interpretation.

It should be clear from the foregoing analysis that even though AA undoubtedly participates to a very high degree in the uniformity of American English, its similarity to certain aspects of General American English is more illusory than real. As similar as AA verb forms are, on the surface, to SE forms, the system in which they operate is quite different in that it allows a variety of non-tensed forms to directly follow the subject. Indeed, the labels assigned to the predicate patterns just discussed indicate that the SE grammatical tense feature has absolutely no role in the AA TMA system.

When a Type I predicate directly follows the subject it has a present tense and noncompletive aspect interpretation as a consequence of that very fact. Since it has such an interpretation by default, the information that would be conveyed by the present tense forms of *is* and *are* in SE is redundant. Similarly, since a Type IIa, or Unmarked Nonstative, predicate has a completive/past tense interpretation by default, the etymological past tense of a verb such as *lost* in example 46 below plays no role in its TMA interpretation, and the absent –ed morpheme of *stop* in example 47, were it present would be redundant and add nothing to the TMA interpretation of the sentence.

46. *I lost my wallet.*
47. *We stop yesterday at six.*

Such facts as the above offer a principled explanation for the frequent absence in AA data, not only of such forms as *is* and *are*, but also the –*ed* suffix. It also helps explain variable occurrences of the verb suffix –s, by clarifying its function as a marker of non-completive/habitual aspect interpretation from context. Occurrence of the stem form unambiguously marks it non-completive/habitual aspect, and lends transparency to the parallel TMA interpretation of sentences like 48, and 49, in which the verbs *hurry* and *works* are instances of the same non-completive/habitual aspect construction as the verb *be*, e.g.:

48. *When I be workin' on the assembly line, I don't hurry.*
49. *I works fast.*

Previous analyses based on the list of features approach only recognize *be* as distinctively habitual, and treat *(don't) hurry* and *works* as present tense forms. From the DeBose and Faraclas perspective all three verbs are instances of V(+s) which differs from the SE present tense form in that the –s suffix optionally attaches to all verb stems, including *be*.

As a final example of AA verb forms that resemble SE tensed forms but function differently in the AA system, consider the forms *was*, *had* and *yusta* which are preposed to Type I, Type IIa and Type IIb predicates respectively, and assign anterior aspect/tense to the predicated event; that is, they locate the event in a time frame before an established time of reference. Since the Type I predicate has a default non-completive/present aspect/tense interpretation, the anterior marker *was* places the event in a time before the present. Similarly, the marker *had*, locates a predicated event in a time frame before the established time of an event marked completive/past. We should note that although the reference to time before the present is semantically equivalent to past tense, it operates in a system in which marking predicates plus or minus anterior is more congruent. The reason this is so is because minimally marked forms in this system may be interpreted present or past tense based on the classification of the predicate. If *had* were interpreted as marking past tense rather than anterior aspect, there would be no difference in the interpretation of pairs of sentences such as 50 and 51.

50. We ate breakfast.
51. We had ate breakfast.

Likewise, sentences 52 and 53 would mean the same thing.

52. When they arrived we ate breakfast.
53. When they arrived we had ate breakfast.

Finally, the marker *yusta* locates a predicated non-completive/habitual event in an anterior frame of reference, e.g.:

57. They be sweatin' they finals.
58. They yusta be sweatin' 'em but not anymore.

C-selection and s-selection properties of AA Predicate Types

Having noted the types of syntactic structures that occur in AA as complements of the subject of the sentence, the criteria for their sub-classification, and the system by which they are assigned tense-mood and aspect, we may now turn our attention to how predicates differ in their ability to take complements of their own and/or assign semantic roles.

What was said above about SE main verbs generally holds for AA, that is, with the exception of the copula *be*, they assign theta roles, and have c-selection properties corresponding to their sub-classification as transitive, intransitive, linking, etc. What was said above about SE nominal, adjectival and locative complements also generally holds for AA in that they function as semantic predicates and assign theta roles. What is distinctive about these complements in AA, as noted above, is their optional occurrence directly after the subject.

The tense-mood aspect markers *gon, done* and *be*, do not assign theta roles. They c-select but do not s-select. The future marker *gon'* takes Type IIb complements; The habitual marker *be* takes type I complements, as well as type IIa complements headed by *done*. The completive marker *done* itself takes V+EN complements; e.g.:

59. *We gon be takin our time.*
60. *Paul be mad.*
61. *I be done got mixed up.*
62. *I done seen that movie.*

Sequences of two or more TMA markers are possible as a consequence of embedding of one predicate type within another in accordance with their respective c-selection properties, e.g.:

63. *They playin in the yard.* [V+in]
64. *They be playin in the yard.* [be+V+in]
65. *They gon be playin in the yard.* [gon+be+V+in]
66. *You gon be done got hurt.* [gon+be+done+V+EN]

The foregoing discussion has called attention to a number of ways in which AA participates in the overall uniformity of American English, measured by correspondences of basic vocabulary, phonemic inventory and basic syntactic patterning. Numerous ways were also noted in which AA language is endowed with a distinctiveness that permeates a number of different particular systems and subsystems of the overall grammar, a distinctiveness that tends to be masked or overlooked by descriptions based on lists of features.

In a more thorough and detailed account which available time and space does not permit, many other dimensions of the distinctiveness of African American language would be included. Without going any further, however, it should be clear that scholars engaged in any aspect of the academic study of African American language can benefit from an accelerated pace of contributions to the study of the grammar as an autonomous system that values the intuitions of native speakers as sources of data, insight and critical reflection.

Implications for language planning

Numerous observations have been made in the foregoing discussion of the multiple ways in which corpus planning, status planning and other types of language planning decisions mutually inform and strengthen one another. Any effort launched with the ultimate goal of full recognition of AA should give high priority to production and dissemination of an autonomous grammar for mass consumption by teachers, writers, artists, scholars and members of the general public motivated by the intrinsic interest aroused in the emergence of a language variety from a former status of stigmatized to that of medium of expression of the thoughts, musings and creative products of an amazing people that is making its mark as a leading contributor to national and world culture.

11
The Standardization of African American Language: Just do it!

> Before points (3–7) of the program can be implemented the codification of the status of BE as a national policy may have to occur. It would appear ill-advised to undertake ... production of grammars, textbooks and other printed matter in an atmosphere wherein varying conceptions exist of the nature of BE and its status ... in the national linguistic repertoire. The task of codification, because of its technical complexity and political sensitivity might best be entrusted to a nationally-based commission on the status of Black English ...
>
> (DeBose 1979)

In this chapter, I assume a visionary role, and invite the reader to join me in an imaginary journey from the status quo of American educational policy to a possible future in which African American language is seen by the average person as it is presently seen by linguists: as an instance of normal language. Imagine if you will, a futuristic scenario in which the idea of "Ebonics being taught in the schools" no longer generates the outrage that was frequently heard in the aftermath of the Oakland School Board resolution.

In the future world at the end of our imaginary journey, books will be available on library shelves to which teachers and other interested parties may resort for authoritative descriptions of the Grammar of African American language. Children of all ethnic backgrounds will have access to published literature in the language of Black America, and persons interested in learning to speak Ebonics as a second language will have access to courses, textbooks and audio-visual aids on the subject.

Envision a world in which African American language is recognized as a language in its own right. Not necessarily a different language than English, although such a possibility should not be ruled out; for in the final analysis – it is the speakers of a language variety who have the final say so in determining whether it is considered a dialect, or a separate language. Just as the different dialects of Chinese are considered dialects because such is the consensus of its speakers, and for the same reason Norwegian, Danish and Swedish, though mutually-intelligible, are regarded as different languages; African American language could attain the status of a separate language as the result of a successful campaign to mobilize speakers in support of the idea. The subtitle, "Just do it!" represents my sincere belief that the prospects for a future high level of standardization of AA depends crucially upon the initiative of persons who would like to see it come about.

For the sake of the present discussion, standardization may be defined as

> any and all of a diverse array of steps, measures and proposals that promise to affect the status of African American language in a manner that decreases the extent to which it is stigmatized, and, furthermore, which expands the range of societal domains in which it is accepted; i.e., from that of Black home and community life, and the performing arts – where it is presently accepted, to the spheres of education, government and the professions.

The present level of AA standardization

African American language is presently at a relatively low level of standardization, i.e.:

1) There has yet to be established a tradition of publishing – for general consumption – books, magazines, newspapers and the like that are consciously written in African American language; and
2) Authors writing in Standard English frequently have occasion to represent spoken language attributed to particular persons whose speech is markedly dialectal; and respond to the challenge by modifying the conventional spelling of words in order to convey a sense of particular marked features of the person's speech – influenced in varying degrees by an established tradition of dialect spelling.

A vast body of African American literature presently exists in which such immortals as Langston Hughes, Richard Wright and Zora Neal Hurston are canonized. Although it is typically about the Black Experience, it is normally written *in Standard English*. More precisely, the *voice of the narrator* of fictional works in the Black tradition tends to be in Standard English, while the characters are typically represented in dialogical sequences speaking in what is traditionally referred to as *dialect*.

In addition to the Black literary canon, there is an established African American journalistic tradition consisting of newspapers and magazines that focus on issues that tend to be neglected or marginalized by mainstream media. They too are written in Standard English. It is not surprising at all that such is the case in view of the fact that Black Americans participate in a social reality in which the notion of literacy is based on Standard English grammar and spelled according to a complex and highly irregular system of conventional orthography.

DeBose 1979 proposes an eight point program that – if successful – would result in a high level of standardization of AA. The basic strategy – to "spread ... the linguist's non-prescriptive attitude [toward AA] among teachers, parents, community organizations, civil rights groups and the general public" – is supported by the rationale that

> The current state of language planning technology renders such an attitudinal shift perfectly feasible, within the span of a single generation, through the implementation of such intervention strategies as the following.

> 1. Calling for an end to the enforcement of prescriptive grammar rules;
> 2. Adding "dialect" and sociolinguistics course offerings to the English curriculum
> 3. Development of a "normative grammar" of AA.
> 4. Reconstruction of "prototypical" AA "as a central aspect of the Afro-American cultural heritage."
> 5. Development and testing of "suitable initial reading texts" in AA to determine their relative effectiveness ... in comparison to traditional texts."
> 6. Promotion of serious literature, newspapers, films, etc. "in vernacular language."
> 7. "Standardization of BE orthography.

The eighth and final point calls for "Reform of teacher training and licensing practices in keeping of the above objectives." The excerpt from DeBose 1979 quoted at the head of the chapter, sets "the codification of BE as a national policy" as a precondition to the implementation of points 3–7. In the following pages, I characterize the strategies corresponding to those points as *long term objectives*. The reference to the desirability of entrusting the task of codification

> to a nationally-based commission on the status of Black English made up of ... linguists, educators and community leaders.

is also a long-term goal. The strategies corresponding to points 1, 2 and 8 are self-explanatory and require no further comment. Anyone who is interested, and has the means or authority to move any of those objectives forward is encouraged to "just do it!" I continue to feel that it will take the authority of a national commission such as the one called for in DeBose 1979 to move the long term program forward.

Several short-term measures, in addition to those alluded to in points 1, 2 and 8 were mentioned in the foregoing discussion of issues currently facing scholars of AA language that qualify as language planning issues. They are further discussed below as steps that linguists might take. I also discuss some other measures, both short and long term in nature, that may lead to significant gains toward the ultimate goal of full and vigorous standardization of AA. Before directly addressing those issues, however, in the following sections I make some observations of a general nature regarding some of the technical parameters of language planning as it relates to the issues at hand. A good deal of the discussion focuses on choices in the area of orthography, partly in anticipation of continued study of some of the specific concerns raised in the introductory chapter.

Much of the material discussed in Chapter Ten informs the corpus planning issue of how the grammar should be described, comparing and contrasting the list of features approach to that of a paradigmatic approach that seeks to make explicit the distinctiveness of AA at all level of linguistic analysis. When choosing between the two options for a grammar, one should, simultaneously, be mindful of the implications of either choice for status options under consideration. Similar implications attend the available options for an orthography.

Orthographic options

In the short term, the most practical options for addressing the standardization issues identified in the introduction are particular types of *modified conventional orthography*, discussed in the following paragraphs as *etymological spelling; inventive spelling*, and *dialect spelling*. Phonemic spelling should also be given serious consideration as a long term option. There are also some short term benefits for planning a phonemic AA spelling system that I address further below.

If a word has come into the language from an external source, through a process such as borrowing, retention, or relexification – it may continue to be spelled according to the established conventions of the source language. An example of etymological spelling is the French derived word *hors d'ouvres*. Although it could be more consistently spelled according to English principles as *orr durves*, the etymological French spelling is codified as correct. Another relevant example is the choice often made by parents to give a child a name that has a correct spelling based on the language from which the name is derived etymologically. It is common for an American boy to be given the etymologically French name *Antoine*, with the spelling *Antwan*, or the etymologically Irish name *Sean*, with the spelling *Shawn*. The non-etymological spelling in each of the above cases has a high likelihood of being correctly decoded by someone who knows the oral word. As such, they may serve as examples of *inventive spelling*.

The existence of variation in the pronunciation of certain words of a language that has an accepted spelling of such words – often associated with some notion of its "correct" pronunciation – engenders the need for alternative, or modified, spellings of such words for use at times when a writer may wish to convey the idea of the variant pronunciation. The first time that an author attempts such a feat, it qualifies as inventive, and its success depends, either upon the reader's prior experience hearing the nonstandard pronunciation, or the inherent propensity for an existing orthography to be extended to novel cases.

An example of inventive spelling in the case in which a reader's prior experience is crucial, is the word, that I spelled "bougie," in the introductory chapter – to represent an African American in-group expression that became popular in the sixties. The spoken form represented by my inventive spelling happens to be r-less. In an earlier draft, however, I made a conscious decision to retain the "r" of the etymological source, and spelled it "bourgie," in the hope of increasing the likelihood that non-Black readers would correctly decode it, aided by the increased similarity to the etymological source afforded by the presence of the "r" in the spelling. My wife, when reading a draft of my manuscript, noticed the discrepancy between my r-ful spelling with the typical spoken form, and proceeded to suggest that she would have spelled it "bougie." I noted that her accuracy in retrieving from my spelling the intended spoken form (represented phonetically /bužie/) speaks to the effectiveness of my spelling.

An example of inventive spelling that depends on the inherent properties of conventional English orthography for extension to novel applications involves the distinctive African American pronunciation of the pronoun form derived from the Standard English contraction, *it's*, pronounced /Is/. The distinctive African American pronunciation of the form, in which the /t/ sound of the etymological source is absent, has a high likelihood of being correctly decoded by literate English speakers from the spelling *iss*. Without proceeding to the problem of trying to decide how best to spell the form, let it serve for the present as an example, along with "bourgie," of the option of inventive spelling.

Spellings that originate inventively may come to be used with a high degree of consistency among members of a language community, and eventually attain the seal of approval of tradition – as in the case of so-called dialect spelling. A more significant generalization for the issues at hand, however, lies in the classification of inventive spelling, and dialect spelling in such cases as the examples just given, as particular forms of what may be termed *modified conventional orthography*.

Modified conventional orthography

When issues of standardization of a stigmatized variety of a language such as English are viewed from the perspective of immediate concerns of application to such sensitive work as the citation of linguistic data in technical writing and the attribution of folk speech to fictional characters, there is a predictable tendency for practical options for representing the variety in print to be limited to etymological spelling or – modified conventional spelling. In the case of the typical AA pronunciation of *it's*, possible choices are to spell it etymologically, with or without the apostrophe, i.e., *it's*, or *its*, or to opt for an inventive spelling such as *iss*; which alone of the three has a good chance of conveying the typical pronunciation to a non-native speaker. It runs the risk, however, of wrongly signaling an intention to stereotype Black language by calling undue attention to certain of its distinctive features.

Dialect spelling and stereotypes

Many examples may be cited of a tendency for conventional orthography, by its very nature, to engender stereotypical representations of typical speech patterns of a particular group. A case in point is the tradition of spelling the definite article, *the*, as it is sometimes pronounced in African American language, with an initial alveolar stop, /d/, by substituting the letter "d" for the diagraph "th."

The common "dialectal" spelling of *the* as *de* tends to be read, not with the neutral schwa vowel, common to standard and dialectal pronunciations, but with the vowel of *we*, which is inauthentic, and encourages a stereotypical conception of Black language that is divorced from reality. Clearly, a significant factor in the whole development is the association of a single letter "e" with a variety of sounds, represented by the words, *the*, *we*, *wet*, etc.

The stereotypical dialect spelling of *the* as *de*, and *more* as *mo'* are just two of a considerable number of words that have come to be spelled traditionally in a stereotypical manner, and used in contexts intended to demean or make fun of Black people; if not to exploit ingrained positive complimentary stereotypes of their culinary genius in the marketing of such products as Uncle Ben's rice, and Aunt Jemima pancake mix. They include, *this* and *that* spelled with "d" substituting for "th," *child* spelled "chile" by analogy with words with which it rhymes when pronounced without the final "d" of the standard pronunciation, and spelling of one of the biblical names of the deity in a typical African American manner, i.e.: *De Lawd*.

One traditional genre in which the kind of dialect spelling just illustrated frequently occurs is that of the Negro Spirituals – highlighting, as such, the dynamic tension that is ever present between authentic portrayal of distinctive cultural traits of an ethnic group, and stereotypical distortions of the same. A recently published collection of Spirituals (Warren 1997) contains many noteworthy examples.

One has to go no further than the title of the book, *Ev'ry Time I Feel the Spirit*, to find conventional spelling modified to give the impression of dialectal speech. The replacement of the second vowel of *every* with an apostrophe, supports the contention that what the writer intended to communicate to the reader was a folksy aura, more so than to accurately represent nonstandard pronunciation. The second syllable of the spelled word *every*, is rarely pronounced in Standard English speech. Interestingly, the listing of the song from which the title of the book is derived in the table of contents has a slightly different spelling, i.e., *Ev'ry time I feel de spirit*, with the word *the* spelled *de*, in accordance with traditional dialect spelling of Black folk speech. An interesting case of standardization involving a project to translate the Bible into Gullah, with implications for the standardization of AA is briefly summarized in the next section.

Lessons from the Gullah Bible translation project

Several years ago, it came to my attention that a project was under-way to translate the Bible into Gullah. In 1997, while attending the annual Heritage Days celebration of Sea Island culture, at the Penn Center on Saint Helena Island, South Carolina, I acquired copies of the recently-published Gullah translation of Luke's gospel, (American Bible Society 1995) entitled *De Good Nyews Bout Jedus Christ Wa Luke Write*. I attended another Heritage Days in 2002, at a time when I was actively developing scholarly interest in biblical translation, including plans to do an MA thesis as a case study of the Gullah translation project. The Sea Island Translation and Literacy Team is a cooperative effort of the Summer Institute of Linguistics, the Wycliffe Bible Society, and native Gullah speakers, to translate the Bible into Gullah. The close look at the project occasioned by completion of the thesis (DeBose 2003) brought to my attention several interesting aspects of the translation project that involve literacy, and contribute to the ongoing standardization of Gullah.

In their entirety, the issues lie beyond the scope of this work. One aspect of it, however, that informs the questions presently under study, is the way in which the project approached questions of orthography related to the translation effort. At the most general level, there are a number of interesting observations that can be made regarding the fact that the project decided against the option of developing a phonemic orthography for the translation product; and opted instead to use con-ventional English orthography, modified at times for reasons specified below.

As far as standardization is concerned – Gullah, in comparison to other creole languages, is relatively low on the scale of standardization, measured by such features as published literature, a stable orthography, dictionaries and grammars and use in the mass media. Two popular publications available at the Penn Center, and addressed primarily to visitors curious to know more about Gullah, are a dictionary by

Virginia Geraty,[6] and a combination vital-facts and phrase book by Laila Olela Afrika.[7] Both books are written in Standard English, and all Gullah expression are translated into English. Both books are available for purchase by visitors to the Penn Center, as is the Gullah-Luke translation, and to that extent they are an integral part of ongoing efforts to revitalize Gullah language and Sea Island culture. (2003: 13)

A major continuing challenge lies in the orthography, mainly because comparison of the translator's spelling with other published works by authoritative authors such as Geraty, Afrika and others indicates a great deal of variability. For all of the variation, however, the biblical spelling of Gullah is consistent with the principle articulated by the translation team in the preface of deliberately adjusting the writing of Gullah toward conventional English orthography. This is perhaps inevitable, as desirable as a phonemic system might be for aesthetic reasons, or the aim of promoting a distinctive Gullah identity, for the reason given by the translation team:

It is, or course, most easily read by the many speakers who read regular English.

The translator's next point, that "It is also considered to help provide a bridge between the two languages as people learn to read and write," is debatable, however. The English spelling system in its standard form is extremely complex, and adjusting it to the special features of Gullah adds more levels of complexity. I suspect that such points were debated by the translation team before deciding on the system chosen.

A number of the idiomatic features of Gullah involve distinctive pronunciations. Although the translators adopted a strategy of using modified conventional English orthography, spelling Gullah words the same as their English counterparts as long as they are similar in pronunciation, they made a conscious effort to write "the most prominent phonemic features." Hence if a word had a characteristically Gullah sound, the spelling was modified accordingly. Some results of this noted in the preface include *soona* "sooner," and *bof* both. Other special spellings that frequently occur in the text are *hongry* for "hungry," *scrait* and *scretch* for "strait" and stretch, and *ooman* for "woman."

---

[6] Virginia Mixson Geraty, *Gullah fuh Oonuh (Gullah for You): A Guide to the Gullah Language.* (Orangeburg SC: Sandlapper Publishing Co. Inc 2002).

[7] Laila Olela Afrika, *The Gullah: People Blessed by God* (Brooklyn NY: A&B Publishers Group 2000).

Some spellings reflect a desire to represent certain distinctive Gullah phonemes, such as the palatal nasal at the beginning of words such as *nyoung* "young," and the bilabial fricative which resembles /w/ and thus is spelled w̲ in such words as *wide* in verse 15.12b *So de man wide e propaty tween e two son* "So the man divided his property between his two sons." (2003: 33,34)

Several general observations about the case of Gullah that are relevant to ongoing decision-making regarding the spelling of African American language are

1. In considering whether or not to use a modified form of conventional orthography, an important criterion is whether the intended users are persons already literate in Standard English.
2. Expanding on the first point, whether on not the target readership is literate in the hegemonic Standard, it is worth considering the option of a phonemic orthography for other reasons, such as the esthetic quality, or overall appearance, of the text.
3. The effects that the translators sought to achieve by modifying conventional orthography in the direction of distinctive Gullah pronunciations would have been an automatic consequence of having opted for a phonemic system. In the light of such a tension, serious attention should be given to investing in alternatives to conventional orthography for representing specific instances of spoken language in print.

Short term issues involving orthography

I take the occasion in this section to summarize some of the issues noted above concerning the current lack of standardization of AA spelling and the effect that it has on the work of writers, and linguists faced with the need to accurately represent AA on the printed page. A common element of all of the issues is the established status of standard English literacy. A fiction writer assumes a reader literate in Standard English does not have the technical ability to decode phonetically transcribed representations. Linguists, although they may safely assume a more technically-adept reader with some proficiency in deciphering the phonetic alphabet, still face some pressure to opt for modified conventional orthography because of the larger audience that has access to their work, and the greater reader-friendliness of conventional spelling in either case. In opting for audience size and reader-friendliness, however, they also risk demeaning and stereotyping African American language in the process.

Linguists may play a useful role in moving the issue forward by engaging in constructive dialogue on such questions as,

1. What rational criteria are available for deciding whether or not to use apostrophes?
2. How do the answers to question (1) inform the issue of how to spell *it's*, *that's*, and *what's* in a manner that best conveys their typical AA pronunciation?
3. What about the AA future marker spelled dialectally *gon'*? What are the options for standardizing its spelling in representations of AA, and what principles inform those options?

Beginning with question (1) one important guiding principle – perhaps the most important – is the potential for the particular form in which an apostrophe occurs to convey a stereotype. One form which I suggested above to be positively stereotyped is the spelling of an r-less pronunciation of *more* as *mo'*. In the case of words like *it's*, the presence of an apostrophe does not appear to be stigmatizing. The reason, apparently, is the fact that it is in accordance with codified practice for spelling a contracted variant common to all varieties of English. To that extent it might be considered in accordance with the etymological principle. Without the apostrophe, it may be perceived as incorrect spelling. With or without the apostrophe, it is not an authentic representation of the typical AA pronunciation in which the "t" is not pronounced. I have seen in the literature where a scholar has chosen to spell *it's* as *is*, or *i's*, which are both difficult for a reader to retrieve the intended pronunciation from. That leaves the options of spelling it inventively, *iss*, and risk conveying a stereotype. In the light of available options, it might be just as well to follow the etymological principle.

Regarding the issue of the AA future marker spelled dialectally *gon,'* it has been noted that scholars have opted variously for spelling it with and without an apostrophe, as well as by substituting the more general American form, *gona*. A literate reader familiar with Southern speech would retrieve an accurate and authentic AA pronunciation from *gon.'* One who is unfamiliar with Southern or Black speech might erroneously pronounce the "n," and mispronounce the form as homophonous with *gone*.

One point that may come through from the above example of spelling issues is the value of scholars at least thinking about and sharing ideas regarding the development of a phonemic AA orthogra-phy. A possible strategy for proceeding might be to explore ways of standardizing the spelling of selected words, especially members of par-ticular high-frequency closed classes such as pronouns, qualifiers and determiners. Some preliminary conclusions that I have reached as a consequence of thinking about that issue are sketched in below.

Phonemic orthography

A phonemic alphabet, designed specifically for a particular language variety, should have a different symbol set aside for each of the distinc-tive sounds that combine in different ways to represent the pronuncia-tion of different words. The following discussion of possible choices for a phonemic orthography of AA is based on the assumption that AA participates fully in the uniformity of American English in having the same inventory of 39 phonemes commonly attributed to American English. Furthermore, it strives to meet the basic criterion of a phone-mic orthography, i.e., *one sound one symbol.*

There is no need to "reinvent the wheel," to get a set of symbols that will serve the purpose at hand. The following plain consonantal letters used in conventional English spelling could be retained,

   b, d, f, g , h , j, k, l, m, n, p, r, s, t, v, w, y, z

While some of those letters have more than one value in the conven-tional alphabet, they are adopted to the phonemic system with the understanding that each letter is limited to a single sound, which is encoded in the name of the letter. The traditional letter names presently used in reciting the A, B, C's could suffice for all of the above-listed letters except "g," and "h." In order for the sounds represented by those letters to match their names, the name of "g" will have the sound that it bears in the word *go*, and the name of "h" will corre-spond to the sound of "h" in *he*. The new name of "g" could be *go*, or better, perhaps, *ga*, and "h" may be renamed *ha*. The letters leading up to those letters could have rhyming names like, *ba, da*, and *fa*. Having names that encode the sounds to which they correspond makes them easy for new learners to acquire.

The consonantal diagraphs *ch, ng, sh*, and *th*; of conventional orthography may be retained in the AA system, corresponding to the sounds with which they are presently associated, in words like <u>*chip*</u>, <u>*ring*</u>, <u>*ship*</u> and <u>*thick*</u>.

The five cardinal vowel letters, *a, e, i, o,* and *u,* will correspond, for reasons made clear below, to the sound they represent in the words w*a*sh, b*e*t, b*i*t, l*o*ve, and p*u*t. The vowel diagraphs, *au, ow,* and *ei,* will consistently be used to represent the vowel nuclei of the words c*au*ght, sh*ow* and *ei*ght, respectively. The diphthong in the vowel of words like *boy,* will be consistently spelled *oy.*

New consonantal symbols

So far we have accounted for all but eight of the 39 phonemes common to most varieties of American English. That includes all but two of the consonantal sounds. One is the voiced interdental fricative at the beginning of words like *the*, and *this*. Since the diagraph "th" is dedicated to the voiceless interdental fricative of words like *think*, the phonemic principle dictates that it not also be used to represent the other (voiced) sound. The need for a different letter to represent the voiced "th" sound is minimized by the fact that AA speakers frequently pronounce such words as *this* and *the* with the stop consonant /d/ instead of the interdental sound of standard English pronunciation. Whenever such words are pronounced in the distinctive AA manner, the letter "d" may be used to represent the initial sound, e.g., *dis* "this" and *da* "the."

Since many AA speakers do not pronounce words like *the*, consistently, writers of the future will have to be prepared to spell it differently than *da* when the need might arise to represent the fricative sound of standard pronunciation, in which case a new letter or diagraph is required. Possible options are to select one of the unused conventional letters; i.e., *c, q,* and *x,* another is to create a new diagraph by analogy with the conventional *th,* by substituting "d" for "t" as the first member, "dh." The spelling of *this* under each of the above options is – *cis, qis, xis* and *dhis.*

If we tentatively select "dh" to represent the voiced interdental fricative, we have a unique symbol for every consonantal phoneme except the voiced palatal fricative represented by the letter "s" in the spelling of *plea*s*ure.* A likely choice for representing it is another new diagraph, "zy" which is motivated by the fact that the phoneme /z/ is sometimes pronounced as a palatal fricative as a result of assimilation to the palatal articulation of a following word such as *your,* as in the phrase *close your eyes.* The set of consonantal symbols for the envisioned phonemic AA orthography is displayed in Table 11.1.

Table 11.1   Consonantal Symbols for a Phonemic AA Orthography

	bi-labial	labio-dental	inter-dental	alveolar	palatal	velar
			Point of Articulation			
Stop:						
Voiced	b *bit*			d *dip*		g *gate*
Voiceless	p *pit*			t *tip*		k *cake*
Fricative:						
Voiced		v *vine*	dh *this*	s *sip*	zy *pleasure*	h *help*
Voiceless		f *fine*	th *thin*	z *zip*	sh *ship*	
Affricate						
Voiced					j *jar*	
Voiceless					ch *chair*	
Nasal	m *map*			n *nap*		ng *ring*
Liquid				l *lip*		r *rip*
Glide	w *well*				y *yell*	

New vowel symbols

In addition to the sounds indicated above for the five cardinal vowel symbols, and the diagraphs "ei," "ow" and "au," there are four more vowel phonemes still in need of orthographic symbols corresponding to the vowels of s*eat*, sh*oe*, b*at* and the unstressed schwa vowel of the first syllable of *about*. One option for representing the high tense vowels, i.e., of *seat* and *shoe*, which I would argue against is to retain the conventional diagraphs, "ee" and "oo," as in *feed*, and *food*. The reason is the lack of symmetry they introduce into an established pattern of associating the letters "i" and "u" with high vowels, and "e" and "o" with mid vowels. I would prefer the option shown in Table 11.2, below, of doubling the symbol for each of the high lax vowels, i.e., "ii" and "uu," to stand for their tense counterparts. A third option would be to represent them as diphthongs, i.e., "iy" for the vowel of *seat*, "uw" for that of *shoe*. Examples of how the sample words would be spelled with either of the three above options are *seet*, *siit*, and *siyt*, for "seat." *shoo*, *shuu*, and *shuw*, for "shoe."

The low front vowel of words like *cat* may be represented by doubling the simple letter "a" set aside for the low back unrounded vowel

Table 11.2   Orthographic Symbols for Vowels

		Front	Back
High:	lax	i *sit*	u *put*
	Tense	ii *seat*	uu *coop*
Mid:	Lax	e *set*	o *love*
	Tense	ei *date*	ow *show*
Low:	Round		au *Paul*
	Unround	aa *bat*	a *wash*
	Neutral	a *about*	

of words like *wash*, e.g., k<u>aa</u>t, "cat." The schwa vowel represented by the first vowel of *about* is best handled as a special case of a generalization about English pronunciation: the tendency for differences among English vowels to be neutralized when they occur in unstressed positions. At the end of words, for instance, the sounds represented by the proposed vowel symbols "i" and "u" rarely occur. Instead, they tend to either be tense if stressed, and neutral (schwa) when unstressed. Hence the spelling of the words *he*, and *she*, as *hi*, *shi* is sufficient, and the doubling of the vowels, i.e., *hii*, *shii*, is redundant and unnecessary. Similarly, the pronoun *you*, is adequately spelled with the simple vowel "u," i.e., *yu*. For similar reasons, the vowel of *wash*, never occurs in unstressed syllables, such as the beginning of *about*, or the end of *sofa*. There is no reason, therefore to reserve a different symbol for the unstressed schwa sound that is represented by "a" in such words. The appearance of the letter "a" twice in Table 11.2, corresponding to two different sounds, is not a serious breach of the phonemic principle, and it is preferable to other options that might require modifying the letters of the conventional alphabet with accent marks, superscripts, etc.

Diphthongs

In addition to sounds like the vowel nucleus of *boy*, which will be spelled in the future AA orthography straightforwardly "oy," the other two sounds commonly treated as diphthongs in linguistic accounts of American English pronunciation, corresponding to the nuclei of *ride* and *house*, will be represented in the future AA orthography as "ay" and "aw" respectively, as shown in Table 11.3.

Table 11.3 Diphthongs

Low-back front upgliding	Low-back Back upgliding	Mid-back Front upgliding
ay *ride*	aw *house*	oy *boy*

Short-term applications of phonemic spelling

Because of the deeply-entrenched and seemingly immutable status of Standard English orthography, it may take a long time and a great deal of dialogue to make any progress toward even partial implementation of phonemic spelling.

A strategy worth exploring is a phased introduction of phonemic spelling of selected words. It could start with closed lexical categories, selected in accordance with the extent to which they contain words with distinctively AA pronunciations, such as the possessive pronouns, e.g., *ma* "my," *yo* "your," *hiz* "his;" etc. Interestingly, the future marker remains a problem, for it requires a way of phonemically spelling the nasalized /õ/ of its second segment.

One solution that has occurred to me for representing nasalized sounds, not only in *gon'* but other words as well, such as *ain't*, which may be pronounced in AA without the final "t," is to adopt the conventional apostrophe sign as a marker of nasalization of a preceding vowel. As such the phonemic form *go'* would be pronounced /gõ/.

Time and space do not permit a fuller examination of the issues regarding standardization of AA orthography in any greater depth or detail than the foregoing. In the remaining paragraphs of this opus, I sketch in a few other short-term projects that appear to have some possibility of successful implementation. Following that, I summarize some of the conclusions or generalizations that emerge from the issues raised above.

Other short-term projects

The creation of an alphabet for a language variety that has previously existed only in spoken form, i.e., a vernacular, has vast implications for literacy. Imagine, for instance, the possible application of the envisioned phonemic orthography of AA in an adult literacy program addressed to speakers of AA language. Assuming the availability of adult reading material in the variety, learners could begin to independently decode such material as quickly as they could internalize the alphabet. Once they are literate in AA, it could serve as an effective bridge to literacy in Standard English, and the access to opportunity and mobility that it affords.

Another idea that is presently being explored is to organize a formal creative writing course on the subject of *Writing in Ebonics*. Several other ideas of that nature include a grammar book, written in AA, which describes the phonology, morphology, and basic patterns of phrase and sentence structure in non-technical language.

I am extremely optimistic about the prospects for the publication of this book to serve as a catalyst for action

- by linguists, interested in exploring the kind of language planning issues listed in the introduction; and sharing the fruits of their inquiry through existing media of academic dialogue, as well as new venues that may emerge in the future;
- by creative writers considering innovative ways of writing AA-medium stories, plays, novels and poems;
- by theologians, intrigued by the prospects of translating the Bible into African American language;
- by journalistic entrepreneurs interested in launching new publications that serve as the vanguard of a new age of AA literacy, and bear the distinction of being the first AA medium newspaper, magazine, or other specific type of publication; and
- by ordinary members of AA speech community and their civic, religious, cultural and political leaders, motivated by a spirit of cultural revitalization to honor respect and preserve the language of their ancestors, in a form that will best serve the needs and interest of present and future generations.

In the final analysis, after all is said and done, it is up to the speakers of a language variety to decide what status they want it to have. Given the socially-constructed nature of reality, what seems immutable is subject to change, concomitant with what is believed by a given generation to be real. If enough speakers of African American language decide that they want their language to have a written form, and the inevitable consequence of recognition as a *sho nuff* language, there is nothing that can prevent it from coming to pass. The operative word is: "Just do it!"

References

Afrika, Laila Olela 2000. *The Gullah: People Blessed by God*. Brooklyn, NY: A&B Publishers Group.

Alim, H. Samy 2002. Street Conscious Copula Variation in the Hip Hop Nation. *American Speech*. 77. 288–304.

Alleyne, Mervyn C. 1980. *Comparative Afro-American: an historical-comparative study of English-based Afro-American dialects of the New World*. Ann Arbor: Karoma.

Anderson, Roger (ed.) 1983. *Pidginization and Creolization as Language Acquisition*. Rowley: Newbury House.

Bailey, Beryl Loftman 1965. Toward a New Perspective in American Negro Dialectology. *American Speech*. 40: 171–77.

Bailey, R. W. 1983. Education and the Law: The King Case in Ann Arbor. In J. Chamber Jr. (ed.), *Black English Educational Equity and The Law*. Ann Arbor: Karoma Publishers: 1–28.

Baratz, J. and R. Shuy (eds) 1969. *Teaching Black Children to Read*. Washington D.C.: Center for Applied Linguistics.

Baugh, J. 1998. Linguistics, education and the law: Educational reform for African-American language minority students. In S. Mufwene, J. Rickford, G. Bailey and J. Baugh (eds), *African American English: Structure, history and use*. London and New York: Routledge, 282–301.

Baugh, J. 2000. *Beyond Ebonics: Linguistic Pride and Racial Prejudice*. New York: Oxford University Press.

Bereiter, C. and Engelmann, S. 1966. *Teaching Disadvantaged Children in the Pre-school*. Englewood Cliffs, N.J.: Prentice Hall.

Berger, P. and T. Luckmann 1966. *The Social Construction of Reality: a Treatise in the Sociology of Knowledge*. Garden City NY: Doubleday.

Bickerton, Derek 1977. Pidginization and Creolization: Language Acquisition and Language Universals. *Pidgin and Creole Linguistics*, ed. by Albert Valdman, Bloomington: Indiana University Press. pp. 49–69.

Burling, R. 1973. *English in Black and White*. New York: Holt-Rinehart.

Burling, R. 1992. *Patterns of Language: Structure, Variation, Change*. San Diego: Academic Press.

Campbell, James T. 1998. *Songs of Zion: The African Methodist Episcopal Church in the United States and South Africa*. Chapel Hill: The University of North Carolina Press.

Chambers Jr., J. 1983. *Black English Educational Equity and The Law*. Ann Arbor: Karoma Publishers.

Chomsky, N. 1965. *Aspects of the Theory of Syntax*. Cambridge: MIT Press.

Chomsky, N. 1995. *The Minimalist Program*. Cambridge MA: The MIT Press.

Clyne, M. G. 1975. German and English Working Pidgins. Paper presented at the International Congress on Pidgins and Creoles, Honolulu.

Comrie, Bernard 1981. *Language Universals and Linguistic Typology*. Chicago: University of Chicago Press.

Cooper, R. L. 1989. *Language Planning and Social Change.* Cambridge: Cambridge University Press.

Curtin, Phillip D. 1969. *The Atlantic Slave Trade: A Census.* Madison: The University of Wisconsin Press.

DeBose, C. E. 1975. Papiamentu: a Spanish-based Creole. Ph.D. Dissertation. Stanford University.

DeBose, C. E. 1977. The status of native speaker intuitions in a polylectal grammar. *Proceedings of the Third Annual Meeting of the Berkeley Linguistic Society*, 465–74.

DeBose, C. E. 1979. Language Planning in the United States: The Status of Black English. Intervention Paper. Conference on Theoretical Orientations in Creole Studies. St. Johns, Virgin Islands.

DeBose, C. E. 1983. Samaná: a dialect that time forgot. *Proceedings of the Ninth Annual Meeting of the Berkeley Linguistic Society*, 47–53

DeBose, C. E. 1984. A Reanalysis of the Black English Verb System as Decreolization. Unpublished Paper. Presented at 1983 Meeting of Conference of African Linguistics, April 7–10, Madison, Wisconsin.

DeBose, C. E. 1988. be in Samaná English. *Society for Caribbean Linguistics, Occasional Paper No. 21*, St. Augustine, Trinidad.

DeBose, C. E. 1992. Codeswitching: Black English and Standard English in the African-American Linguistics Repertoire. In C. M. Eastman (ed.), *Journal of Multilingual and Multicultural Development: Special Issue on Codeswitching. Vol. 13: 1&2*, 157–67.

DeBose, C. E. 1994. A Note on Ain't versus Didn't Negation in African American Vernacular. *Journal of Pidgin and Creole Languages 9.1*, 127–30.

DeBose, C. E. 1995. Creole features in Samaná English. Society for Pidgin and Creole Linguistics, Annual Meeting, New Orleans, January 1995.

DeBose, C. E. 1996a. Creole English in Samaná. *1994 Mid America Linguistics Conference Papers*, (ed.) by Frances Ingemann. Lawrence: The University of Kansas. Vol. II: 341–50.

DeBose, C. E. 1996b. Question formation in Samaná English Paper. Presented at NWAV 25 Las Vegas Nevada.

DeBose, C. E. 1999. Factors affecting the rate of language change: The case of Samaná English. Paper presented at the Ninth International Colloquium on Creole Studies, Aix en Provence, France.

DeBose, C. E. 2001a. The African American Literacy and Culture Project. Parasession on Reading and Dialect. 2001. Annual Meeting of the Linguistic Society of America.

DeBose, C. E. 2001b. The Status of Variety X in the African American Linguistic Repertoire. NWAV 30, Panel of the Sociolinguistics of Hip-Hop. Raleigh North Carolina October, 2001.

DeBose, C. E. 2001c. Patterns of complementation in African American predicates. Symposium on Recent Directions in the study of African American language. 2001 Annual Meeting of the Linguistic Society of America.

DeBose, C. E. 2003. Translation as cultural revitalization: The case of Gullah. M.A. Thesis, Pacific School of Religion.

DeBose, C. E. 2004. Manifestations of double-consciousness in the translation of Luke into Gullah. Annual Meeting of the Western Commission for the Study of Religion. Whittier, California, March 21, 2004.

DeBose, C. E. and N. Faraclas 1993. An Africanist Approach to the Linguistic Study of Black English: Getting to the Roots of the Tense-Aspect-Modality and Copula Systems in Afro-American. In S. S. Mufwene (ed.), *Africanisms in Afro-American Language Varieties*. Athens: University of Georgia Press. 364–87.

DeCamp, David 1971. Toward a generative analysis of a post-creole speech continuum. In Dell Hymes (ed.), *Pidginization and Creolization of Languages*. London: Cambridge University Press, 349–70.

Dillard, J. L. 1971. The Creolist and the Study of Negro Non-Standard Dialects in the Continental United States. In D. Hymes (ed.), *Pidginization and Creolization of Languages*. London: Cambridge University Press, 393–408.

Dillard, J. L. 1972. *Black English: Its History and Usage in the United States*. New York: Vintage Books.

DuBois, W. E. B. 1999. *The Souls of Black Folk: Authoritative Text, Contexts, Criticism*. Edited by H. L. Gates Jr., T. H. Oliver. New York: Norton.

Fasold, Ralph W. 1969. Tense and the form Be in Black English. *Language 45*, pp. 763–76.

Fasold, R. W. and W. Wolfram 1975. Some Linguistic Features of Negro Dialect. In P. Stoller (ed.), *Black American English: Its Background and Its Usage in the Schools and in Literature*. New York: Dell Publishing Co., pp. 49–83.

Fennell, Barbara 2001. *A History of English. A Sociolinguistic Approach*. Malden MA: Blackwell.

Ferguson, C. A. 1959. Diglossia. *Word. 15*: 325–340.

Ferguson, Charles A. 1971. Absence of copula and the notion of simplicity: a study of normal speech, baby talk, and pidgins. In D. Hymes (ed.), *Pidginization and Creolization of Languages*. London: Cambridge University Press, 141–150.

Ferguson, Charles A. and Charles E. DeBose 1977. Simplified Registers, Broken Language, and Pidginization. *Pidgin and Creole Linguistics*, ed. by Albert Valdman, Bloomington: Indiana University Press, pp. 99–125.

Fishman, J. A. 1980. Bilingual education, language planning and English. *English World Wide: A Journal of Varieties of English. 1.1*, 11–24.

Fishman, Joshua. 1964. "Language maintenance and language shift as a field of inquiry." *Linguistics 9*: 32–70.

Fishman, Joshua; Ferguson, Charles A. and Das Gupta, Jyotirindra (eds) 1968. Language Problems of Developing nations. New York: John Wiley and Sons.

Gates, Jr. Henry Louis 1988. *The Signifying Monkey: A Theory of African American Literary Criticism*. New York: Oxford University Press.

Gearty, V. M. 2002. *Gullah fuh Oonuh (Gullah for You)*. Orangeburg, S.C.: Sandlapper Publishing Co.

Gethridge, Carolyn 1996. Schools' standard is quality English instruction. *Oakland Tribune*. December 29, 1996.

Goss, Linda and Marian E. Barnes 1989. *Talk that Talk: An Anthology of African-American Storytelling*. New York: Simon and Shuster.

Gilbert, G. G. 1993. Historical Development of the Creole Origin Hypothesis of Black English: The Pivotal Role of Melville J. Herskovits. In S. S. Mufwene (ed.), *Africanisms in Afro-American Language Varieties*. Athens: University of Georgia Press, 458–75.

Gramsci, A. 1971. *Selections from the Prison Notebooks*. New York: International Publishers.

Green, Lisa 2002. *African American English: A Linguistic Introduction.* Cambridge University Press.

Hale, Janice E. 1982. *Black Children, Their Roots, Culture, and Learning Styles.* Provo UT: Brigham Young University Press.

Hall, Robert A. Jr. 1966. *Pidgin and Creole Language.* Ithaca: Cornell University Press.

Hancock, Ian F. 1970. A Provisional Comparison of the English-Derived Atlantic Creoles. *African Language Review. 8.7–72.*

Haugen, Einar 1966a. *Language Conflict and Language Planning: The Case of Modern Norwegian.* Cambridge: Harvard University Press.

Haugen, Einar 1966b. Linguistics and Language Planning. In Bright (ed.) 50–71.

Haugen, Einar 1969. "The analysis of linguistic borrowing." In Roger Lass (ed.), *Approaches to English Historical Linguistics: an Anthology.* New York: Holt Rinehart and Winston, 58–81.

Herskovits, F. S. (ed.) 1966. *The New World Negro: Selected Papers in Afroamerican Studies by Melville J. Herskovits.* Bloomington: Indiana University Press.

Herskovits, M. 1930. Review of *Black Genesis* by Samuel G. Stoney and Gertrude M. Shelby. *Annals of the American Academy of Political and Social Science.* July, 1930. 313–14.

Hoetink, H. 1962. Americans in Samaná. *Caribbean Studies Vol. II, No. 1:* 3–22.

Hollins, E. R., L. R. McIntyre, C. E. DeBose, K. S. Hollins and A. G. Towner 2005. Literacy Development in the Primary Grades: Promoting a Self-Sustaining Learning Community Among Teachers. In B. Hammond et al. (eds), *Teaching African American Learners to Read: Perspectives and Practices.* Newark DE: International Reading Association. 233–52.

Holloway, J. E. and Vass, W. K. 1997. *The African Heritage of American English.* Bloomington: Indiana University Press.

Holm, John A. 1988. *Pidgins and Creoles. Volume 1. Theory and Structure.* Cambridge: Cambridge University Press.

Holm, John A. 1989. *Pidgins and Creoles. Volume 2. Reference Survey.* Cambridge: Cambridge University Press.

Howard, D. L. 2004. Silencing Huck Finn. *The Chronicle of Higher Education.* August 6, 2004.

Hughes Langston and Arna Bontemps 1958. *The Book of Negro Folklore.* New York: Dodd, Mead.

Hymes, D. (ed.) 1971. *Pidginization and Creolization of Languages.* London: Cambridge University Press.

James, C. L. R. 1963. *The Black Jacobins: Toussaint L Ouverture and the San Domingo Revolution.* New York: Random House.

Kovecses, Z. 2000. *American English: An Introduction.* Ontario, Canada: Broadview.

Labov, W. 1972. *Language in the Inner City: Studies in the Black English Vernacular.* Philadelphia: University of Pennsylvania Press.

Labov, William. 1969. Contraction, Deletion, and Inherent Variability of the English Copula. *Language. 45.* 715–62.

Labov, W.; Cohen, P. and Robbins, C. 1965. A preliminary study of the structure of English used by Negro and Puerto Rican speakers in New York City. *Cooperative Research Project 3091.* Washington D.C.: Office of Education.

Levine, L. W. 1977. *Black Culture and Black Consciousness: Afro-American Folk Thought from Slavery to Freedom.* New York: Oxford University Press.

Lockward, George A. 1976. *El Protestanismo en Dominicana*. Santo Domingo: Editora del Caribe.

Low, W. Augustus W. and Virgil A. Clift (eds) 1981. *Encyclopedia of Black America*. New York: Da Capo Press.

Luckmann, Thomas 1975. *The Sociology of Language*. Indianapolis: Bobbs-Merrill

Martinus, Frank 1988. Guene: The connection between Papiamentu and African. *International Round Table on Africanisms in Afro-American Language Varieties*. University of Georgia Athens, February 25–27, 1988.

McKay, Sandra Lee 1996. Literacy and Literacies. In McKay and Hornberger (eds), *Sociolinguistics and Language Teaching*. Cambridge UK: Cambridge University Press: 421–445.

McPhail, Irving Pressley 2005. On Literacy and Liberation: The African American Experience. In Hammond et al. (eds), *Teaching African American Learners to Read: Perspectives and Practices*. Newark DE: International Reading Association. 9–23.

Mesthrie, Rajend, Joan Swann, Andrea Deumert and William L. Leap 2000. *Introducing Sociolinguistics*. Philadelphia: John Benjamins Publishing Company.

Miner, Barbara 1998. Embracing Ebonics and Teaching Standard English: An Interview with Oakland Teacher Carrie Secret. In Theresea Perry and Lisa Delpit (eds), *The Real Ebonics Debate: Power, Language and the Education of African American Children*. Boston: Beacon Press. 79–88.

Mitchell-Kernan, C. 1971. Signifying and Marking: Two Afro-American Speech Acts. In J. Gumperz and D. Hymes (eds), *Directions in Sociolinguistics: The Ethnography of Communication*. New York: Holt-Rinehart. 161–179.

Morgan, M. 1993. The Africanness of Counterlanguage among Afro-Americans. In S. S. Mufwene (ed.), *Africanisms in Afro-American Language Varieties*. Athens: University of Georgia Press, 423–435.

Morgan, M. 2002. *Language, Discourse and Power in African American Culture*. Cambridge University Press.

Morris, William (ed.) 1976. *The American Heritage Dictionary of the English Language*. Boston: Houghton Mifflin.

Mufwene, S. S. 1983. *Some observations on the verb in Black English vernacular*. Austin: African and Afro-American Studies Research Center, University of Texas.

Poplack, Shana and David Sankoff 1987. The Philadelphia Story in the Spanish Caribbean. *American Speech 62(4)*. 291–314.

Reinecke, John 1971. Tay Boi: Notes on the Pidgin French of Vietnam. In D. Hymes (ed.), *Pidginization and Creolization of Languages*. London: Cambridge University Press, 48–56.

Riessman, F. 1962. *The Culturally-deprived Child*. New York: HarperCollins.

Rickford, John and Russell Rickford 2000. *Spoken Soul: The Story of Black English*. John Wiley and Sons Inc.

Rickford, J. and A. Rickford 1995. Dialect Readers Revisited. *Linguistics and Education: An International Research Journal*. 7.2, 107–28.

Rickford, John R. 1977. The Question of Prior Creolization in Black English. *Pidgin and Creole Linguistics*, (ed.) by Albert Valdman 190–221. Bloomington: Indiana University Press.

Rosenthal, R. and Jacobson, L. 1968. *Pygmalion in the Classroom*. New York: Holt, Rinehart and Winston.

Rubin, Joan and Bjorn H. Jernudd 1971. *Can Language Be Planned? Sociolinguistic Theory and Practice for Developing Nations.* The University Press of Hawaii.

Ruiz, R. 1984. Orientations in Language Planning. *NABE Journal, 8.2*: 15–34.

Schuman, John H. 1978. *The Pidginization Process: A Model for Second Language Acquisition.* Rowley Mass: Newbury House.

Simpkins, G. and Simpkins, C. 1981. Cross-cultural approach to curriculum development. In G. Smitherman (ed.), *Black English and the Education of Black Children and Youth: Proceedings of the National Invitational Symposium on the King Decision.* Detroit: Center for Black Studies, Wayne State University.

Simpkins, G., Holt, G. and Simpkins, C. 1977. *Bridge: A Cross-Cultural Reading Program.* Boston: Houghton Mifflin.

Smith, E. 1975. Ebonic: A Case History. In R. L. Williams (ed.) 77–85.

Smith, E. 1992. African American language behavior: A world of difference. In P. H. Dreywer (ed.), *Reading the World: Multimedia and Multicultural Learning in Today's Classroom.* Claremont CA: Claremont Reading Conference.

Smith, E. 1998. What is Black English? What is Ebonics? In. L. Delpit and T. Perry (eds), *The Real Ebonics Debate: Power, Language and the Education of African American Children.* Boston: Beacon Press.

Smitherman, G. 2000. *Talkin that Talk: Language, Culture and Education in African America.* New York: Routledge.

Smitherman, G. 1994. *Black Talk: Words and Phrases from the Hood to the Amen Corner.* New York: Houghton Mifflin.

Smitherman, G. 1977. *Talkin and Testifyin: The Language of Black America.* Boston: Houghton Miflin.

Spady, J. G., Lee C. G. and Alim, H. S. 1999. *Street Conscious Rap.* Philadelphia: Black History Museum Umum/Loh Publishers.

Stewart, W. A. 1967. Sociolinguistic factors in the history of American Negro dialects. *Florida Foreign Language Reporter 5*: 1–7.

Stewart, W. A. 1968. A Sociolinguistic Typology for Describing National Multilingualism. In J. Fishman (ed.), *Readings in the Sociology of Language.* The Hague: Mouton, 531–45.

Thomason, Sarah Grey and Terrence Kaufman 1988. *Language Contact, Creolization and Genetic Linguistics.* Berkeley: University of California Press.

Tollefson, James W. 1991. *Planning Language, Planning Inequality: Language Policy in the Community.* New York: Longman.

Tsuzaki, S. 1971. Coexistent systems in language variation: the case of Hawaiian English. In D. Hymes (ed.), *Pidginization and Creolization of Languages.* London: Cambridge University Press, 327–339,

Turner, Lorenzo Dow. 1949. *Africanisms in the Gullah Dialect.* Chicago: University of Chicago.

Van Keulen, J. E., G. T. Weddington and C. E. DeBose 1998. Speech, Language, Learning, and the African American Child. Needham Heights MA: Allyn and Bacon.

Warren, G. S. 1997. *Ev'ry Time I Feel The Spirit.* New York: Henry Holt and Co.

Weinreich, Uriel 1953. *Languages in Contact.* New York: Linguistic Circle of New York.

Whinnom, Keith 1971. Linguistic hybridization and the "special case" of pidgins and creoles. In D. Hymes (ed.), *Pidginization and Creolization of Languages.* London: Cambridge University Press, 91–116.

Wiley, T. G. 1996. Language Planning and Policy. In S. L. McKay and N. H. Hornberger (eds), *Sociolinguistics and Language Teaching*. New York: Cambridge University Press, 103–47.

Williams, G. 1992. *Sociolinguistics: A Sociological Critique*. London: Routledge.

Williams, R. L. (ed.) 1975. *Ebonics: The True Language of Black Folks*. St. Louis: Williams & Associates.

Williams, R. L. and M. Brantley 1975. Disentangling the Confusion Surrounding Slang, Nonstandard English, Black English and Ebonics. In R. L. Williams (ed.), *Ebonics: The True Language of Black Folks*. St. Louis: Williams & Associates. 133–138.

Williams, S. W. 1991. Classroom use of African American language: Educational tool or social weapon? In C. E. Sleeter (ed.), *Empowerment Through Multicultural Education*. New York: SUNY Press. 199–215.

Williams, S. W. 1993. Substantive Africanisms at the End of the African Linguistic Diaspora. In S. S. Mufwene (ed.), *Africanisms in Afro-American Language Varieties*. Athens: University of Georgia Press, 406–22.

Wilmore-Kelly, Martha Leticia. Personal communication. Tape recorded interview in Samaná.

Wolfram, W. 1969. *A Sociolinguistic Description of Detroit Negro Speech*. Washington, D.C.: Center for Applied Linguistics.

Index

Printed in the United States
64401LVS00001B/133